Doris "Nina" Myrick

# Nina's Book of Days

*Nina's DearDiary entries from 2001-2005.*

COMPILED BY JORDAN SINCLAIR

*I humbly ask you Father God
to always hold my hand
and keep me ever close to you
help me, O Lord, to stand
I cannot walk without Your help
no good thing can I do
my efforts are all doomed to fail
unless I trust in You*

*-Doris "Nina" Myrick*

## 18 Feb 2001 - Starting at last

I think that writing down memories, putting thoughts on paper (or on a screen) takes a discipline that I intend to try to develop. I've always enjoyed sharing my thoughts with my children, but it has taker a long time to get around to this recording of past events.

Let me introduce myself. I'm called Nina (a nickname begun by my oldest grandson.) I am 66 years old, and a wife, mother, grandmother, even a great-grandmother. Am I not blessed?

I'm doing this as a gift for my children. They have probably heard most everything I'll write here, because I've always enjoyed talking and sharing with them. But the little ones may want to know about these things someday. So I'll probably begin tomorrow with some early memories.

## 18 Feb 2001 - In the beginning

My parents met when Mother was 16 years old and Daddy was 24. Mother lived in a small mountain town, and Daddy had recently moved there and was operating a pool hall. I guess Mother was fascinated with this "man of the world" who had done so many things and been to so many places. He was good at spinning tales too. So it wasn't long until they eloped to the adjoining city and were married by a justice of the peace. The next day Mother said to her brother and his wife, "guess what we did last night." Well, you know no one was going to guess. Then Mother said, "We smoked cigarettes." I've always loved this little story. It shows how naive and innocent she was. She grew up very poor in a family of 10 children, had never been anywhere out of her county, and knew almost nothing of the ways of the world. Her life really changed after that. I'll probably talk about this more another day. I had a special day today. I drove to Statesville (about 75 miles from here) and visited my Aunt Flora in the nursing home. She will be 95 in July, and it was so good to spend a little time with her. When she first saw me her face lit up and she reached out her arms and called me by my mother's name. But she knew who I was in a moment. Then when I left there I went to my cousin's wedding. She is 66 like me, and has been a widow for about 5 or 6 years. We were very close as children, spent lots of time together. Today I told her new husband how she used to bite me, and she says she can't remember doing that. I guess that proves that pain makes us remember better. But I did enjoy the day so much.

## 19 Feb 2001 - After the Wedding

Just 11 months after the wedding, I was born. Mother had gone back to the mountains to visit her family, thinking she was not due to give birth for a couple of weeks at least. So on a Saturday about noon, she had a great big baby. The doctor estimated 10 1/4 pounds. She was a very small woman, probably 90 or 95 pounds, so this was a rough experience for her. Daddy always told me that the doctor brought me in his bag. Of course I believed that. He also told me that I belonged to the doctor because Daddy never paid him. This all took place at my aunt Bert's house. What a surprise when Daddy arrived to pick Mother up and take her home. So we went back to Statesville and lived there until I was 7 years old. Lots of things happened during those years, but I think I will save those stories til later. I'm not sure yet just how to present all of this. So I'll just jump around part of the time. We moved to Asheville after I finished the first grade, so I had to go to a different school to start the second grade. Then in the middle of that year, we moved to Swannanoa and another school. I remember that was hard because the class had already learned to write in cursive, and I only knew how to print. So Mother had to teach me that at home. After the second grade, we moved to Charlotte and another school for third grade. But then we stayed in Charlotte til I was grown. But it's difficult for children to change schools often and not know anyone there. But I guess I must have been pretty tough because I survived. And third grade was good in many ways. The teacher let me help others with their reading, and she even appointed me to be the class president. That's one of my special memories.

## 20 Feb 2001 - Just Rambling

When we moved to Charlotte, Mother had to go to work, after being at home with me for my first 8 years. This was hard, but necessary. Daddy could always find work easily, but most of his money was wasted, so he was never a good provider. So I was left on my own most of the time I wasn't in school. Then began my love of the movies. I went to just about every movie that came to town. If Mother gave me a quarter, I could go to the movies and buy popcorn. Some theaters charged nine cents and others were twelve cents, so at the cheaper ones I could also afford a candy bar. And if I really liked the movie, I'd stay and see it again. I fell in love with Alan Ladd and Van Johnson and Gene Kelly and others. Once I had a terrible scare at a theater. I fell asleep and when I woke up, the place was dark and I was all alone. I managed to feel my way out to the lobby, then went to the front and stood there crying til someone passed by and saw me. This was probably after midnight. The police came and let me out and drove me home. When we arrived, no one was home because my parents were out looking for me. They were really relieved when they got home and found me there. I don't think I ever fell asleep at the movies anymore.

This is one of my creepy memories.

## 21 Feb 2001 - Days of Radio and Rummy

A comment I received yesterday got me to thinking about how big a part of my life the radio was. When I was growing up, our only sources of entertainment were the movies and the radio. Of course, there were some other occasional things like going skating or swimming, but we couldn't afford these often. I still remember my parents and me sitting by the radio and listening to many different programs. We always listened to "Mr Keane, Tracer of Lost Persons" and there was "Life with Luige" and "Inner Sanctum." We really enjoyed the comedy shows, like "Burns and Allen" and "Baby Snooks" and "Amos and Andy" and "It pays to be Ignorant." There were so many that I enjoyed so much. And always on Saturday night, there was "Your Hit Parade." It was so exciting to hear which song was number one. And we always listened to championship boxing. I remember Joe Louis and Billy Conn. The other thing my parents and I enjoyed together was playing Rummy, and I still enjoy that. I've taught two of my granddaughters to play it and they are good at it. Well, so much for entertainment tonight. That's all folks.

## 22 Feb 2001 - Free as a Bird

Soon after we moved to Charlotte, I began to go everywhere I wanted to go. As I talked about before, I went to the movies as often as I could get a quarter. But I also went into the stores just looking at everything. I discovered the first escalator I ever saw in Efird's Department Store. I had the grandest time playing there. I'd walk up on the down side and down on the up side. But after awhile a man (probably the manager) came to me and told me I'd have to stop it because I might get hurt. That was disappointing and a little embarrassing. But even more embarrassing was the time I went to town and was looking around Kress' 5 and 10 when a nice lady came up to me and whispered "Honey, your dress is unbuttoned all the way down the back." I had buttoned the top button and evidently forgotten about the rest of them. One very memorable experience was the day I was walking around in Kress' and not looking where I was going when suddenly I bumped into this big man. He was amused at the expression on my face, because I was awestruck to see Tex Ritter in person! I don't know how many know who this was, but he was one of the cowboy stars I had seen at the movies. (He was the father of John Ritter. You all probably know him. but of course this was before he was born, I would imagine.) But I don't know whether I spoke a word to this very nice man. I think I was speechless for once. But this was memorable indeed. And sometime later, at the Carolina Carousel Parade (It was always on Thanksgiving Day) I got to see Hopalong Cassidy riding a big horse and leading the parade. He was the grand marshal, and I believe that was the first Carolina Carousel Parade. I really loved Hopalong Cassidy in the cowboy movies, so that was quite a special day. Well, I guess that's enough remembering for tonight. I'll probably be back tomorrow.

## 23 Feb 2001 - Music Hath Charm

Music has always been a very important part of my life. My mother taught me to sing when I could barely talk. Then I got to sing in several talent shows in Statesville. One newspaper article called me the "Statesville Songbird." They said that after I finished singing, I tap-danced. This was so funny because I never could tap-dance. I just didn't want my time on stage to end so I started doing a dance we called buck-dancing. I loved being on stage. Once I won the prize of ten dollars and we bought my first doll with hair. I think that was the same contest where a little boy won first prize and got to go to New York to be in a big radio contest. We really felt cheated because the boy played a song on the harmonica, and only knew one song, whereas I could have gone on and on. Oh well, I guess that's show business. Mother taught me to sing harmony with her and we spent so much special time singing gospel songs. She was never too busy to sing with me, even after working all day, and then having to fix our supper and do dishes and lots of other things. Mother couldn't read music and we had no instruments, so I think it was amazing how she could teach me so much. There are so many things I could tell about music in my life, but for now I'll just briefly tell how I was asked to be the choir director at my church when I was about 32 years old, and couldn't read music. So I started taking night courses at a nearby college learning all I could about music, and finally earned an associate degree in church music. My mother was there to see me graduate (with honors) and I think she was proud of me. I owe her so much for teaching me so much about music. She was my first and most important teacher. And I thank God often for the gift of music, and that special mother who took the time to sing with me.

## 24 Feb 2001 - First Love

My first-love. It was so sweet. I had known him nearly all my life. In fact his sister married my uncle so our families were somewhat connected. When I was 13, I took the bus and went to Swannanoa to visit my grandmother. On the way from the bus station (walking), I passed his house. He was standing in the front yard with his parents. We said hello, and I found out that my grandmother was away. So I went instead to my uncle and aunt's house. This aunt was his sister. He later told me that he said to his parents after I passed by that I was the girl he would marry. He was 16 years old at that time and really very handsome. Well, I stayed with my uncle's family for about a week, and Bobby was there every day. I thought that was his usual routine, but they said he hardly ever visited them as a rule. So I was flattered. In a couple of days, he asked me to go to the movies with him, and of course I was delighted. We had to walk a long way, because he had no car at that time, but it was great. And he was a perfect gentleman. After that, he came down to Charlotte to see me whenever he could, and whenever I went there to visit relatives, we would see each other. I really fell in love with him, and he with me. Those were special days in my memory. When the Korean War began, he was 19 and of course joined the Marine Corps. He was sent to Korea and took part in the Inchon landing. He was gone for a little over a year and I missed him terribly. He got back in August and we were married in September. I was so happy, but soon realized that he was different. He had begun to drink, probably because of things he had experienced in Korea. Our first child, Paulette, was born while we were living at Camp Lejeune, N. c. She was a wonderful blessing to me. She gave me a reason to live during the next few years while our marriage was in such trouble. We were transferred to San Juan, PR, and lived there for two years. Well, I don't think any good purpose would be served in going into any more details, but it was heartbreaking to lose him. I still loved him. But a few years later, after our second daughter was born, and our son was nearly due to be born, he left me. And that was the end of a large part of my life. He died a little over two years ago. What a tragedy. But I have been so richly blessed, because a wonderful Christian man came into my life when my son was about 8 months old, We've been married now for 34 years, and I could never have asked for a better husband and father for my children. He is outstanding!

## 25 Feb 2001 - Tell a child the truth

I want to tell you a story about a dog named Popeye, and a lesson I learned. I was about 6 or 7 years old when I got this little female dog that we named Popeye. I know that's a strange name for a female, but she had a black circle around one of her eyes and this reminded up of Popeye the Sailor. He often had a black eye. Well when Popeye had puppies, I was allowed to keep one of them, and I chose the smallest one and named her Suzie. I really loved these dogs and enjoyed playing with them. We gave one of the puppies to my cousin, Nancy. She named hers Wimpy. We loved to play house with Suzie and Wimpy. We'd dress them in doll clothes and they'd be our babies. Sometime later, we moved away and left the dogs with my grandmother. I missed them so much and could hardly wait to see them again. So when we went back to visit, I hurried straight to the backyard, and they weren't there. Grandma told me that they ran away. This was terrible, but there was nothing to be done about it, except to cry. And I cried so much and worried about them, and I kept hoping I might find them someday. I guess it was several months later that Mother realized that I needed to be told the truth, so that maybe I could begin to get over it, because I often cried at night in bed. She told me that the dogs had started having what we used to call "fits" and Grandma had to call the sheriff to pick them up. I don't know what they did to them, but they probably either shot them or put them to sleep. This was hard for me to hear, but after that I was able to stop worrying about them and soon stopped crying about it. I think children need to be told the truth, in a gentle way. They can handle it. Grandma had the best intentions but she caused me to hurt a lot longer than I needed to. This is one of my sad memories, but I learned from it, so I guess it was for my good.

## 26 Feb 2001 - Temporary Housing

For most of my life, until I married Irving, I lived in so many places that it is hard to count them all. From the time I was born until we moved to Charlotte when I was eight years old, we had lived in at least four different places. Then I can count about eight houses or apartments until I was seventeen and married for the first time. Then, since my husband was in the Marine Corps, we lived in six places in just a few years. So there is not much feeling of home or security in one's life in a situation like that. We often had to move when I was a child because Daddy didn't pay the rent. That's not a good way to live, but Mother always did the best she could to make each place seem like home. I think that wherever your mother is it is home. But since Irving and I have been married, I have felt so secure knowing he would always provide for me. We started out in a trailer with two rooms built on the front of it. It wasn't much to look at but we were comfortable and it was ours. After thirteen years, we were able to build a nice brick house. I was so proud of it, and we paid for it as we went along, so that when we moved into it, it was all paid for. I thought that was fantastic! We lived there for twenty-one years, and last June we bought a smaller, but very nice house in town. And I am enjoying it so much. We still have our other house. It's rented and they have an option to buy it after a year. But I wrote all this just to show the contrast in my life since I met Irving. What a great provider he has been. I thank God for him. And the security I have experienced, knowing that our home is our own, and that we can stay as long as we want, if it's in God's will.

## 27 Feb 2001 - I Remember Jimmy

Since I started writing about all of these memories, I've spent a lot of time thinking of the past, and maybe it's good for me to exercise my mind and to put these things down for others to read. I'm kind of enjoying it, so far. When I was in the first grade in Statesville, there were several things that I like to remember, some of them funny, some serious. My cousin Nancy was in my class and she was so shy that I felt that I had to look after her. For example, if she had to go to the bathroom, she would whisper and tell me. Then I would raise my hand and announce to the teacher what Nancy needed to do. And I would always accompany her and help her. Once I guess we were talking too much, and Mrs. D. told Nancy to pick up her chair and move it to the other side of the room. I immediately picked up my chair and followed her. I was so surprised when Mrs. D. told me to put my chair back, that I couldn't sit by Nancy. We had a play that year that was about dolls and wooden soldiers and various toys. All of the girls were dolls, and we all wore such pretty dresses, all of them different pastel colors. Jimmy was the leader of the soldiers, and at one point was supposed to say, "I will blow my whistle and my soldiers will come and march for you." Well, when the time came he just stood there for a few moments looking dumbfounded, then he said "I forgot my whistle and left it at home." I wonder if Jimmy remembers that. He was my boyfriend, and now and then he would walk me home, but only after I walked home with him for him to get permission from his mother. Sometimes she would say yes, and sometimes not. And so sometimes I ended up just walking him home, and then going on home by myself. After the first grade, we moved to Asheville, so the romance ended. But I still remember Jimmy.

## 28 Feb 2001 - World War II, as I saw it

The War started when I was seven years old and lasted til 1 was eleven. I didn't really understand a lot of it, but I'll just share a few of my memories about it. For one thing, I had four uncles who were in the service; three in the Navy, and one in the Army. I'm sure the adults in the family were very worried about them, but I didn't hear much about that. I remember that Daddy almost got drafted, and we were so upset about that. He had to go down to Fort Bragg, but was back in a day or so. He said he was just barely over the age to be drafted. Every child knew who Hitler was, and who Tojo was. Also Mussolini. (I'm not sure how that should be spelled.) And we often drew pictures of the three of them, not complimentary pictures, but easily recognizable. Hitler had that unique hair, straight and combed over to one side of his forehead. Tojo had large buck teeth and squinty eyes. And Mussolini had very fat jaws, and always looked like he needed a shave. So this was the evil trio. Every child hated and feared them. There would be air raid drills at night. The wardens would patrol the neighborhoods and make sure that every light was turned off. It seems that I was often alone when these things took place and I was scared to death. Not only from being in the dark, but I was always afraid that there might be a real air attack. A lot of things were rationed in those days, like coffee, sugar cigarettes, shoes. I might be mistaken about some of these things, but that's the way it seems to me. Mother would have ration stamps for these different things. I think that nylon hosiery was hard to get, maybe impossible. And one thing I remember well was that elastic was really scarce, because my underpants had strings to tie them, instead of elastic. One thing that we couldn't get was bubble gum and this was a terrible hardship or so it seemed. Mother worked with a woman whose relatives owned a candy making company, and this lady gave Mother some bubble gum for me which was a good-sized block of totally white gum. But it had that wonderful bubble gum flavor, and I thoroughly enjoyed it. I remember the day that President Roosevelt died. Everyone I saw was so sad. It was like a death in the family. Then I remember the day that my uncle Billy came home. My mother worked in a café at that time, and she said that when she saw Billy come in she was so thrilled and so surprised. She thought he was still fighting in Germany. He was her baby brother. And she said she didn't remember how she got over that counter, that she probably jumped over it. That was a very happy day for us. And soon all of my uncles were home again. None of them got hurt in the war, but not too long after that Billy was killed in a terrible accident, but we were so thankful that he did get home safely from the war. Well, I guess that covers the main part of my memories of World War II. I didn't know him at the time, but my husband was in the Navy, serving in the Pacific.

## 1 Mar 2001 - One Wonderful Day

I'll tell you tonight about one of my experiences in high school. It was probably the very best ever. I guess I was fifteen years old, because I was in the ninth grade. I was a member of the choir, and we were learning an operetta which we would perform soon. It was titled "The Sunbonnet Girl" and it had a really good story, and some beautiful music in it. One of the characters was a girl named Miranda Meadows, and I wished with all my heart that I could have that part, but I didn't dare ask for it, for fear that I would embarrass myself. Well, the last day came for trying out for a part and the teacher asked if anyone wanted to sing this particular song, which would be sung by an older woman in the play. I didn't really want that part, but it was better than nothing. So I stood up and said that I would like to try. I was so afraid, but I sang the song. And I think it must have been pretty good. A little later, Mr Cook went to the blackboard and began to write down his choices for all of the parts. I held my breath. When he came to the name of Miranda Meadows, He wrote my name beside it. I don't know how to express how thrilled I was. At that point in my life I felt so inferior, I couldn't believe my good fortune. But for a few weeks I was Miranda, and that was one of the greatest times of my life. I loved it. And would you believe I now have a granddaughter named Miranda, after me. Isn't that the coolest thing? O yes, one other thing that I treasure. After class that day, I stopped to thank Mr. Cook for giving me that part, and he said, "You deserve it." Wow! I walked on a cloud out of that room. "

## 2 Mar 2001 - Jeep

When I was about nine years old, I came home after school and Daddy surprised me with a little puppy. He was only five weeks old, but needed to be sold, because his mother couldn't feed him. I don't remember why, she may have died. He was the most adorable puppy I had ever seen. Daddy was able to buy him for very little money since he was so young, and I guess there was a good possibility that he wouldn't survive. But he was a full-blooded Eskimo Spitz, the toy size. He was a little white ball of fluff, with shiny black eyes, and I dearly loved him from the start. He thrived and was very healthy. and was so much company for me. I never had a brother or sister, but I felt like I loved him like a little brother. He was so smart and learned to sit up on his hind legs, and would stay there until he was told to get down. He never allowed anyone to hit anyone in his presence. Sometimes we would pretend that we were going to hit each other, and he would growl and warn us to stop. Once he got hit by a car, and I thought surely he was going to die. We couldn't afford a vet for him, so we just kept him lying on a quilt and we took care of him the best we could. Now and then he would yelp with pain, and I would cry with him. But after a week or so, he began to mend. He never again went into the street. I had a little boyfriend who would come to see me, and we would read comic books together. He knew how to win my heart; He would bring a candy bar for Jeep. (Yes, I've heard lately that you should never give chocolate candy to a dog, but it never hurt Jeep. He loved it.) One day, we got a message that Daddy was in jail, and that someone needed to come and pick up the dog. I hurried there and found Jeep in the cell with Daddy. Daddy loved to take Jeep with him and that day he drank too much. So when the police arrested him, they had to take Jeep with them. It's a funny picture in my mind, even after all these years, to think of Jeep in jail. Of course, I took Jeep home but had to leave Daddy there. He probably got out the next day. Later when Jeep was about five years old, we moved out into the country. A female dog who belonged to a family down a little dirt road behind us was in heat, and although we always kept Jeep in the house, that evening when we got home he dashed out the door past us and headed down that dirt road. Well, Daddy went after him, and in just a few minutes came carrying him in. He was dead when Daddy got to him, and we never knew what caused it. We wondered if some other, larger male dog might have broken his neck. But there were no marks on him or any blood. We thought he might have had a heart attack. But I was devastated. I don't have words to express how heart broken I was. I cried long into the night, and the next day I had a funeral for him. I wrapped him in a shirt of Daddy's and put him in an orange crate and buried him in our back yard. But I'll never forget Jeep. He was the greatest dog I ever knew. You might think I'm silly but I'm sitting here on the verge of tears as I tell his story.

## 3 Mar 2001 - The Runaway

One day I got really mad at Daddy. I think he had spanked me. I was probably about four years old. So while Mother was busy hanging out her wash, I left. Mind you, I didn't have to walk, I had my own vehicle. It was called a "Kiddy Kar" and it drove just like Fred Flintstone's car does. You know, with the feet on the pavement or the dirt. Well, when Mother and Daddy discovered that I was missing, Daddy took off to a nearby store and asked the owner if he had seen a little four year old girl around there. He said he had seen a little girl pass by a little while before, riding in some kind of a little car. He told Daddy the direction I was going in, and Daddy hurried up the road in hot pursuit. Before long, he caught up with me and asked me where I thought I was going. I told him that I was going to Oklahoma to be a cowboy, then I was going to come back and shoot him. I don't really remember this, but I must have been very angry indeed. But I am thankful that he made me go back home. And I'm really very, very glad that I didn't shoot him. I don't think I ever considered running away again. Once was enough.

## 4 Mar 2001 - Great-grandparents

My father's grandparents (last name Wilburn) had a rather hard life. They didn't have much in the way of material things, but they had a large family, I think it was eight children. I can't remember his first name, but hers was Dovey Jane. Her husband really treated her badly after the children were some size. He left them with nothing except a lot of hard work. Then later when the crops were in, he reappeared for a little while, just until the crops were sold. Then he took all of the money and left again. I don't know any more details about how they survived, but I guess they just worked really hard to grow more crops. He seemed to be a very cruel man. No one knew where he was after he left, until one day his body was found in some other town in a burned up house. They said his head had been cut off, but his family never knew any more about what happened. Obviously someone had murdered him. And there was a small boy in the house with him, also dead. We wondered if it was his son. Dovey Jane lived to be very old, and I remember a little bit about her. We lived near where she was living with her daughter. We didn't have an indoor bathroom at that time, and I would often ask to go to Great-grandma's to use her nice white pot. I guess it was nicer than our pot. And sometimes Mother would take me there for that purpose. I think I was about five years old when Great-grandma was dying, and she asked me to sing her a song. She really had a hard life but at least I suppose her last years were peaceful. I hope so.

## 5 Mar 2001 - S.A.L.T.

I thought for a change I would write tonight about something current in my life. Some of you might be interested in what I started today. I read in the paper a week or so ago about a volunteer program called S.A.L.T. (Seniors and Law Enforcement Together.) Five weeks of training, every Monday afternoon, started today. I'm kind of excited about it. After I complete the program I'll be able to help out at the Sheriff's Office, in a lot of different areas. I feel like it will be good for me to learn some new things and meet some new people. Today, the sheriff spoke to us, then a captain, then a detective. And it was interesting. Some of the things that seniors can do are to work at the desk where visitors come in to the jail, or fill in at different office jobs, or help in the detective area with entering information into the computer. There is one man who even loads the guns for the target practice. Each Monday, different officers will speak to us about their areas and hopefully we will soon have a pretty good understanding of the work there. I'm looking forward to it. We'll see how it goes. And I'll let you know more about it later after I know more.

## 6 Mar 2001 - The Accident

I keep going back into the past to think of something to write about, and I think I'll tell about my terrible accident when I was just a toddler, I think about eighteen months old. We had an open fireplace, and while my mother went into the kitchen to see about something she was cooking, I picked up a belt and threw one end of it into the fire. Of course it caught fire, and when I pulled it back out it set my nightgown on fire. When Mother heard me scream, she rushed into the front room and found me lying on my back with my nightgown burned off except for a little bit around my neck. The doctor said later that if 1 hadn't fallen down, the flames would have suffocated me. Well, Mother picked me up and carried me around in the room trying to comfort me, and she told me that there were bits of flesh falling in the floor from my legs. Some neighbor boy ran to the mill where Daddy was working and told him that I got burned up. Daddy said that he went out through a window and fairly flew home. Well the doctor bandaged me up, and I healed after several weeks, but I was left with ugly scars on my legs. This really bothered me when I was growing up, to feel that my legs were ugly, but after I got older it didn't matter. I just have always been so thankful that the fire didn't get to my face. That could have really been a hard thing to bear. And I've always felt sorry for Mother about the accident. I know she must have felt so guilty, but she was only about seventeen years old at the time, and just didn't think about the danger. She was a wonderful mother. I don't consciously remember anything about this incident, but I've always been afraid of fire. That makes me think that somewhere in my mind, maybe I do remember it. This is a very depressing thing to tell about, but it was an important part of my life.

## 7 Mar 2001 - Snuff and Sacrifice

I remember when I was very young, my mother used snuff. We called it "dipping snuff," and I was always asking Mother for it. One day she decided she would give me a dip, thinking it would make me sick and I wouldn't ask for any more. Well I put the snuff inside my lower lip and stood on our back porch where I could spit when I needed to. In the meantime, Mother went to visit the next door neighbor. Pretty soon, I came to the door asking for more snuff. I really liked it, and it didn't make me sick at all. Needless to say, I didn't get any more. I also remember Mother cooking mush for us, and I loved it. If you don't know what mush is, it's made with cornmeal, salt, and water. It's cooked like grits, and I've always loved it. I didn't realize at the time that this was the only food in the house, and I thoroughly enjoyed eating it with Mother. We would share a bowl, but we would each have our own spoon. Mother made even something like that enjoyable. Sometimes, she would send me to my grandmother's house to play with my cousins just before lunchtime. I didn't realize until much later that she did this knowing that Grandma would ask me to eat lunch there. What breaks my heart is that Mother would stay at home and do without lunch. She wouldn't ask for anything for herself, but she would make sure that I had something. She probably didn't want to tell Grandma that we didn't have food in the house. This grandmother was my daddy's mother, but she loved Mother dearly, and would have given her anything she had if she had known. Well, this was another one of my sad stories, but it's one of my memories, and maybe it has value. It really demonstrates the love and sacrifice of a mother. But she still wouldn't give me any more snuff.

## 8 Mar 2001 - A School Volunteer

I am so frustrated. For the second time lately, I have been finished writing my entry and before I pushed the button to enter it I hit the wrong key and lost the whole thing. I'm not sure my entry was very interesting anyway, but I guess I'll try again, but I think I'll sort of condense it. I worked for about fourteen years in the library at an elementary school, part-time, and also substituted a lot. The children's behavior got really hard to handle through the years. There was very little discipline or respect for adults. (This does not apply to all the children. There were always a few who were behaving well and trying to learn.) But I was ready to resign, and glad to be through. This was about five years ago. Well a dear friend at my church, who works for the school system, asked me last week if 1 would do a favor for one of the schools in the county. They had been unable to find enough volunteers to act as proctors for the seventh grade writing test. Of course, I couldn't say no. So this past Tuesday I went to this middle school, and was directed to a seventh grade classroom. Well, I had forgotten how tough it can be to walk constantly around in the room, watching all the students to be sure they were following all the directions. But I survived, and the students impressed me with their good behavior. They all paid close attention to their writing, and obeyed all the rules. When I left the school, I was exhausted, but I felt a sense of satisfaction in knowing that I had helped. But I surely wouldn't want to do that every day.

## 9 Mar 2001 - Grandma

I want to tell you about my paternal grandmother, "Grandma." She grew up in a very poor home with several brothers and sisters. Then she married my grandfather, who was at that time a widower with two young children. She had eight children, pretty close together. One of her children, Gracie, slept in the bed with Grandma. She was just a few months old, and one morning she was dead when Grandma woke up. When Daddy told Mother and me about this, he said he always thought that Grandma rolled over on her and smothered her. What a tragedy. Certainly Grandma never meant to hurt her. Later, during the Flu epidemic, (I think about 1917 or 1918) Her son Fred, who was about two years younger than Daddy, probably close to eight years old, died. This caused Daddy grief all the rest of his life because he had talked mean to Fred the day before they both took sick. Daddy said he and Fred were in bed together, and while Daddy had a high fever and was out of his head for a few hours, Fred died. Then just a few years later, her husband died, still a relatively young man. I never knew him, but they say he was a really good man, but I never thought he was a good provider, because Grandma had to take in boarders to make ends meet, on top of all her other work for her family. Later she married a man who was mean to her and at times mean to the grandchildren. There were times when he would stick out his cane and trip us on purpose. And when he would get mad at me, he would take my cousins, Nancy and Terry, to the store and buy them candy. Or if he was mad at them, he would take me and buy me candy. He never caused any of us to like him. Grandma had a house when they married, and he borrowed money against it and caused her to lose it. Soon he died and Grandma never had a home after that. She had to divide her time between her children. Whenever she came to our house in Charlotte to stay awhile, she would always have some candy or gum in her pocketbook. I liked that. Also, she always slept in long flannel gowns that were so nice and warm. She would always give me one of them. She would clean and cook while Mother was at work. The only trouble was that she thought I should do housework too, and she thought she should be my boss while Mother wasn't there.

Well, that didn't suit me, because I was used to being on my own during the days and didn't think I needed a boss. And I never had to do housework. So that caused a little friction, but I always felt like I was her favorite grandchild. She would take me to see cowboy movies, then in the evening she would tell Mother all about what Roy Rogers or Gene Autrey did. She spoke of them as if she knew them personally. And I've seen her eat a whole box of chocolate-covered cherries during one movie. She really was a good cook, and we ate well while she was there. She could do so much with nearly nothing. I learned to make potato fritters and bean fritters, out of leftovers. And these are still favorites of mine. And she made the best fried apple pies I've ever tasted. She has been gone now for many years, but I won't forget her as long as I have my mind. She was a good one.

## 10 Mar 2001 - Mamaw

Yesterday, I wrote about my daddy's mother, so tonight I'll write about my mother's mother. We called her "Mamaw," and she was priceless. Her life was always hard. When she was about eleven or twelve years old, her mother died. Mamaw was the oldest of about six children, I think, and she had to take over running the house and taking care of her brothers and sisters. I'm not sure how old she was when she married my grandfather, but I would guess maybe fifteen. My grandfather was a widower, much older than Mamaw, and he had several children, some of whom were as old or older that Mamaw was. Some of my aunts said he was mean to Mamaw, kind of treating her like a hired servant. Well, she had to work very hard during those years, and she had a baby every two years, until she had ten children. Then she had a miscarriage and never got pregnant again. She had to work in the fields, then go to the house and cook large meals for her family, and her laundry must have taken one whole day a week to do, not counting all the ironing and mending.

Of course, I'm sure her children all had to work hard as soon as they were old enough. I don't know what year it was, but Mamaw wanted a sewing machine so badly that she took in washing and ironing for other families until she earned enough money to buy herself a new Singer sewing machine. I believe she paid fifty dollars for it, but I'm not sure. But I know that it was a treasure to her, and it was a tremendous help to her. After all of her children were married, my grandfather died, and Mamaw had no means of support. She had to just depend on whatever her children were able to give her. Later on, she began to receive a small monthly pension check of about fifty dollars a month, and she really took care of that money. At one time I was living in Iowa, and Mother asked Mamaw to go with her to visit me. Well, this was probably the biggest adventure of her life, and she had saved up fifty dollars and insisted that Mother let her pay that much on the trip. 1 was impressed that she had been able to save that much money out of such a tiny income. She was a committed Christian, and her church was a vital part of her life. I'm really proud of her, and could tell more of her story but maybe that's enough for now. Maybe another time I'll write about her again. One more thing I want to mention is about her sewing machine. She chose to give it to my mother years later, and I now have it. What a treasure it was for her, then for my mother and now for me.

## 11 Mar 2001 - More About Mamaw

There are a few more things I wanted to share about Mamaw. She lost her son, Billy, in an accident soon after he returned from the war. Billy was so full of life, and so much fun to be around, and suddenly he was gone. I remember him well. I think everybody loved him. He was Mamaw's youngest son. Well, the thing that I noticed during those days of loss and during the funeral was Mamaw's quiet acceptance and peace, even though her heart was broken. Others in the family were crying loudly or having to be sedated, but not his mother. She just sat quietly, and this showed me what strength she had. And I think about another time when my mother had surgery. I was grown then, and Mamaw came to Charlotte to be with us during the surgery. There was a tumor which might have been malignant, and it was a scary situation. But again, I noticed Mamaw sitting quietly, worried of course, but showing that same strength and peace. She was a devoted Christian who loved God and her church. And she cared deeply for her family. She left behind a great testimony of faith by the way she lived her life. These were just two simple instances in my memories of Mamaw, but important to me.

## 12 Mar 2001 - More Training for SALT

1 went today for my second session of training to be a volunteer for the sheriff's department and it was really interesting. We heard four different speakers, each sharing a different aspect of legal things. There was the staff attorney who is responsible for seeing that the officers all know exactly what the law says about the situations they might find themselves in. Then there was an officer who talked about gun safety. I learned some things that were new to me, although I don't know much about guns anyway. Later the Clerk of Superior Court spoke to us about her office and what they do. I had met her before and was already impressed with her. She is really one sharp and likable lady. We learned a lot from her. Then last we heard from an officer who conducts classes in the schools, educating children about drug abuse. So this was a most interesting day. I think that this will be beneficial for me, just to help keep my mind active.

Maybe I won't get senile very soon. I hope.

## 13 Mar 2001 - Visiting Aunt Pearl

1 used to really love to visit at my Aunt Pearl's house. She lived in Swannanoa, and she and Uncle Tom worked for many years at the mill where they made blankets. They always treated me just like they treated their own daughters, and I knew that I was welcome there. They had four daughters. Three were older that I was, and one was about eight months younger. Their house was never dull or boring. I loved playing with these cousins. Sometimes the youngest one and I would go into the woods and make us a playhouse by spreading rocks around the area that we chose for our house. And there was plenty of moss to use for carpet. We could even make cups to drink from by folding a leaf a certain way. Someone told us that crawfish had pearls in their heads, so we spent some time looking for pearls, but even though we killed several crawfish, we never found a pearl. I loved it when all five of us would go up on this hill called the cow knoll. Some people kept cows there. There were grapevines there, a little like the ones that Tarzan swung on. These were great fun, and we spent a lot of time swinging on them. The oldest girl would always carry a knife with her, just in case any of us got bitten by a snake. So we felt very safe, and knew that Hazel would take care of us. She loved taking care of people and later became a nurse. On Friday nights, Aunt Pearl would go to the grocery store after work, and we would always have hot dogs. They were always good, just as everything was at Aunt Pearl's house. Well, Uncle Tom died many years ago, but we still have Aunt Pearl. She is now ninety years old and still has a sense of humor, even though she had to sell her house a year or so ago, and go to live with her youngest daughter. She doesn't see well anymore, but she can still enjoy the Atlanta Braves' baseball games on television. She is a really unique person, and has always

been like a mother to me.

## 14 Mar 2001 - The Café

    Mother worked for a year or two at a café owned by a Greek man we called Mr. Tom. I spent a good deal of time there. Mother would have me come there and have something to eat very often, and I always enjoyed that. One Sunday, Mr. Tom invited our family to have lunch there with him, even though the café was closed on Sundays. I remember that meal. It was Greek food and it was delicious. I liked Mr. Tom, although sometimes he was a little gruff, and I remember he ate raw garlic everyday, so that he really had a strong odor about him. One really humorous thing that happened at the café was the day that this man who often ate there came in and ordered a piece of pie. When it was placed on the counter, he picked it up and ate it from his hand, rather than to use his fork. Mother knew him, and teased him about this, asking him if he had been raised in a barn. (She really felt bad when she found out that his mother had died when he was very small, and that he had not had a good upbringing.) But here's the good part of the story. Soon after Mother teased him about the way he ate his pie, I came in. He offered to buy me a piece of pie, and when I got it I picked it up and ate it just the way he had done. He had a good laugh, and Mother was really embarrassed.

## 15 Mar 2001 - Puerto Rico

    When I was married to my first husband, we traveled a lot, because he was in the Marine Corps. The first big trip was when our first child was only four months old. He went ahead, then sent for us to join him. This was so exciting for me, but it was terrible for my mother to see her only child and only grandchild board the plane to go so far away. On the flight from Miami to San Juan, P.R., the flight attendant demonstrated how to use the life jackets. I was sure that we were going to crash, and they were preparing us. I couldn't imagine how I could protect my little baby in the water. It was a really frightening time. (I later learned that they always showed this when the flight is over water.) But we made it safely, and I was so glad to see my husband meeting me at the airport. But I soon realized that he had been drinking, and this was to continue for the rest of our marriage. But anyway, It was interesting to see Puerto Rico, and we stayed there for two years. I was able to come home once for a visit at Christmas, and Mother came to visit us once for about two weeks. I made a few good friends there, two of whom I'm still in touch with. One lives in Deer Park, N.Y., and the other lives near St. Petersburg, Fl. Now this has been about forty-seven years ago, and I think it's remarkable to stay in touch for that long and to remain friends. Puerto Rico is a beautiful island with the nicest beaches and the most wonderful flowers. But there were also lizards of all different sizes. The little ones might be on the screen of the porch or maybe even in the house, but you get used to them. They actually get kind of cute. I didn't get to do a lot of things there, but we did get to come back on a Navy ship. A few of our friends saw us off, and two of them were crying. This was a mother and a daughter who were really devoted to Paulette, and wished they could have her. (She really was an adorable little girl with her pretty eyes and blond curly hair.) We sailed to New York City, saw the Statue of Liberty, spent the night, then came to Charlotte by train the next day. I always thought that I would like to go back to PR someday as a visitor, and I got to do just that about three years ago. Our nephew and his wife were living there due to his work, so my granddaughter, Hannah, and I went down to visit them. We stayed for four or five days and we had a wonderful time. Debbie was the greatest hostess, and planned so many interesting things for us to do. We pretty much stayed busy. I got to see more than I had seen in the two years I had lived there. The development where I had lived was gone and seemingly forgotten. But that was an adventure for sure.

## 16 Mar 2001 - A Few of the Things I've Learned

I've been thinking a lot lately about many of the little things that happened during my childhood. Since I started writing in this diary, I keep trying to remember as many of these events as I can, so I'll have something to talk about. A couple of the things I've had on my mind today are kind of funny, so I'll recall how I've learned a few things by personal experience. I got a bicycle when I was about ten years old and I was determined to learn to ride it the next day, even though there was no one to help me. So I tried and fell, and tried and fell, until I finally was able to balance myself. And by the time my parents came home, I was skinned nearly from head to toe, but I could ride that bicycle. From that experience I learned that it is probably better to wait until there is someone to help you with learning to ride a bike. At least, it would have saved me a lot of falling. I learned another good lesson around that time. I had a nice cat named Dixie, and I decided one day that she needed a bath. So I proceeded to give her one. Boy, was that a battle! Even though she was nice, she scratched me all over my arms and hands, in self defense. When my parents came home that day, they were shocked to see how badly scratched I was, and they explained that cats are afraid of water, and that they keep themselves clean. I've never forgotten that lesson. There was a man who lived about two blocks from us who had two monkeys, one named Jacob, one named Beulah. He kept them outside in a cage, and I liked to go and watch them. One day I went with a couple of other children, and we teased Beulah. I know we didn't hurt her, but I remember we gave her some bubble gum that one of us had chewed, and we laughed at the way she played with it, stretching it out and then chewing it. It was really funny. Well, the man took Jacob out of the cage and I asked if I could hold him, and he handed Jacob to me. Boy, that monkey bit my finger and wouldn't turn loose. It felt like he had bitten all the way through. The man finally got him to turn loose. We couldn't figure out what caused him to bite me, unless he was mad because we had teased and laughed at Beulah. Since then I haven't held a monkey. I learned the hard way how hard they can bite. Well, those are just a few little unimportant things I've remembered, but maybe my grandchildren will get a laugh one day from this entry, and maybe they will even learn from my mistakes.

## 17 Mar 2001 - My First Chinese Food

When I was about ten or eleven years old, a man named Mr. Brown became a friend of our family. I don't know where he came from or anything about him. It seems like he might have stayed at our house for a while. But the big thing I remember was that he took Mother and me out to eat at a Chinese restaurant, called The Oriental. This was such an adventure to me that I still think about it, even after fifty-five years have gone by. I think that was the only time in my whole childhood that I ever got to eat at a nice restaurant. Well, I was allowed to choose what I wanted, and I chose chicken chow mein with almonds. It was delicious. But now I practically never go to a Chinese restaurant. I don't think it could ever quite compare to that time at the Oriental. Well, this is short but it's late, and I must sign off.

## 18 Mar 2001 - Another Small Memory

One day after school! when I was in the first grade, this little girl who was very timid asked me if I would walk home with her. I told her I didn't want to, and she told me that she was afraid of this dog who lived near her. She held out her hand and offered me a penny if I would walk with her. Well this really got to me. I felt so sorry for her that I walked her home and didn't take the penny. It's strange how little things like that can stick in your memory and you don't know why. But I've always been so glad that I helped her. I don't remember her asking me again, so I don't know what happened to the dog. That same year, I had a birthday party. It was one of only two I ever had. I was seven and the only guests I remember were three of my cousins; Nancy, Terry, and Mary Faye. I remember Daddy took us all for a walk in the woods,and that was a real adventure. Then we had cake and lemonade. Terry was about five years old, and he got really upset and cried because he thought he didn't get as much lemonade as the rest of us. That put a damper on the party, but it is still a nice memory of mine. Just a small thing.

## 19 Mar 2001 - Another SALT Session

Today I went for my third class of study to be a SALT volunteer. It is interesting to hear about how the sheriff's department works, and to meet these interesting speakers. We heard talks about crime prevention, communications, criminal histories, the civil bureau, traffic safety, and school resource officers. I can't begin to grasp or remember all that I heard, but I did get a pretty good overview, something to build on. I don't know if I told this before, but we will get to ride a shift with a deputy. As one of my granddaughters would say, "How cool is that?" And I didn't know until today that the school resource officers work directly with the students, helping them to understand the consequences of breaking the law, and also letting the students see that officers are real people and can be their friends. They also help to keep the schools safer, and we all know how vital that is nowadays. They even sponsor a graduation party, which can provide safe entertainment for the students. Well, I believe that "Honey" asked in a comment if I knew whether other counties and states had programs like this one. I asked about that today, and they thought that some had similar things but possibly by other titles. So I would just recommend that you contact your local sheriffs department, and see what they have available for volunteers. One of our speakers today talked about the number of motorcycles in use in the county. I told him that I really hope that our ride along with a deputy wouldn't be with one on a motorcycle, because I rode on one about fifty years ago, and I decided that if I got off of it alive, I wouldn't get on another one. One of our speakers gave us a test afterwards, and it consisted of riddles, so funny. For example, Johnny's mother had three children, the first was named April, the second was named May. What was the third one's name? Another one was, Can a man in California legally marry his widow's sister? I think there were twelve questions, and who do you think answered them all correctly? Only one, yours truly. So I had a very successful day.

## 20 Mar 2001 - Golly

He's my uncle, and we've always called him Golly. His name is really Clifford, but when he was a young boy he loved to hold his sisters down and make them say "Golly." Now in their family, this was close to a curse word. Their father was an itinerant preacher, and very strict. But they started calling him Golly after that. I don't know whether they let their father hear it or not. Golly and his younger brother Billy were the two youngest boys in a big family of ten children. One sister was younger than they were. One time Golly and Billy decided to cut off a grasshopper's head, and Billy had to hold the victim on the chopping block while Golly swung the axe. Well, Billy got the end of his finger cut off. What a funny pair they must have been. Years later, after Golly was married and had one child, my parents and I stayed with them for awhile, maybe six months or so. They were so good to me, and I loved to work with Golly in the barn, shelling dried corn. This was rough on a little seven year old's hands, so someone gave me a pair of heavy work gloves for Christmas. I sure was glad to get them. I remember Mother made Golly a purple hood to keep his head warm, and he wore it proudly, although I thought it looked funny. Then the war started and Golly joined the Navy, and Billy joined the Army. They both came home safe and sound, for which we were so thankful. I wrote a while back about Billy's death not too long after he got back, but I'll save writing more about him for another time. Well Golly has worked so hard all of his life and never had much, but I think he has been pretty happy. He and my aunt raised three children. His oldest daughter wrote me yesterday that his driver's license will expire in April, when he will be 82 years old. His son has taken him to take the test twice and both times he has failed to pass it. He told my aunt that it seemed like every time he sat down, his mind went blank. He just couldn't identify the signs. So he says he won't try anymore. That is probably for the best, but it seems so sad to me when I think about that young and happy man he used to be. I love him, and I hope he can adjust to this new phase of his life. Maybe there will be lots of happy days for him yet. I think he deserves it.

## 22 Mar 2001 - Uncle Bill

I want to tell about my uncle Bill. Now this is not Billy, who was my mother's brother, and whom I've talked about some before. This is my dad's brother, the baby of the family. I would assume that he was petted as a child, and possibly not disciplined much, because of the way he lived his life. But he was always special to me, kind of like a big brother. I think he was only about twelve years older than I, but in actuality he acted about the same age. I don't really think he ever grew up. Well, he slipped off and married a woman with a bad reputation who was about thirty-five, when he was only sixteen. Needless to say, that didn't work out. I think Grandma got it annulled. Then, not too long after that he joined the Navy, I think to avoid being drafted into the Army. He couldn't stand this kind of life, so he kept going A.W.O.L. They would always find him at home, and take him back and lock him up in the brig. As soon as he would get out, he'd come back home. I guess they finally gave up on him, and they discharged him. Now please don't think too hard of him, just remember his background, and his youth. He was always my buddy. He would come to our apartment often to visit with me. I remember when I was probably twelve or thirteen, he would buy the sheet music to some popular song and bring it to me, and we would enjoy singing together, although he couldn't carry a tune. It was fun. And if we got hungry we would toast some slices of bread in the frying pan. What a treat that was. We were two children playing together in a way. One special memory I have was when Grandma was staying with us for awhile. This one day Bill was there too, asleep. Well, Grandma got mad at me and really embarrassed me in front of one of my girlfriends. Bill heard all of this and he raised up and said, "Aw Mom, leave her alone." This probably sounds so small and unimportant, but it meant so much to me, that he would take up for me against his own mother. I never forgot that. Well, Bill married again not too long after that, to a woman who adored him. She had Polio as a young girl, and had one leg that was shrunken and short. She always wore a brace, yet she was strong and worked hard. They had one son, and soon after, Bill's health began to fail him. He had trouble breathing, and many health problems. He died at the age of fifty-three or fifty-four, I think. But he still lives in my memory, almost a Peter Pan, always young and boyish. I really enjoyed and loved him.

## 23 Mar 2001 - I Love Baseball

Daddy loved baseball, and went to see it as often as possible. Charlotte has a basketball team named the Hornets, but when I was sixteen, our baseball team was the Charlotte Hornets. I was not the least bit interested in seeing a game, but Daddy said he wanted to take me for my birthday. I hated to hurt his feelings by refusing to go, so I went with him. And it was fantastic! I quickly learned to love the game and all the players. I even went by myself on the Fourth of July and had a ball. One of my favorites hit a grand slam homerun, and I cheered my head off. But after that season, I didn't get to go anymore, and soon lost interest in the game. Except for the World Series every year. But that wasn't as good as when you follow one team and know all the players. Well, after Daddy died and Mother broke her hip, I stayed with her for awhile at night, and began to watch the Atlanta Braves on television. This was Daddy's favorite team, and Mother enjoyed watching them, too. Well, pretty soon I was totally taken with the Braves. I learned all the players, and never wanted to miss a game. So now for about ten years I have considered myself to be their number one fan. They are all my boys. And a few years back when they won the World Series, I was absolutely thrilled! Last Spring, Irving and I went down to Kissimee, Florida, and saw two of their exhibition games. That was really exciting. Well, their season opens on April 2nd, and I am ready. I so hope this will be a great year for them and for me. Go Braves!

## 25 Mar 2001 - Put Off The Bus

This was a very, very embarrassing experience. I think I was probably nine or ten years old. Daddy and I went to the bus station, got our tickets, and headed for Statesville to visit relatives. Daddy was pretty drunk, and after we got about five or ten miles out of town the driver stopped the bus and made us get off. Daddy was causing some kind of disturbance, but I can't remember what he was doing. It's a terrible feeling to get put off a bus. We started walking back towards Charlotte, and very soon a police car stopped and picked us up. This really scared me, but Daddy was pretty belligerent, and when the police asked me where we lived, Daddy said,"Don't tell them a d..... thing." Well, I was afraid not to tell them, so I did. They dropped me off at the corner near where we lived, and took Daddy on to jail. Instead of going on home, I walked all the way across town to where my mother was working and told her what happened. I guess they let Daddy out the next day after he sobered up, and I doubt if he ever remembered what happened that day. He had a terrible time with alcohol for many years and ruined his health. I really do feel sorry for the way he wasted so much of his life. He was gifted in many ways but never realized his potential. It's sad.

## 26 Mar 2001 - Another SALT Class

Today was our last class, and it really was interesting. Our speakers talked about gun laws and permits, the jail, and juvenile procedures. It's probably different in each state, but in our state you need a permit to buy a handgun. It only costs $5.00. To get a permit to carry a concealed weapon is much more expensive and complicated. It costs $90.00 plus you have to take a gun safety course, which costs about $100.00. I'd feel better if 1 knew other people weren't carrying concealed weapons. I learned a lot about the jail, too. The deputy who is watching the prisoners must see each individual twice each hour. They must clean their own cell each morning, and they have the opportunity to go outside three times each week. The cooking is contracted out to a food service, and it is done there at the jail. There is a canteen available to them if they have money, where they can buy candy or chips or soft drinks, lots of snacks. Visitors can leave money for their use at the desk, when they sign in. The juvenile procedures deal with all children who are involved in crimes plus the children who have been victims of abuse, either sexual or physical, and those who have been neglected. I think these officers have a terribly stressful and often heartbreaking job. Well, we will have our graduation next Monday at a local restaurant, and I'm really looking forward to it. Then I'll be ready to do some volunteer work. This should be very interesting. By the way, I think I told you last week about the little fun test we had, and that I was the only one who knew all the answers. Well, today I was presented with a nice travel mug with a sheriff's badge on it. I'm proud of that. Sometimes it pays to be good with silly riddles.

## 27 Mar 2001 - I Enjoyed Charlotte

When I was a child living in Charlotte, there were so many things to do. I really liked to get on a city bus and ride to the end of the line and back. I believe it cost seven cents, but I can't remember if I had to pay for the return trip. I don't much think I did. But this was a real adventure for a child, and I always did this alone. Another thing I always enjoyed was window shopping. Mother and I would often walk uptown on Sunday afternoons and just go from store to store looking in all the windows. Of course, the stores were all closed on Sundays. There was one large store, Ivey's, which always covered its windows with curtains or some kind of cloth to prevent window shopping on Sundays. I remember one year during the Christmas holidays when there was a contest where you had to guess a lot of song titles, and each store would have a spot in their window with clues for a particular song. That was fun to try to guess them all. But

I never hear of anything like that anymore. And Charlotte is so different now. I don't think there is any shopping there now, because everyone prefers the malls. But I remember how it used to be, and I really loved it.

## 28 Mar 2001 - Responses to Comments

I wanted to respond to a couple of comments I received recently. One of them was from WWI, and I don't know where to answer him, except here. He asked me what I remember about a few different aspects of World War II. Well in my entry for February 28, I talked about that as I remembered it. So if you are interested, WWII, I'd love for you to read it. But as for the handsome guys at the USO, I only know about them through the movies. I was eleven when the war ended. Thanks so much for leaving a comment. And Honey left a comment which I think merits a reply. It concerned abuse by a father towards a mother. Yes, Honey, that is a hard thing for a little child to deal with. I've experienced a lot of that as a child, and I may talk about it at some point. But I feel a little bad to write down things like that. I've said a good bit about Daddy drinking, but I'm not ready to say how he treated my mother. Because I feel sorry for him, when I think about him as an old man, and I know he wished he could go back and change things. He did so much for my children, always buying them toys and candy and taking them places. And I always knew he was trying to make up for what he failed to do for me. If I know my heart, I have forgiven him a long time ago. But one can't ever really forget.

## 29 Mar 2001 - Scary Things

I don't understand this, but as a child I enjoyed scary movies, and I'm sure I saw all of them that came to Charlotte. There was Dracula, Frankenstein, The Wolf Man, and some about people being turned into zombies. And I usually went to these alone and often at night. Then I'd walk home in terror. I remember one of the Wolf Man movies had a person dressed up to look like him who would run out from behind the stage and continue up and down the aisles. This was just too much for me, and I got down in the floor under my seat and stayed there until I knew he was gone. In the process, I even tore a button off my coat. I was scared to death, but would you believe I went back to see it another day? And one of the apartments we lived in then was about half a block off the main street I walked on, which was better lit. And there were bushes all along the sidewalk. Well, when I turned onto my street after seeing these movies, I would panic and start running down the middle of the street. 1 wouldn't have dared get next to those bushes in the darkness. And once I started to run, I could just feel some kind of monster gaining on me. And after I got inside, I wouldn't dare to look at a window, for fear that something might be looking at me. Then I would sleep with my head under the covers. I don't know how I breathed. It sure makes no sense to me that anyone could enjoy that sort of thing. I certainly couldn't stand it now. The last thing I watched that was scary was years ago. Jami and I watched a movie called "Carrie," and that scared me at the end so badly that I screamed. So I'm all through with that, thank goodness.

## 30 Mar 2001 - Extra Innings

I just finished watching a Braves game which lasted for 12 innings, and the Indians won the game at last. But I was still so glad to see my team after so long. I am so excited that the season will begin for the Braves on Monday. But the game lasted so long that it's time to go to bed, but I'm determined to write something every day if I can, at least for awhile. Yesterday was a big day for me. I got my driver's license renewed, and this time it is good for five years. I always get a little nervous when I have to identify the signs, even though I did study them earlier, but I didn't miss any. What a relief. Well, I hope I didn't bore any one too much tonight. Maybe tomorrow I'll come up with something interesting to tell.

## 31 Mar 2001 - Ladies' Jubilee

A church in our county held their third annual Ladies' Jubilee today. It is for women and girls from sixth grade and up, and it is a wonderful event. I've been to all three of them. There is a goodie bag given to everyone who comes, and I am like a child with that. We had all kinds of neat little presents, like notepads, pencils and pens, kleenex, shower caps, magnets, samples of hand lotion, calendars, etc. Then during the program there was some really good music, a lovely older lady who was the speaker. She talked about Martha and Mary who were friends of Jesus, and the difference in their priorities. You may remember how Martha was busy preparing the meal when Jesus visited their home. When she realized that her sister Mary was sitting at the feet of Jesus, listening to him, it made her a little angry. Jesus considered that Mary was doing a good thing. Our speaker said that Martha put work first, and Mary put worship first. Something to think about. Then a lot of prizes were given away. I won something, a birdhouse, and my granddaughter, Hannah, won a nice fancy tin of nuts. They gave away many donated items and this was fun for everybody. After that, there was a fabulous meal, with barbecue, marinated turkey, fried chicken and all the trimmings. Plus a great variety of wonderful desserts. So it was a very special afternoon. I'm already looking forward to the next Ladies' Jubilee.

## 1 Apr 2001 - Mary Faye

I like to tell about different relatives from time to time, because every one has a story that I find interesting. So this is about my cousin, Mary Faye. She was an only child like me, and we often played together when I was a child in Statesville. Most of the time we got along fine, but I remember a few times when we couldn't agree on what to play and she would go home mad. She lost her father when she was about nine years old, so it was just her and her mother alone after that, but her mother did a wonderful job raising her. She grew up to be a lovely young woman, with a great personality. Everyone loved her. Here's an example of her sweet nature: When I was pregnant with my first child at the age of eighteen, she came to visit us at my parents' home. Daddy wanted to take us to a ballgame, and I was embarrassed to go wearing a maternity smock. Well Mary Faye told me to get her one of my smocks and she put it on and wore it to the ballgame so that I wouldn't feel self-conscious. After that we often laughed about what people must have thought about Daddy bringing two pregnant girls with him to the game. She married a very special young man when she was about nineteen, and they seemed to always have a great relationship. They had three sons, and after they were born, she decided to go back to school. I believe she went for two years to a junior college in Statesville, then for two years she drove back and forth to Charlotte until she got her degree and became a teacher. She was a great teacher and loved it. After a few years, she was attacked by cancer, first a spot on her upper leg, later a bout with leukemia, which was arrested after a terrible fight. Then it attacked her lungs. Over the next few years, she had three lung surgeries and so much chemotherapy that her heart was damaged. She fought that cancer so bravely, and showed so much faith in God, she was an inspiration to me and to countless others who knew her. She died nearly two years ago, and in one sense she lost her battle, but in reality she won a great prize. Her suffering is all over now, and I am fully convinced that she is now happy in Heaven. But I really miss her. She and I were so much like sisters. I was so proud of her.

## 2 Apr 2001 - SALT Graduation!

Today was our graduation day. We met at a local restaurant and had a really special lunch. I enjoyed the fellowship with the other volunteers. After lunch, we were presented with certificates of graduation, and the sheriff spoke to us. He really appreciates our group. I signed up to work this coming Thursday morning, and I'm looking forward to learning more. I hope to be a big help to the department before very long. We have really had a beautiful day today, very Spring-like. I feel so thankful that I was able to enjoy it. I realize that many people are shut in and unable to do the things they would love to do. So I need to remember to always be grateful to God for special blessings. A small group of folks from my church began to deliver "meals on wheels" a few months ago, and this has been such a blessing to us. And it has made us all aware of how wonderful it is to be able to drive and do the things that we want to do. One day we may be on the receiving end, and shut in, so for now we want to be as much help as we can to these dear people. One of them is 100 years old, and she still has a good mind, but she can't see well any more. But she has a sweet spirit, and it's always good to see her. Well I guess that's enough for tonight.

## 3 Apr 2001 - Mother Loved To Fly

Mother always was fascinated by airplanes. For a while, when I was very young, she and Daddy both took flying lessons. We would all go to this small airport for them to take their lessons, and I even got to take a ride once or twice. It was really nice. Mother was about ready to fly solo, when she quit taking the lessons. I never knew why she quit, but it was probably because she didn't have the money. But she would have loved to be a pilot. She flew down to Puerto Rico to visit me once and enjoyed the trip. Then many years after that, when she was probably about 60 years old, Irving gave her a trip to Bermuda. He was a York Heating and Air Conditioning dealer and he used to earn trips now and then. He let Mother go in his place with me, and she was delighted. This was during a time when she had no income, a year or so before she began to draw social security. Her job had been done away with at Swift and Company. So when we went to the airport, she had no spending money. Irving handed her forty dollars, and that was a wonderful moment. It added so much pleasure to the trip and she of course bought gifts for everybody. That meant so much to me when Irving gave her that money. But she enjoyed the flight and every day of our time in Bermuda. She and I always enjoyed each other's company. But after that trip, she never wanted to fly again. I think she got scared of it. But it is a precious memory for me.

## 4 Apr 2001 - A Few More Pleasant Memories

When I was around nine or ten years old, there were two men who came to our neighborhood regularly and added fun to the day for the children. One of them was the man from the cleaners. He delivered dry cleaning and laundry in a panel truck. All of us were always glad when he stopped near our houses, because he was always willing to entertain us, with his ventriloquy. He would open the back of his truck and throw his voice so that the packages of laundry seemed to be talking to him. This always delighted all the children. He was really kind to do that, I thought. Then there was the ice man. He would stop and cut big blocks of ice for every house or apartment where it was ordered. I remember that we had a sign of some sort to put in the window when we needed ice. Well, this man would give us small chunks of ice every time he stopped and what a treat this was on a hot day. It is so pleasant to remember the people who were nice to me and the other children.

## 5 Apr 2001 - Two Very Interesting Hours

I went to the sheriffs department today to observe the work in the console. I had no idea how busy this office is. The dispatcher was amazing. He could keep up with one phone call after another, while answering communications from the deputies. They contact him about checking on people's driver's licenses, and about whether a person might have an outstanding warrant against him. He then gets on the computer and pulls up all kinds of information, then passes it on to the deputy who requested it. And all this time there are people coming to the window, to get a gun permit or to see someone who works there, or various things. Then there are faxes coming in that he has to get to the right person. I don't think I'd want his job. Too stressful. But he is great at it. I only stayed for two hours today, but I hope to go back soon for two more hours, then I'll be ready to ride with a deputy. I expect that to really be awesome!

## 6 Apr 2001 - Special Times With Children

I was thinking yesterday about something that my grandma used to do for me that I enjoyed so much. She used snuff which she bought in large cans, then she would put a small amount in a small can to carry in her apron pocket to use for that day. Sometimes she would mix a spoonful of cocoa with some sugar and put it in a small snuff can for me. This was a wonderful treat for me. It was delicious snuff, and I remember it so clearly. And this memory made me think of a little tradition which my granddaughter, Lauren, and I used to enjoy together. I have this beautiful small china tea-set which my daughter, Jami, gave me. And I often made hot tea using this set just for Lauren and me. She was so cute sipping her tea and chatting with me. She was probably around four or five when we started doing this. I've never really liked hot tea much, but it was a pleasure to sip it with Lauren. And I hope that maybe she will think about those times after she is grown, and enjoy the special memories.

## 7 Apr 2001 - His Eye is on the Sparrow

I've thought a lot of times about telling of some close calls I had as a very young girl, about some of the sexual perverts I came in contact with. I've hesitated about whether it would be in poor taste to talk about ugly things like that, but I decided to write about a few incidents. And I have a definite purpose in mind. More than once I had some man to sit beside me at the movies with bad ideas. I always managed to dodge them. Once I went out and got an usher and told him about what this man had done. He went down the aisle with me and I spotted the man in another seat and pointed him out. The usher asked him to come out to the lobby, and when I confronted him, he of course denied all of it. I was crying when I told him that if I ever saw him again and if my mother was with me, he would be sorry. But an even more close call happened one night when I was at the café where Mother worked. We lived just about two or three blocks away from the café, and when I was ready to walk home, this man offered to walk with me. Mother and I thought it was nice of him, we had no clue that he was really evil. When we got to my house, I told him thanks and started to go inside. He asked if he could go inside with me and I said I didn't want him to. I didn't know anything about things like that, except that it was ugly. He kept on until I was really scared and I just hurried into the house and got away from him, and locked the door. I told Mother about this later and she was furious. The man had the audacity to go back to the café another night, and Mother told him off. I never saw him again, thank goodness. Probably the worst time of all was when Daddy had brought this man that we didn't know home with him. He and Daddy had been drinking together and Daddy used very poor judgment. I don't know where the man was supposed to sleep, but we all went to bed. After awhile, I woke up to find this pervert in my bed and with his hand on my leg. I was so scared I didn't know what to do, so I just quickly rolled over and fell out of the bed, jumped right up and hurried to my parents' bed. This was not unusual, because I had always gone to their bed if I had a bad dream. So I slept there the rest of the night, and in the morning he was gone. I never told Mother or Daddy about that. I was too embarrassed. I don't think I've ever told anyone about that as far as I can remember. It was so ugly. But I said at the beginning that I had a definite purpose in writing about these things, and there were more, but I think I've told enough for now. Here is my purpose: I want to give God the glory for protecting me from these terrible men. I didn't understand much, but God was always there for me. There's a beautiful song that says, "His eye is on the sparrow, and I know He watches me." And I just want to thank Him tonight.

## 8 Apr 2001 - My Uncle James

I don't remember telling about my uncle James. He was never wild nor into any mischief. He was just a good honorable man. He was the only one of my daddy's family to finish high school. That made everyone proud of him. He never, to my knowledge, smoked a cigarette or drank any alcoholic beverage. He joined the Navy during World War II, and served honorably and well. He was a radioman and good at it. After the war, he came home and married a wonderful girl. They had a son and a daughter, and a good life together. He had a long career with the Post Office, from which he retired a good many years ago. It seemed like a fairy tale life until Parkinson's Disease struck him about sixteen years ago, and that terrible sickness has nearly destroyed him. It made him an old man rather quickly, and it has been so sad to see him this way. And now he is in a hospital bed in his home and has to be cared for like a baby. His joints seem to be frozen, and if he tries to say a word, it is almost impossible to understand him. It appears that he still has his mind, but that just makes it more tragic. His wife, Mary, is absolutely precious. She loves him and never complains, but I know her life is so hard. James is eighty years old now, and I'm very proud of him. Inside, he is still that good honorable man that I remember.

## 9 Apr 2001 - A Few Fun Things

I used to live very near the railroad tracks and the train station, so I spent a lot time playing on the tracks. I loved to walk on the rails and pretend I was walking a tightrope, and I would run on the crossties, usually skipping over every other one. And it was fun to stand at the station and watch a train go by. If you stand very still, it feels like you are moving instead of the train. And there was a large cemetery just a little ways past the tracks and I enjoyed going there pretty often to play. But there was one monument that was tall with a head in the top part of it, and if I looked at it, I imagined that it was looking at me and following me with it's eyes. I don't know how many times this happened, but every time it would scare me and I would run as fast as I could til I was away from that cemetery. For some reason, I would go back again and again. I guess it was fun to be scared. And one other thing that I really enjoyed was this man who used to come and sit near my front yard on Saturdays and play a banjo. The unique thing about him was that he only had one arm. He had a contraption rigged up where he could press the strings with his shoulder, and pluck the banjo with his one hand. Passers-by would give him money, and I just loved to sit there beside him and watch him and ask him questions. He was always nice to me, always patient with my questions. So these were just a few things that I enjoyed as a child. It was kind of fun growing up in Charlotte.

## 10 Apr 2001 - The Salvation Army

I have some very fond memories of the Salvation Army. When I was between eight and twelve, we lived near their building. (I don't know whether it would be called a church or a temple or headquarters.) The people there were so kind and a child was always welcome. They used to wear uniforms, sort of military-looking, and the women wore bonnets tied under the chin. They were often seen on street corners singing and preaching, and I always admired them. I don't know what it is like now, but I used to go there a lot. They would teach the children how to play instruments, and I chose a very large horn. I only tried long enough to learn how to get the sound to come out, then gave up. They had a club for children called the Red Shield Club, and everyone was welcome. There was an indoor pool, and we all loved that. And I was a member of the Sunbeams and had a special uniform-type dress. I remember once they gave all the children gifts for Christmas, the girls all got dolls, and I was delighted with mine. Once we were out of coal to heat our apartment, and Daddy asked them for help, and they gave him a bag a coal. I've remembered these things for a long time, and even though I am a Baptist fully committed to my church, I'll always have a special spot in my heart for the Salvation Army. That's where I was when the news came out that President Roosevelt had died. Lots of people there were crying. It seemed he was well loved. Well, I just wanted to compliment this group for their kindness, and I wish them well.

## 10 Apr 2001 - I Nearly Forgot

Today is Jami's birthday, and I think she has had a good day. She really deserves the best. Happy birthday, Jami. I'm proud of you.

## 11 Apr 2001 - China is not our Friend

During World War II, China was our friend and Japan was our enemy. Now that is totally reversed. Strange, isn't it? China is now a place where people are treated badly, and baby girls are often thrown away, or raised in places where they get very little attention or kindness. I don't understand why China was given "favored nation" status. And I don't understand why we do any business with them. I'm so glad that our people who have been detained for the last several days are being sent home, but now I think we should break all ties with these Communists. We have nothing in common with them. They are not our friends any more, and we might as well face that fact.

## 12 Apr 2001 - Still Thinking of China

Yesterday I talked about the fact that China is not our friend, and Jami pointed out in her comment that I might have given the impression that I didn't care for the Chinese people. I appreciated the comment, because I wouldn't want anyone to think that I dislike the Chinese people in general. I should have made that clear in the first place. What I really hate is that the people are being oppressed and that women are being forced to either have abortions or to get rid of their babies, after the first one. I saw a television program about two years ago, I think, which showed how badly some babies were being treated in the orphanages there. If I remember right, these were unwanted little girls. I saw how they were seated on potty seats, and strapped in them for the main part of the days, so as not to have to change diapers. And when one of them got very sick, they would be placed in a separate room and left there to die alone, with no help or comfort given. This is so outrageous and I don't know anything we can do about it, short of declaring war on them. And of course, war would be horrible too. I can't remember much more about that program, but it really showed how heartless the government is over there. I really wish there was a way to help these people. I hope I haven't offended anyone with this entry, but this was on my mind.

## 13 Apr 2001 - Mustard Sandwiches

My firstborn, Paulette, was always a very finicky eater. When she was in first grade, her school had no cafeteria, so I had to send her lunch every day. The only kind of sandwich she would eat was a mustard sandwich. I wanted her to eat something else so badly that sometimes I would put some kind of meat in her sandwich, hoping that maybe she would be hungry enough to eat something different, but that never worked. She would just bring it back home in the afternoon. So I just finally accepted the fact that she wouldn't eat anything else, and she did need something to eat, so I quit trying to change her mind. Well, one year at Vacation Bible School, they were going to have a picnic lunch, and they asked all the children to bring a sandwich. I naturally fixed Paulette a mustard sandwich. When the children arrived, they were instructed to put their sandwiches on a large table. Paulette didn't much like that, but had no choice. Later, all the children got a sandwich from the table, and of course Paulette didn't get her own back. She got a normal type of sandwich which she absolutely would not eat. I later overheard a mother telling someone that her child got a sandwich that had nothing on it but mustard. I was a little embarrassed, but said nothing. This has always been a funny little story for our family. Paulette, do you still like mustard sandwiches?

## 14 Apr 2001 - I Never Got Enough

So many of my memories have to do with food. I wonder if this means anything. I was thinking tonight about how I never got enough dumplings. Mother said I used to say that I could eat a dumpling a mile long. And I never got enough of my daddy's fudge. He really could make the best fudge I've ever tasted, and he'd never let me eat all that I wanted. He said it would make me sick. Boy, I wish I could have some of that now, but I don't know anyone who can make it like Daddy did, and his recipe was all in his head, never written down. One more thing I couldn't get enough of as a child was watermelon. I remember holding it in my hands, and burying my face in it, and just letting the juice run down off my elbows. It sure made for sticky arms, hands, and faces but that never bothered me. I loved it, and I still do, but it isn't quite as good with a fork. And now I can have all I want of dumplings and watermelon, but never of my daddy's fudge.

## 15 Apr 2001 - Easter Sunday

This has been a special day. We had a sunrise service at church. I always love these. I think we had about sixty people there. Afterwards, we had breakfast together. Then at the usual time, we had Sunday School and worship service, which was most enjoyable. I was delighted with the song Jami sang, He's Alive. She printed the words to the song in her diary this morning and it has an incredible message. Well, Easter is such a wonderful time when we remember that Jesus won the victory over death for us. And I want to share another precious Easter memory with you. My daughter, Paulette was an only child for a long time and she wanted a baby sister more than anything in the world. Well, on the Easter Sunday when she was about nine-and-a-half, she received Jesus as her Savior. And on the following Easter, we brought her little sister home from the hospital. Some will say that this was simply a coincidence, but in my heart I accept this as an evidence from God that Paulette's prayers were heard and answered. And it was beautiful to see the love that she had for Jami. Even though she had been the only child, and the only grandchild on my side of the family, there was never even a hint of jealousy. So we often say that Paulette is the reason that Jami came to us. We have been so blessed. Thanks be to God.

## 16 Apr 2001 - A Little About Daddy

Daddy was a most unusual person. He was incredibly talented, even though he wasted most of his life. He could have been an artist if he had been given the opportunity to study. He loved to sketch scenery, like snow-capped mountains, fenced pastures, and scattered pine trees. He could have been a very good comedian, and did a good bit of that sort of thing with a traveling side show as a young man. It was hard to know how much to believe when he told of his adventures, because he often told outlandish stories. But I saw some of the special things he could do. He talked about being a good swimmer and diver, then when he was at the swimming pool with me once, he climbed up on the high diving board, and jumped into the deep water with me holding around his neck. I was impressed. He said he was a good skater, but we didn't necessarily believe that, until one day he went skating with me. He hadn't been on skates in years, but he was outstanding. He could do really unusual athletic tricks, like walking on his hands, and I've seen him hold a broomstick with one hand on each end of it and jump over it flat-footed. That really was awesome, I thought. He became a carpenter, and was an excellent one. He could have been a wealthy man if he had been able to manage his money. But drinking and gambling ruined him. He spent his money on beer and whiskey, and never was able to have much of anything else. It's a tragic thing when a person is so gifted but wastes his talent.

## 17 Apr 2001 - A Big Adventure

There's a popular talk show on the radio in Charlotte each afternoon, hosted by Richard Spires and Brad Krantz. Last Friday, I called in to the show and won a prize for answering a couple of questions. Then I learned that I would have to drive to Charlotte to pick up my prize, which was dinner for two at a new place: Chicago Dogs and Deli. It was a long trip but I just had to get what I had won. My granddaughter rode with me, and said that maybe we would get to meet Spires and Krantz. I said that I doubted it, because we would be picking up the prize at the front desk. Well, when we got there I told the receptionist how far we had come just to get the free meal which turned out to be two hot dogs, two fries, and two drinks. She felt sorry for us, and offered to take us on a tour of the station. This was really neat. She showed us where the television news was broadcast, where the weather forecasts were done, and the places where the radio programs were done. And guess who we just happened to run into. Richard Spires! And he was so friendly and showed us more things, and he took us downstairs to meet his partner, Brad Krantz. Hannah was fascinated, because to her these were real celebrities. She hears them on the radio at her home nearly every day. So this was a big adventure, and on the way back home, we stopped and ate hot dogs for free. A nice day.

## 18 Apr 2001 - The Yard Sale

My son's entry yesterday reminded me of something funny that happened about fifty-seven years ago. I went to Statesville to visit my cousins and I found that Nancy was having a sale. I don't know whether they called it a yard sale in those days but I just know that she had mainly clothes that she had outgrown all hung up to sell. It was a chilly day, and I was wearing my coat, but I really wanted to sell something too. It looked like a great way to make money. So I took off my coat and quickly sold it. I think I got about two or three dollars for it. But I was really blessed when the person I sold it to gave it back to me, and I don't remember having to give the money back. I'm not sure about that part of it, but 1 do know that Mother would not have been pleased if I had come back home without my coat. That sale was not one of my best ideas.

## 19 Apr 2001 - The Free Puppy

Today my granddaughter went to the grocery store with me, and as we started in to Bi-Lo, there was a man holding an adorable puppy. He had two more in a small cage, and he was trying to give them away. Hannah was delighted with them and wanted one so much, but didn't think her parents would let her have one. So when I took her home, I told her to go in and start begging. Well, I had been home for maybe twenty minutes when Hannah, her mother, and her two brothers appeared at my door, so excited. They just had to show me their new puppy, and it is a darling little dog. It is a mix of beagle and Jack Russell terrier. My husband raised beagles for a long time , so we know how sweet they are. And the last dog we had was a Jack Russell terrier. She was precious. So I'm fairly confident that the combination will make a nice pet. I told them that this was my new "grand-dog."

## 20 Apr 2001 - Believe it or Not

This story will sound unbelievable, but it is true. Or at least 1 saw a part of it with my own eyes. My great-grandfather was plowing and somehow the rope got twisted up around his thumb, and the mule who was pulling the plow got spooked at something. Well, this accident caused my great-grandfather to lose his thumb. That doesn't sound so eerie, does it? But here is the odd part that happened later: One of his sons was born with two thumbs on one hand. (This was my great-uncle Ernest.) As if that wasn't strange enough, another son who was my grandfather was born with two thumbs on each hand. I never knew my great-grandfather or my grandfather, but I actually saw Uncle Ernest's extra thumb. So I accepted the whole story as true. I sure can't explain it, though.

## 21 Apr 2001 - House for Sale

We are trying again to sell our other house. After trying for awhile last Summer, we rented it, and now our renters have moved after about seven or eight months. We were so glad that they left it nice and clean, but my husband has spent many hours repainting every room and having new carpet installed in the living room. So now it really looks nice and we have two possible prospects to buy it. It will be a great relief to be done with it, but in a way it seems hard, because we really loved that house for a long time. But we would like to have the money out of it. Tonight my little grandson, Alex, is spending the night with us. He really is sweet when he is here alone with us. But he does get scared in the night and usually ends up in the bed with me. So I told him I will leave the kitchen light on tonight, so maybe that will help if he wakes up. He will go to church with us in the morning and I always enjoy that. Well, it's bedtime. I hope to write again tomorrow.

## 22 Apr 2001 - Two More Overnight Guests

Last night, my grandson Alex spent the night with us, and he was so good. This morning, after breakfast, he went out for a long bike ride before church. I think he really enjoyed the visit. Now tonight, Jami's two boys are going to spend the night. We have a trundle bed in the guest room, and they just pull out the under bed and then there are two beds for them. We had popcorn awhile ago, and now they are watching television. They get along so well it's amazing, and when I tell them goodnight, I don't hear another peep out of them. So we'll do fine tonight. And Jordan usually makes up the bed without being told to. I think that's kind of remarkable.

## 23 Apr 2001 - A Long Evening

Our ladies' prayer group was invited to a dinner held in honor of volunteers at a nursing home. We went there a while back and held our devotions and Bible reading with the residents. These were mostly Alzheimer's patients, and they love to have people come to visit them. We sang several songs with them, and they nearly all joined in. It's kind of a mystery how people can lose most of their memory but they can still remember so many of the hymns they learned as youngsters. Our group is looking forward to going back soon. We were blessed by being with them. After I left the dinner, I went to the funeral home to visit with the family of a young man who killed himself Saturday night. They all used to go to our church, but something went wrong with the parents' marriage. They divorced, and later the man remarried and none of them came to our church anymore. I don't know why Jason killed himself, but I know that it broke a lot of hearts. I just pray that those parents and the two brothers can find peace about it.

## 24 Apr 2001 - Rebecca

As I was leaving the funeral home last night, I ran into a friend who works at the school where three of my grandchildren attend. She happens to be the teacher assistant in Rebecca's first grade class. I was so amused at some of Rebecca's antics, and so proud of her ability to read. My friend told me that she was reading on a third grade level, but I have to disagree with that. I would estimate that she reads on a much higher level. In fact she reads better than a lot of adults, and she understands what she reads. My friend said that Rebecca is very smart and I agree. She told me that Rebecca chose the word "acknowledgment" for her bonus word this week. Mrs M. asked her if she knew what the word meant and she said, "I'll tell you tomorrow." And the next day she gave Mrs. M. a sentence using the word. Of course, I think her parents helped a little bit, but that's fine. Rebecca's sister, Lauren, has always been an excellent reader too. I'm really proud of them. But then I'm also proud of the two precious boys in that family. They have special gifts too. Four great children!

## 25 Apr 2001 - The Journal Jar

Jami sent me a list of things that might give me some ideas of what I might write about. I read through them all, and there are a lot of good possibilities, although I've already written about a lot of these things. But one suggestion caught my attention today. It said to tell the most important word in living successfully. That was a little hard for a few moments, but then I remembered the advice my pastor gave to Irving and me just before we married. He said that the key word in building a good marriage is "consideration." It was really good advice then, and still is. If one has consideration for another's feelings and for that person's likes and dislikes, that makes a great foundation for building a marriage or a friendship or any relationship. It's a lot like the scripture which we call the Golden Rule: As ye would that men should do to you, do ye even so to them. So I choose the word "consideration" as the most important word in living successfully. It has worked well for Irving and me, because we have had a very good, strong marriage. Of course, most of the credit should go to God, because I believe that He brought us together.

## 26 Apr 2001 - My Favorite Writers

I thought I'd talk about my favorite writers. I don't know how interesting this will be to anyone, but it might give you some ideas about some books you might want to read. I have three favorites at this time: Janette Oke, Lori Wick, and Francine Rivers. Janette Oke has written several series and I love them all. The first one I read was the Love Comes Softly series. This had about eight books in it, I think. Her characters are such great people, I loved them all. My favorite book of Lori Wick's is Sophie's Heart. It is wonderful. And I love everything I've read by Francine Rivers. The first one I read was The Atonement Child, and this is an outstanding book. I nearly forgot that I have another favorite, Gilbert Morris. He wrote the Winslow series, and they are all very special. If you are looking for something wonderful to read, try one of my favorites. And I really hope you will enjoy it as much as I have.

## 27 Apr 2001 - Mother Had A Fur Coat

I have no memory of where or when Mother got it, or whether it was new or used, or what type or quality it was. I just know that Mother had a fur coat when I was around nine or ten years old. It was dark brown and so soft, it felt wonderful and warm. And she looked so beautiful in it. I remember once she came to my school to talk to my teacher about some problem, and the other girls were so impressed and I was so proud of her. We were so poor, we had almost nothing, but you would never guess that when Mother wore that fur coat. And, too, my mother was younger than most of my classmates' mothers. So I felt that they envied me, and I liked that, because I surely wasn't envied often. I remember walking uptown with Mother at night when the weather was really cold, and she would let me put my hand in her pocket as we walked. That was so nice and it was so warm, and that is a special memory of mine. I really liked that fur coat.

## 28 Apr 2001 - It Was Scary The First Time I Saw It

If you are under fifty years old, this will be hard to comprehend, but I actually remember the first time I saw television. I think I must have heard of it, but I guess I didn't really believe it. (In a way, I still can't believe it.) I went to visit neighbors one day when I was about fifteen, and when I walked into their den, they were all looking at this strange thing. When I looked at it, I saw two very fat, ugly men trying to kill each other, and they weren't even fully dressed. It was awful and scary. I'm sure you've guessed that it was wrestling that I saw. Well, it was quite a while before we had a T.V. at my home, but I don't thing I was in any hurry. I remember after that my uncle, James, got a set and my parents went to his house occasionally to watch something that was of interest to them. But at that time, the radio was still enough for me. I loved the radio. But nowadays, without a television how could I see my Atlanta Braves? What a thought!

## 29 Apr 2001 - Mother's Shoes

I thought of something really funny to share in this entry. My mother was very conscious of people's shoes. She always noticed whether shoes were clean or if they needed polishing. If a man at church was wearing dusty shoes, that really bothered her. Well, this incident took place maybe thirty years ago, when Mother was the Director of Training Union at her church. These meetings took place on Sunday nights. That particular afternoon, Mother walked around in her little garden, which was slightly muddy at the time, wearing old work shoes. Later, she freshened up and went to church. While she was standing up in front of the crowd leading the assembly program, she looked down at her feet, and she was mortified to see those old muddy shoes. This was probably one of her most embarrassing moments, but it gave us a funny story to enjoy for all these years.

## 30 Apr 2001 - One Of My Lessons

This happened between twenty-five and thirty years ago. I sat down at the counter of a drugstore to have a sandwich or something. I soon noticed a woman sitting nearby with a couple of people. I kept hearing her laughing and talking, obviously having a great time. And she was very attractive. I didn't have nearly as much self-confidence as she did, and I think I was even a little jealous of her. She just seemed to have everything that I didn't. Well, when I left the drugstore, you can imagine the shock I felt when I saw her heading for the parking lot, limping badly on an artificial leg. Then I was able to see her inner beauty that I hadn't seen before. And I was reminded of how blessed I was. There is an essay or poem that I had read years before that. It talked about a person complaining about his situation when he saw a man with no legs. He then said,"God forgive me when I whine, I have two legs. The world is mine." That was a big lesson for me. Something to think about. I often count my blessings and I thank God.

## 1 May 2001 - What A Nice Compliment

I was so excited this morning to learn that my last entry was chosen to be the entry of the week. How nice. I am really enjoying writing in DearDiary. I feel that it is helping me to sharpen my thinking, at least I hope it is. I find myself thinking more and more about the past, and trying to remember all I can, hoping it might benefit someone, or at least entertain someone. And I believe I may be gaining some insight into myself because of this. But regardless of anything else, there will be some of my thoughts written down to leave for my children and grandchildren. Jami is printing my entries out for me, so that they can be kept in a journal. Well, I didn't have a story for tonight, but maybe I will tomorrow.

## 2 May 2001 - An Adventure Trip To Florida

About twenty-something years ago, I was invited by a friend of ours who was working at a church in Florida to come down and bring some young people to visit the church and do some work there. So I started getting up a group, which turned out to be all girls. For awhile, there were seven, but when it was almost time to go, one of them backed out. So there were six girls all about thirteen or fourteen years old, and me. I was a little uneasy about being the only one who could drive. But it was an exciting time for all of us as we made our plans. We held an attic sale and we sold doughnuts, and we got up a fair amount of money. Our church helped us some, and I asked each girl to bring fifty dollars to spend on meals. Then we had to find something to ride in. There was a station wagon available, but it wasn't in good condition. So one of our members offered us the use of his almost new pickup truck with a camper top on it. This was ideal, except that it was very warm in the back, even though there was a small window in the back glass of the truck. We planned that the girls would rotate sitting in the truck with me, two at a time, but this didn't exactly work out. Two of them always seemed to get more time in the cool than the rest. But everyone survived the heat, and we had a great trip. We left right after church on Sunday, stopped for the night in Savannah, where the girls swam and had a ball. The next day, we went on down the road, stopped in Daytona Beach for lunch. This was the first time we'd been to a Red Lobster, and it was really nice. Then we went on to Orlando, found the church there, and settled in. Our friend assigned us all some work to do for the next couple of days. I think it consisted of mostly paper work, and one evening we went out with other groups all over the community gathering up young people to come to a Bible study and a pool party. This was a really successful evening. I think they did this sort of thing once a week there. We slept in different Sunday school rooms in the basement in sleeping bags, ate cereal in the kitchen for breakfast, and there was even a shower room for us to use. And we even got to spend a day at Disney World while we were there, courtesy of someone who was a member of that church. On the way back, we stopped again in Savannah for the night, then came on home the next day. What an adventure. The girls who went with me were: Jami, Terri, Leah, Melissa, Gina and Sheila. And I was talking about this trip tonight after church with Terri, and her daughter said she wants to go on a trip like that, and I said I would almost do it again. Almost. It really was a special adventure.

## 3 May 2001 - Prune Whip

I was thinking this evening of how I learned to cook. In Home Economics class at school, I only really learned how to read a recipe and how to measure ingredients. My real lessons came from my mother. She was really a good cook. When I was about thirteen, she taught me how to make biscuits, and how to stew potatoes. So with that much knowledge, all I had to do was open a can of some kind of vegetables and we had a meal. I was really proud that I was able to cook a meal for the three of us, and Mother always bragged on me for anything I did. So from that point, I was able to learn on my own just by reading a recipe and following instructions. Now after all these years have passed, I seldom need a recipe, unless I want to make a cake or something fancy. It seems so strange to hear my family brag on my cooking. I still consider myself to be very mediocre in that field. But back to my first thought on this subject. The first and only thing I ever remember learning to cook in Home Economics class was Prune Whip. I tried that out at home only once, and it just wasn't our kind of food. And I've never since that time heard of prune whip. We've always liked things like beans and potatoes, corn bread and biscuits. Of course fried chicken or pork chops are mighty fine, too. But simple things seem the best to me. No more prune whip.

## 4 May 2001 - A Workshop And A Concert

Today I went to a workshop for musicians at a large church in Charlotte. There were three of us from our church, and we had such a nice time. I attended two classes, and the first one was not a good one at all for me. It was about "How to talk to the sound man," and I didn't understand the first thing about it, since 1 am totally ignorant of the sound system at church. When I talk to our sound man, it's usually just to tell him how many microphones we'll need. And I tell him it's his job to make sure we sound good. The second class I attended was dealing with worship at church, and it was really good. Our leader was just wonderful, an extremely talented musician who happens to be blind. His name is Ken Medema. The biggest lesson I got from that class is that worship is an offering. I'd never heard it expressed that way, but I found it fascinating. When we worship, we offer God praise and honor and love. Later, after we had supper, there was a great concert. There was a group of young musicians and singers who presented praise songs. Very good. Then Ken Medena played the keyboard and the piano, and he sang beautifully. He told some funny stories, did some really amusing things at the piano, and just thoroughly entertained us. He is extraordinarily talented. I'd sure like to see more of him, but he's from San Francisco. I hope to go back tomorrow for the rest of the workshop, and maybe I'll be blessed again. It was a good day.

## 5 May 2001 - Cinco De Mayo

My birthday is celebrated in a big way in Mexico. It's a really important holiday there. There is a song which says, "Cinco de Mayo is holiday time." So today I am 67 years old. It doesn't seem possible that I could really be that old. I surely don't feel it. And I'm very thankful for that. Jami gave me a copy of one of my favorite books today, "Sophie's Heart" by Lori Wick. I had a copy and gave it away about three years ago, so I'm really glad to have another one. Tonight we went out to our favorite fish restaurant, so I've had a very nice day. God is so good.

## 6 May 2001 - A Surprise Phone Call

I had just gotten home from church this evening, when the phone rang. It was a call from my first husband's nephew, whom I! have not seen or spoken to in probably about 36 years. He got my phone number from his sister, with whom I have kept in touch from time to time. He was just a boy when Bobby and I married. His family lived with Bobby's family during most of the years that Bobby and I dated, so I saw quite a lot of him. He had a sister who was about two years younger than he was, and then he had a brother and sister who were twins, about seven or eight years younger. Well, it really brought back a lot of memories talking to him. His parents are both dead now, and his sister who was close to his age died several years ago, and his wife is dead. And now his health has failed him. At the age of 60, he is now on disability, with heart and lung problems. We must have talked for 45 minutes, and he was calling from Florida, where he now lives. It seemed good to talk with him, and at the same time it was a little depressing. But I am so glad that he remembers me fondly, and that he wanted to talk with me.

## 7 May 2001 - Mother Was Right On Time

I'm thinking about two separate occasions when I was around seven years old, and how they kind of fit together. I remember that my cousin, Joan, and I were really upset with one another. We argued about something that made me so mad. We were standing on her front porch, and I called her a fool. Well, it seemed that my mother appeared out of nowhere, and she spanked me soundly and told me never to call anyone a fool again, and I don't think I ever did. What a well-taught lesson that was. The other incident is funny looking back, but it was really serious at the time. I was playing outside while Mother was gone to the store when some other children came by. They pointed out an old man who walked by looking kind of wild to us. A couple of the older ones said that he was crazy and that we should hang him. Well, that made perfect sense to the rest of us, because he was a dangerous man. So one of them found a length of rope and we all fell in behind him following after the wild man. Well, we were maybe two or three blocks from my house when Mother came by on her way home. She spotted me and asked me what we were doing, so I told her. She scolded me and made me go home with her. I never heard any more about the proposed lynching, whether they did it or not, but now I'm glad that Mother kept me from being an accessory. She got there right on time to teach me not to call anyone a fool, and not to take part in a murder. These were two more of my good lessons.

## 8 May 2001 - Billy

My uncle Billy was such a special person. His life was short, but so full. He was my mother's brother, the ninth of ten children, and it would be hard to really describe him, but I want to tell a little bit about him. He didn't get to go to school much, because he had "fits," which I believe were due to epilepsy, but he apparently outgrew whatever caused his problems, because he grew up very strong and healthy. He enlisted in the Army soon after World War II began, and served honorably. We were so excited when he came home. His antics were so wild and funny, and sometimes dangerous. He was married to a sweet girl named Evie, and they lived in the mountains near my grandmother, his mother. I'm not sure what kind of work he did, but I think it involved cutting down trees. He worked with his brother, and they used two big work horses. One day I was there visiting when he came home from work, and I asked him if I could ride his horse. He said "Sure you can," then he helped me onto the horse's back. There was no saddle, so he told me to hold onto the reins, then he slapped the horse on the rump and the horse and I took off. Well, I had a ride such as I've never had since, and I hope never will have again. That horse took me up one road and down the next one and after a few terrifying minutes, he took me back to where Billy was. Maybe Billy knew the horse would bring me back safely, but I didn't. Once he came back from a hunting trip, while Mother and I were visiting at one of her sisters' house. Thinking his gun was empty, he pointed it at Mother's feet to scare her, and it went off and shot a hole in the floor near her. That time he scared himself more than anyone else. But there were too many crazy stunts to tell all of them, and he was just so much fun to be around. Everyone loved him and he loved life. One of the last funny things I heard about him was one morning when he had his little nephew, who was still a baby, on his lap. He had two kinds of applesauce, one sweet and one sour. He would give Roddy a bite of the sweet, then a bite of the sour, and he would laugh his head off at the faces Roddy made. He really enjoyed children but never had any. The last time we saw him alive, we were leaving my grandmother's house and passed him on the road walking. When we stopped to say goodbye, he teased Mother about not coming to his house to visit him while we were there, and she said, "I promise you that the next time I come, I will come to your house first." And we did, but this time he was dead. He had gone to a service station a couple of miles from his home, and noticed some friends gathered around the back of a car where there was some kind of homemade air tank in the trunk. They were filling the tank with compressed air, and when Billy walked up, the man who was standing closest to it stepped aside, and Billy stepped right into his foot prints. Then the tank suddenly exploded. Billy died on the way to the hospital, the only one who was injured. I'll always remember how precious he looked in death. He was almost smiling, as if he was thinking of another joke to play on someone. I can't do justice to his life or his personality by just telling a few things like this, but he really was dearly loved, and he only lived twenty-six years.

## 9 May 2001 - Quilts and Aprons

When I was a child, women used to make a lot of quilts, and mostly the ones I saw were just simple patchwork quilts. These were made from small scraps of material, many times cut from old dresses or shirts which were about worn out. The thing that I really liked was that sometimes there would be a few squares that I remembered from a dress I had worn. These old quilts were so warm to sleep under and it didn't matter that they weren't fancy. How I wish I had one of them now. Well, I do have one old quilt that was my husband's mother's, but it's not the same as one I would have remembered as a child. Then there were aprons. I think probably all the old women I knew wore them, to protect their dresses and to keep them clean. They would all be homemade, just cut from leftover pieces of cloth. Some had bibs, some didn't, but they all tied in the back. And they all had one or two pockets. I loved them, and I have some of my grandmother's on my mother's side. Mamaw always had a handkerchief and a small can of snuff in her apron pocket. And if she needed to go anywhere, all she had to do was to hang up her apron, and her dress was clean and she was ready.

## 10 May 2001 - I Can't Stand Bullies

I was always, and still am, the type of person who is a great target for a bully. I've never been able to defend myself. Well, almost never. I can remember instances in school when another student would treat me like I was nothing, and I would either act like I didn't notice it or I would cry. Once when I was in second grade, during recess, a big boy was threatening to hit me with a snowball that had a rock in it. I was afraid and went inside and told the teacher. She was irritated because I had disturbed whatever she was doing, so she told me to go back outside and not bother her or she would hit me with one herself. That happened about sixty years ago and I still remember it well. And there was a time when I was in sixth grade, when I got out to the playground after the class had started playing kickball. Well, I went to the end of the line, and as each person would come back after taking their turn, they would get in front of me saying that was their place. So naturally I never got a turn. And there were many times that I was picked on for no reason. There was a girl who said she was going to beat me up after school, and I hadn't done anything at all to her. There must be some strange disorder in the bully mentality which tells them who to pick on, and I guess it makes them feel superior.

I went through years of feeling inferior and maybe that's part of the reason that I couldn't defend myself. I would suspect that this sort of thing is still going on nowadays, but I don't hear of it. I really hope that teachers are sensitive to these students who need their support, but I'm afraid that human nature hasn't changed that much and that there are still people like my second grade teacher who don't care. I'm so thankful that I don't feel inferior anymore, but I still can't stand confrontations or hard feelings. I'll always avoid them if it's possible. But I really have this immense dislike for bullies, and in the movies or on T.V. I love to see them get what's coming to them.

## 12 May 2001 - I'm so Thankful

It's such a blessing to be a mother I wouldn't trade places with anyone else in the world. And I really mean that. All the riches, all the pleasures on earth could never be as good as what I have. I have two daughters and a son, and I must have done something right because they turned out so well. Not perfect, but close enough for me. What a privilege it was to care for them as babies, and then to be their first teacher, to see them learn to walk and to talk and to grow strong and healthy. I'm so proud of them, and even though I don't tell them often I think they know how I feel. And they all gave me the dearest grandchildren I could ever have asked for. And now there are even great-grandchildren who are also precious. I am so very blessed and so very rich, I thank God for these children. And what's more, I have two beautiful step-daughters who were grown when I married their daddy, and I'm really proud of them and their children and grandchildren. Life is so good in so many ways, and J am thankful indeed.

## 13 May 2001 - Mother

I've thought all day that I want to write a tribute to my mother, but I don't think I can really do her justice with a few words. The one word that I think describes her best is unselfish. She gave me so much all my life. She never had much money, but whatever she had she just loved to share it. When I was very small we didn't have much food, but she always saw to it that I had something, whether she had anything or not. And it wasn't only me that she gave to. It was anyone that she knew of who needed help. She gave her mother so much when her mother was old. She felt like Mamaw should have as good as anyone else, and she bought her a refrigerator, probably the only one she ever had. Mother and her sister went in together and bought Mamaw a television set. One of Mother's sisters had very little money, and Mother always made sure that her two daughters had winter coats. She bought my children so many things through the years. And when she was old and in a lot of pain, she still loved to cook a big meal for all of us, and she really could cook. And lots of times she'd call me and tell me that she was cooking a big pot of something, and that I could have a bowl of it to go with our supper. If I was sick, she would cook potato soup and send me some of it. I could go on and on telling about things she did for me and for others. She was the most unselfish person I've ever known. She went to Heaven three years ago, and she is sorely missed. What a dear precious mother and wonderful friend. I'm so thankful that I had her for a long time, and she will always be loved and treasured in my heart.

## 16 May 2001 - My Trip To Caraway

On Monday, I went to a conference for senior citizens. There were six of us from our church. The place where it was held is absolutely beautiful, away back off the road in the woods. It lasted until after lunch today. (Wednesday) I've been to many of these and I just love them. The staff always has things planned for us to do, with several opportunities for worship, a good deal of singing, and a lot of good fellowship with other seniors. It was amazing to me the first time I went to one of these to see how much fun older people can have. And it's remarkable that nowadays so many can afford to do things like that. Of course, this particular place belongs to the Baptist State Convention, and the cost is only 91 dollars, including all meals. Last night they had a good movie for us: Remember the Titans. I had seen it before but I enjoyed it again. So I always enjoy going there, but I was glad to get home. Oh I nearly forgot to say that there was a lovely little lady who is 93 years old, and she looked so neat and pretty. And she is an inspiration to the rest of us, to see her still enjoying getting out and enjoying life. I don't know whether she has children, but if she does, aren't they blessed to still have her.

## 17 May 2001 - Yellow Jackets Attacked

I remember a time when I was about fifteen years old that Mother and I were picking berries. I stepped into a nest of yellow jackets, and they started stinging me all over my foot. Well, I started screaming and running and the yellow jackets chased me all over the place. The hilarious part of the experience was that I was calling Mother to "Catch me! Catch me!" And of course there was no way possible for her to catch me, because I was flying. We often laughed about that through the years, and I can still remember how terrified I was, but my first reaction to any frightening thing was usually to automatically call for Mother. I guess I instinctively felt that Mother could fix anything and she often did. Mothers are like that, aren't they?

## 18 May 2001 - About Yesterday's Entry

After I posted my entry, I began to realize that I may have caused some folks to feel bad. I was talking about how I always felt like Mother could fix anything. Well, I don't remember exactly what I said, but it was something along this line. I made the comment that "Mothers are like that, aren't they?" But all mothers aren't like that. Sad but true. I had just read in one of my favorite diaries about both parents being alcoholics and abusive when this person was small. My childhood was terrible in many ways, but I always knew that Mother loved me and would do her best for me. She wasn't perfect but she did the best she could, and I realize that lots of folks missed out on that. And I'm really very sorry if I caused anyone to feel bad. It was kind of strange last night after I went to bed. I fell asleep rather quickly, then I had one of those brief but very scary dreams, and I screamed out for Mother to help me. I guess it seems odd that I would still call for her at my age, but old habits die hard.

## 19 May 2001 - Still Thinking About Mothers

I guess because Mothers' Day was so recent, I keep thinking about mothers and how they are sometimes treated. A friend of mine told me that when she was a young girl, she and her mother were extremely close but that one day when she was about seventeen, and newly married, she and her mother got mad about something and had a terrible quarrel. During the course of the argument, she threw a really hateful comment, saying something about her mother being fat and how she was an embarrassment to her. She then left her mother's house, and that night her mother had a heart attack and died, leaving my friend with no opportunity to ever say that she was sorry. She didn't mean what she said, but that didn't change the fact that she said it. She told me that Mothers' Day was always so hard for her, and I'm sure it was. There is a lesson here for the rest of us. I think if that had happened to me and my mother it would have either killed me or run me insane. I thank God that I never talked mean to Mother, and I have peace about her, but I'm so sorry for my friend. We should all be very careful what we say, because once we say something it can't be unsaid. And we never know when will be the last time we'll see that special person.

## 20 May 2001 - An Answered Prayer

We were talking tonight at church about prayer, and I told the group about a very special prayer that God answered for me. When my daughter Paulette was about two years old, we were living in Puerto Rico. One of my friends, Mary, asked if she could take Paulette to her house so that she and her daughter, who was about eight, could play with her. Mary lived a few miles away and Paulette had never been away from me in any situation like that. I really didn't want her to take Paulette, but it seemed silly not to let her. She and her daughter loved Paulette dearly. So I said she could go, and as Mary was driving away I felt afraid and I stood on the sidewalk and prayed that God would keep my little one safe. A few hours later, when Mary brought her back home, she told me that a strange thing had happened when she was leaving her house. She said that the screen door had caught Paulette's little sandal and pulled it off. So Mary had to take the time to put the sandal back on. At the time that she would have been at the corner near her house, there was a bad wreck. Paulette would have been right in the midst of it, except for her sandal coming off. I still, after all these years, praise God for such a precious answer to my prayer. I won't forget that.

## 21 May 2001 - The Soldiers

During World War II, there were a lot of soldiers around Charlotte, and several of them spent a good deal of time at our house. I guess Daddy would meet them at a café and bring them home with him. I don't really remember how we came to know them, but there were three that I especially liked and have always remembered them. There were two Sammys, both of them Italians from up North. They played with me and I was always so glad to see them. One of them was very handsome and one was not, but they were equally nice, and seemed a little like big brothers to me. Then there was Doug and he was my buddy too. One big thing I remember about him was that he stole a doll from his girlfriend and brought it to me. It was a rag doll, and it had the name "Cookie" written across its forehead in ink. We never met his girlfriend, but I imagine she wondered what happened to her doll. And I wonder what ever happened to these three sweet young men who treated a little girl so kindly. We never heard from them again after they left Charlotte, but I've never forgotten them.

## 22 May 2001 - Bad Language

When I was about four years old, I was playing in the back yard, when the little boy next door started saying "Hey, Baby" to me. This was an insult, so I told him that I was not a baby. He kept on calling me a baby until I finally said,

"I'm not a baby, you blankedy blank blank." I used some pretty bad language which I can't write here, and Daddy said that the little boy's mother heard me and took him quickly into the house, telling him that he was not to play with me anymore. I'm sure that suited me just fine, and I don't think I was punished for talking that way. I probably should have been, but I think Daddy felt like the little boy pushed me into saying what I did. Thank goodness, this didn't become a habit for me, because I really dislike bad language, and feel that it shows a lack of intelligence and a very poor vocabulary.

## 24 May 2001 - Two Really Big Announcements

I was trying to think of some really interesting thing to write about tonight, and started thinking about how I learned about two of my grandchildren. All of my little ones are very special, but these two incidents stand out in my mind. The first happened when I was at work in the elementary school library. I noticed Jami and Calvin walking toward me and wondered what in the world they were doing there. We spoke, then they handed me a Christmas card. I can't remember exactly what it said, but it was something like "To a wonderful grandmother at Christmas." It was signed from Baby Sinclair, and it said something about seeing me in July, I think. I was dumbstruck for a moment, then it dawned on me that Jami was pregnant! That was really an exciting moment, and wasn't that a cute way to announce it? The next outstanding announcement came four months after Hannah was born. My son and his wife lived right next door to us, and early one morning my son called and told me he was taking Annette to the hospital. It was time for their firstborn, and he was trying to get her to hurry, but she didn't see a need to hurry, and of course she was feeling awful at the time. Well, I told Jon that I would leave soon after they did so that I could be with them for the birth, which I did. The trip to Charlotte was about an hour or less, and I naturally expected to be there for quite awhile before the baby came. Well, when I got off the elevator there was Jon waiting for me, and he looked awfully emotional. He told me that the baby was already born, that she had been born in the car outside a convenience store. They had to stop there for Jon to call 911, then a fire truck arrived and a fireman was able to help with the delivery. That was really big news! It even made the front page of our local newspaper, titled "Couple's Camaro becomes birthing room." What an exciting time that was. And now both of those little girls are eleven years old, and their Nina thinks they are pretty special.

## 25 May 2001 - A Big Scare

When my son was very small, he often disappeared if I turned my head. Not so with the girls. They stayed pretty close as a rule. But my little Jon was an adventurer. He had a lot to do and places to explore. This one day in particular, I called him and he didn't come. I looked everywhere, in fact we were all looking for him, but he was nowhere to be found. At times like this, I always thought about our pond, because Jon loved to go there with MawMaw to fish. I was so afraid he had gone there alone, so of course we looked there but still couldn't find him. Well I stopped in the house for something and the phone rang. It was our next door neighbor, and she was just calling to let me know that Jon was there. She said he had just walked in the door, said nothing, then climbed up onto a chair, and just sat there, not bothering anyone. Well, what a relief that was. And later we often thought of how funny it was that he would just decide to go visiting all alone like that. But my goodness what a scare that was. I'm still so thankful I was able to raise him safely. I'm sure that I had special help from above. Don't misunderstand me. He was a wonderful child. He just had a lot of things to see and do.

## 26 May 2001 - More About My Boy

I wanted to clear up a couple of things from my entry last night. It may have given the impression that Jon was hard to raise. Actually I have no complaints whatsoever. He was never demanding, and was always basically a very good boy. Even when he was nearly grown, he would always call me if he was going to be later that eleven getting home. It was so cute the way he wandered around our place all alone, and he loved it. He loved our barn where sometimes he would find interesting things, even kittens. He loved our woods. He would follow his daddy around copying whatever he did. One time he watched Irving pouring out the chicken's water before giving them fresh water, and he followed along behind pouring out the water like he had seen his daddy do. There were so many cute little things he did. But I mainly wanted to be sure that everyone knew that he was a wonderful son. And I am so proud of the man he became. And I'm so thankful that I did have help from above raising him.

## 27 May 2001 - NEPOTISM

All of my children have very good singing voices, for which I am so thankful. As long as I've been involved in the music at church, I've been careful not to have my own children do too much, for fear that it would seem that I was showing them off.

It always bothered me to see a parent who was in charge of something allowing their own children to have major parts, as in a play or something. So I've sort of bent over backwards not to do that. But this morning at church, I had

Jami singing the solo part in the choir song, and then our ensemble sang "I'll fly away." There were six singers in the ensemble, and four of them were Jami, Calvin, Hannah, and myself. And just before church, our pianist suggested that Jami sing a solo during the offertory. He had found a song he thought would really fit in with the morning's program, "I'll tell the world that I'm a Christian." Well, it all turned out just fine, the music was all good, but I keep thinking of the word NEPOTISM, and how carefully I've avoided it, except for today.

## 28 May 2001 - Memorial Day

I had a really nice day. First, my daughter Jami called and invited me to go with her and our dear friend, Terri, to hunch and to a movie. Then my stepdaughter called and asked me to go to the movies with her. I told her that I'd love to but I had already planned to go with Jami and Terri. I suggested that she might like to meet us for lunch and go with us to the movie. She decided she would. Then in a few minutes I had a call from my other stepdaughter telling me that she was going to crash our party. So she met us at the restaurant with her twins, and Hannah had decided to join us, so there were eight of us for lunch. It was nice to be with them, then five of us went to see Pear! Harbor. I guess it was a good movie, but it was also horrible. It has me thinking of the dreadful things so many of our men and women went through during the different wars we have had. They really deserve our thanks for what they've done for our country. They were true heroes.

## 31 May 2001 - A Couple OF Rough Days

I haven't written for two or three days because things here have been kind of stressful. Irving's back has really gotten so much worse, he can't even walk without help, and even then it is so painful he can hardly bear it. I took him to the emergency room Tuesday. They xrayed his back and said he has a crushed vertebrae and severe osteoporosis. This evening our pastor and three others came and brought a hospital bed, so he is in it and I hope he can rest tonight. He sure has had a rough time. And on top of all that, a special friend died suddenly today. She was my age, 67, and had just come through a brave fight against cancer. Her hair has grown back now and she seemed to be fine at our ladies' prayer meeting this Tuesday morning. Her son found her this evening about six o'clock. She was sitting on the couch dead. She had four children and several grandchildren. Betty was a very dedicated Christian and she will be sorely missed at our church. But I'm convinced that she is in a much better place now. I'm only concerned about the pain her children must now endure.

## 1 Jun 2001 - One Day At A Time

My husband is having a really bad time with his back. Right now he is nearly helpless, but we are so hoping that this won't last. This morning he asked me what we were going to do, and I told him that we would just do whatever we have to do, one day at a time. Today was my good friend Betty's day to take the "Meals on Wheels,"so I took them in her place, because she left this world yesterday. Her funeral will be Sunday. My heart breaks for her children. But as I was thinking about this entry tonight, I thought about the phrase "under the circumstances" and how so often folks will use this phrase to describe their situation. Well, I was reminded that we are not "under the circumstances" at all. We are on top of them, and we know that our God will work out everything for our good. One of Betty's favorite songs was "Great is Thy Faithfulness." And He is truly faithful and loving and able to do whatever we need. What a Mighty God we serve!

## 7 Jun 2001 - Bits and Pieces

It's getting late, and I must get ready for bed soon. But I did want to write at least a short entry to keep in touch. My husband has been in the hospital since last Saturday with an injured and very painful back. But he has been improving a lot and yesterday he had a procedure done in which the doctor injected some sort of cement into the crushed vertebrae. Tomorrow we expect him to be sent to rehab for possibly a week until he can gain some strength and better mobility. I'm pretty tired from driving to Charlotte every day and sitting so long, but at least we have hope now that he will be much better soon.

My Uncle James is very near death. Some of you may have read my entry about him. He is a very special man, 81 years old, and has been struggling with Parkinson's Disease for 16 years. It has destroyed his body, and we don't expect him to last more than a day or two. Today was his and Mary's 55th wedding anniversary, and we suspect he may have been hanging on because of that, but we don't know for sure. We will miss him, but I'll be so glad for him to go to Heaven where there will be no more suffering. And last I want to tell about a lady at the gas pump yesterday. I had a bedside commode in my back seat which could easily be mistaken for a walker. After I pulled up to the gas pump, I took a few moments to get out my billfold, and this lady who had just finished getting gas, came up to my car door and said,"Ma'am, are you going to have to use your walker to pump your gas? I'll be happy to pump it for you." I was so touched by her offer, but explained what it was in my back seat. I thanked her over and over, and told her that I hoped that someone would be as kind to her. But isn't it refreshing to realize that there are still people out there who care about others?

## 8 Jun 2001 - Another Long Day

Irving was sent to rehab today. He may be there for a week or so. It depends on how quickly he gains strength and mobility. But he is so much better than he was a week ago, it is just wonderful. Now he is really tired of hospital food, so I told him tonight that I will bring him some Kentucky Fried Chicken for lunch tomorrow. That should do him a lot of good. This evening I showed our other house to a couple and they want to buy it if they can get the financing arranged. She said that she just loved it. So I'm praying for God's will to be done, whether we sell the house or not. It has gotten to be a strain on us, not knowing, but I guess this is where faith comes in. So now we just wait on the Lord.

## 9 Jun 2001 - Uncle James Died

It's hard to realize that he is gone, but I know that he is much better off now. But I think back to when he was young and strong and just back from serving in the Navy. He was one of the most decent men I ever knew, an excellent husband and father. And he was such a good brother to my daddy. When Daddy was old and a semi invalid, James would come to see him and bring him some Dr. Peppers. That was Daddy's favorite drink, and he was always glad to get some. And he was a very good uncle. I'll miss him, but I am so glad he isn't suffering anymore. Now the only one left from Daddy's family is his sister Flora. She's the oldest, will be 95 in July. It must be a terribly lonely feeling to outlive all of your brothers and sisters.

## 12 Jun 2001 - A Very Full Day

Today I did two very important things. First, I went to my Uncle James' funeral, then I went to the Rehab and brought my husband home. James' funeral was a real blessing. That may sound strange, but it is wonderful to know that his suffering is over, and that he left behind good memories for those of us who loved him. The graveside service was beautiful. There were three Navy men waiting for us, and when the casket passed by, two of them stood there at attention and saluted. They were dressed all in white and looked so nice. Then after the preacher said a few words and a prayer, the third sailor played "Taps" on a bugle. Then the first two folded the flag that was on the casket and presented it to my Aunt Mary. This ceremony was so special and paid a great honor to my uncle, who had served honorably and well in the US. Navy during World War II. Later I went to the Rehab and picked up my husband. He has improved so much, and was really wanting to come home. So now he is in his own bed and resting well. This is a great blessing.

## 14 Jun 2001 - A New Kitty

Last night at church, there was a little lost kitten in the parking lot. It was raining, and the poor little thing was soaking wet. The children held it and played with it during choir practice. No one wanted a kitten, including me, so everyone left afterwards. But my conscience really bothered me, even after I went to bed. I felt so mean for leaving that little cat with no one to care for it. So today when I was in the area delivering meals on wheels. Hannah and I stopped to see if it was still there and it was. So after a little debating with myself, I brought it home with me. I stopped at a store and bought a box of kitten chow, and when we got here, I told Hannah that if she would stay on the deck and in the back yard with it, maybe it would stay here, because we can't keep it in the house. But it has been in the house most of the time being held by grandchildren. Jamison just left, and Lauren is due in about an hour. So it has had a lot of attention. I tried to think of a name for it, and Jami suggested that I might ask the folks at DD to give me some ideas. But after I thought about DD, I happened to think of the diarist called Rayne. I love that name, and since I found the kitten in the rain, that name really seems to fit. I don't know whether it is male or female, J can't tell with kittens. It is white with very blue eyes, and is probably about seven or eight weeks old. I hope Rayne won't mind my using her name. I don't think she will. So Rayne is the newest member of our family.

## 19 Jun 2001 - The Words Of My Mouth

As a very young person, I enjoyed hearing jokes. And some of them were not fit for a Christian's ears. Later on, I began to realize that I was wrong to ever listen to things like that, but there were things already lodged in my mind that I can never erase. But I've tried to dodge the dirty jokes, but not always successfully, I'm sorry to say. Years ago, I learned a trick that enabled me to look a person in the eye while he told a dirty joke, and never hear it. I would put my mind on something else while he told it. We had a friend who loved to tell these ugly things and he knew I didn't want to hear them, so he delighted in telling them to me, trying to embarrass me. So when I learned this trick, it soon put an end to his stories. I'd not crack a smile when he finished and that just confused him. I thought that was funny. When I worked in the library at school, one teacher loved to tell vulgar stories in the teacher's lounge, and she loved it if I happened to be in there. She'd laugh and say. "Look at Mrs. Myrick," thinking she'd embarrassed me. Sometimes she would even follow me back to the library to add something she thought was funny. Well, I'm not trying to give the impression that I haven't been guilty of hearing some really ugly things, but I do know that it's not pleasing to God, and I regret that I've ever done that. There's a verse in Psalm 19:14 that says "Let the words of my mouth, and the meditation of my heart, be acceptable in thy sight, O LORD, my strength, and my redeemer." This is my prayer.

## 25 Jun 2001 - An Update

I haven't been writing often lately because too much has been going on. I seem to be pretty busy looking after Irving and doing all my other everyday things. But I thought I would just give an update about a few happenings. First, I'm so glad to say that Irving is doing so well with hardly any pain. That's a miracle. He doesn't even need his walker in the house, but he still has to wear his brace when he's up. I even took him to church yesterday and that was special. Next, I got a call from my daughter about an hour ago telling me that I have a brand new great-grandson. He weighs 6 Ibs and 8 oz, and I'm sure he is very cute and very sweet. His name is Andrew Reed. (Reed is my mother's maiden name.) Pretty, isn't it? I think they will call him Drew. And my last bit of news is that our new kitten, Rayne, is doing well. I still don't know whether it's a she or a he, but it sure is cute, and the grandchildren enjoy it a lot. Well that's about all for this time. Maybe things will slow down a little soon, and I can think of something more to write about.

## 26 Jun 2001 - Uncle

My uncle Clinton is my mother's brother. He's about 86 years old and he really is a dear. We have always called him "Uncle." His first marriage was a disaster but lasted for many years, probably 35 or 40. His wife seemed crazy to all of us, and she made Uncle's life miserable. She would sometimes say something at church to embarrass him, and sometimes she would go to where he worked and say or do something to make him look bad or incompetent. She was extremely jealous of him, even if he was just friendly with his sister, or if he paid attention to one of his nieces. So for all those years we never really got to enjoy his company, because Geneva would spoil it for everyone. I think the worst thing she did to him was during the time that his mother was dying. He would go and take his turn sitting with Mamaw, and Geveva didn't like that. She would always have something hateful to say to him when he got home. She even told him that she hoped his mother would die and that when she did she (Geneva) would laugh. When Mamaw died, we went up for the funeral, and when it was time to go to the church, there was Uncle all alone. He rode with us because Geneva wouldn't come with him. Not too long after that he finally got up the courage to leave her, and we were all glad because we finally got him back. Later, he met a French woman who had come to America as a War Bride. She had also been treated badly in her marriage. I think her husband was dead. Uncle and Elaine hit it off immediately, and soon married. And they have been so happy together these last several years, just like two young people in love. It's really cute to see them together. They travel and have lots of fun, even went to France a few years back to visit her family. Now we can go to their house and feel so welcome and enjoy Uncle's company. Elaine certainly isn't jealous. Geneva died several years ago, and I'm sorry to say she left only bad memories. How tragic that a life could be so wasted, but I'm so glad that it wasn't too late for Uncle to have some happiness.

## 30 Jun 2001 - Daddy Taught Me To Drive

I was staying with my parents while my husband was overseas for a year, and every time I needed to go any place, Mother or Daddy had to take me. And it was not always convenient. So at the age of twenty one, I decided to learn to drive. Daddy said he would teach me, so I got my learner's permit. Most every evening, we would go out for a ride and Daddy would give me instructions. Then he decided that it was time to try driving in the city. Boy, what courage he had. I know I scared him many times, but somehow we made it. When I went to take my driving test, I was so nervous I forgot my name for a moment. I had always been a little afraid of policemen, and having a patrolman riding beside me was almost traumatic. Once we came to a stop sign and I didn't even notice it til I passed it. I thought he would surely not give me a license after that. But he just gently warned me to be careful about stop signs in the future. Another thing that was memorable that day was that he asked me to parallel park, and I had never been able to do that right. But that one time I did it perfectly. Was I relieved! So I got my license and have been driving for 46 years now without a ticket. Not that I haven't ever deserved one for speeding. Now I love that line from the movie "Rainman" and I often tell my grandchildren that "I am an excellent driver."

## 1 Jul 2001 - Daddy's Birthday

Today, if he had lived, he would have been 93 years old. And I've often thought that if he had taken care of himself, he might still have been with us. He was blessed in so many ways, and talented, but he wasted so much of his life. And who knows whether it was all his fault or whether his parents failed him in some way. He ruined his health by drinking for many years, and hurt a lot of people in the process. It's really a tragic story and I won't go into any more details today. But we never said "I love you", until one day when he had been very sick for weeks and in a coma for much of that time. I was able to forgive him for the past, and when he awoke I told him that I loved him, and he said "I love you the mostest." This meant a lot to me, and I think he really did love me, but he didn't know how to show it. He died nearly 12 years ago, and I am not sure he went to Heaven. With all my heart, I hope he did. I'd really love to see him there someday.

## 7 Jul 2001 - Just Rambling

I was just about to turn this off after reading a few diaries, and I tried to think what I could write about, but it's getting pretty late so I thought I'd just ramble a little, just to be in touch with you all. We had a very nice Fourth of July, went to Jami's for a late lunch, then to our daughter Vicki's house, where we visited for awhile and had some cake. The really great thing about all of this is that Irving was able to visit that long and not need to hurry back home because of terrible pain. We've been so blessed by that procedure he had done, and he is still getting more and more back to his old self. Thanks be to God.

## 8 Jul 2001 - Short Stories About Clothes

Today I was telling Jami and Hannah about an incident when I was about 14, I think it was. Jami said I should write about it. My daddy opened a charge account at a clothing store. (I have no idea why because he sure didn't hardly ever buy any clothes.) Well, he told me I could go to that store and buy myself a new outfit and charge it to him. I was delighted. I went there and bought myself a really nice wool plaid skirt and a pretty sweater set to go with it. Well, when Daddy found out how much it cost, he was really irritated at me. But he hadn't told me how much I could spend. As far as I can remember, that's the only outfit he ever bought me, and I was so proud of it. It really did look good on me. But soon after that, Grandma came to spend a week or two with us, and she washed my sweater set in hot water and it shrunk so much it would have fit a baby. I don't guess I'll ever forget that. Another incident concerning clothes was that I needed an evening gown to wear in a operetta at school, and my girlfriend, Alice, said that her sister would lend me one if I would lend her a dress of mine. So I agreed. Now this dress she wanted to borrow was the prettiest dress I ever had. It was two pieces. The top was navy blue velvet and the skirt was red, white, and navy plaid. I loved it. Well, after the operetta, I returned her sister's dress, but she never returned mine. I can still see her walking down the hall at school wearing my dress but I didn't have the courage to ask her for it back. I was probably afraid she would get mad at me. Well, Alice is dead now, so I guess I may as well forgive her for keeping my dress. But I don't think we ever spent any time together after that. Too bad. A dress ending a friendship.

## 14 Jul 2001 - Aunt Flora

My Aunt Flora had her ninety-fifth birthday on the third of July. She is Daddy's only remaining sibling. She's in a rest home in Statesville and doing pretty well. It's kind of odd that she'd be the last surviving one, since she is also the oldest one. I visited with her back in February, I think it was. Her life was mostly lived way out in the country on a big farm, with three children and a really good husband. I didn't get to spend a lot of time with them as I was growing up, but Aunt Flora was always very sweet to me. I remember that she loved to cook and was really good at it. She was always interested in new recipes. She used to make persimmon pudding, and also a great cake which was a lot like fruit cake, but it had those pretty different flavored gum drops in it. As far as I know, she had a good life, but there was one really big tragedy when her oldest daughter got sick with Alzheimer's disease. Aunt Flora was up in her mid-eighties, yet she had to help care for her daughter. That seems so sad when a mother has to see her own daughter destroyed that way, and Irene was always such a bright person and so nice. But of course she became like a child before she died. They had to keep the doors locked at night in such a way that Irene couldn't get out. And they got little rest during that time. They finally had to put her in a nursing home and she died there the very next day. This hurt them even more knowing that if they had just waited one more day, she could have died at home. Recently, Irene's husband died and Aunt Flora grieved for him. He was like a son to her. And last month, her last brother, my Uncle James, died. So she has had a lot to deal with, but she is very strong, and a very special lady. I hope we can keep her for a while longer.

## 15 Jul 2001 - Uncle Claude

I'm trying to include all my aunts and uncles in my journal, so tonight I'll tell Uncle Claude's story. He was my mother's older brother and he really had a hard life as a young man. He married Viola at an early age, and they soon had two sons. Well, Viola really went wild when the boys were about 6 and 8 years old. The war (World War II) was going on and she started dating soldiers. She'd meet them in Asheville and probably take their money. We even heard that she married more than one of them and began to collect allotment checks from the government. I have no idea whether that was true, but we all believed it at the time. Well, after a while Viola took the boys and left Uncle Claude, and he didn't know where they were for some time. Somehow he found out where they were staying and went there to bring them home. He found them huddling together behind the stove in the kitchen, scared to come out. This was a boarding house where they were staying, and they told their daddy that at night men would come into their bedroom and their mother would make them cover up their heads til after the men left. Well, he took the boys home with him, but I think they were always scarred by their early life. They started drinking early, and a few years ago the younger one killed himself. But after Uncle Claude divorced Viola, he married again, and they had six children. I guess his life turned out to be pretty good, not perfect because he still had to worry whenever his children had problems. He died a few years ago with cancer.

## 18 Jul 2001 - Aunt "Buppie"

Her name was actually Bertha, but I never called her that. She was my mother's sister, probably about eight years older that Mother. She was a wonderful woman, a Christian and devoted to her church. She had two children and a very good husband. They both worked hard to provide for their family and were just very decent people. There were some pretty hard things that happened to them. One of their granddaughters has had a lot of trouble in her marriage, including having her husband mistreat her little son, who was about two years old when they married. Aunt Buppie's son even went to court to try to get custody of the little boy, but that failed. But this really was so painful for Aunt Buppie and Uncle Stewart, and of course there was nothing they could do. They had another grandchild who had a rough life, all kinds of problems, and at the end he was found dead in Florida on a railroad track. Their only daughter was a wonderful woman, happy in her marriage, and active in her church. At about the age of fifty, she had a sudden brain aneurysm and died almost instantly. This was extremely hard to bear, but their faith in God carried them through, although they naturally never got over losing her. Then Uncle Stewart died several years after that, and it seemed that Aunt Buppie's mind was never right after that. She died about two years ago, at about ninety years of age. And it was a great blessing when she was released from this world. But she left behind some really good memories. If we were visiting in the mountains on a Sunday, we could always feel welcome at her house after church. She always had a lot of food ready for anyone who might drop in, and she loved to see folks eat. She was precious.

## 19 Jul 2001 - Uncle Clyde

I wanted to be sure to write about all of my aunts and uncles in this journal, mainly so that my children and grandchildren would get to know more about my family background. I will write tonight about Uncle Clyde, Mother's oldest brother. I never got to know him very well, so I don't really know much to write about his life. He married Aunt Lucy, who had a daughter before they met, then they had four daughters together. I always felt a little sorry for the one who wasn't his daughter, because she never called him Daddy. She always called him Clyde, while her four sisters called him Daddy. She never knew any other daddy, and she was very small when Uncle Clyde came into her life. I feel like he loved her but she must have never felt like she was really part of the family.

Uncle Clyde was always teasing and being funny, but he was also very tender-hearted and would cry easily. One little aside bit of information that I've always found amusing was the names of my mother's brothers. There were five of them: Clyde, Claude, Clinton, Clifford, and Willard (Billy). I never figured out why Mamaw didn't name Billy something that started with Cl, like maybe Clarence or Cleveland or Clayton. Well, now I've written something about all of Mother's brothers, and two of her sisters. So there are two sisters left to write about, so I'll try to get that done pretty soon.

## 20 Jul 2001 - The Choir Social

Tonight at church, we had a choir social, and it was a lot of fun. There were about twenty people there, and we had a good meal, a catered affair. Barbecue (It was to have been chicken, but the caterer said they had burned that), mixed steamed vegetables, potatoes, salads, rolls, and peach cobbler. We just had a nice time being together and after we ate, we played bingo. This was really funny. We laughed the whole time. And after all the prizes had been won, we were going to quit, but someone suggested that we play for the gift bag that the prizes had been brought in. Well, guess who finally won a game and got to bring home the bag that says Happy Birthday on it. Me. And Terri, who had won two prizes, felt sorry for me and gave me the crossword puzzle book. This was nice, because I work crossword puzzles a lot. So I'll enjoy that. But it was a nice evening, good fellowship with dear friends.

## 21 Jul 2001 - July Birthdays

July really is an important month in my family. The first day is my daddy's birthday, the third is my Aunt Flora's. Then begins a parade of grandchildren. Rebecca is now seven. I remember her daddy telling me, with tears in his eyes, that he had another daughter, Rebecca Marie. What a beauty she is. Then there is Andrew, who is now thirty-one. I can hardly believe it. Where have the years gone? I remember him looking right at me just after he was born, with those big eyes, even though people say newborns can't see. He now has three wonderful sons of his own. Today is

Hannah's birthday. She is twelve, and that's also hard to believe. She is almost as tall as I am. It seems no time at all since she was a tiny newborn, and, like Andrew, she had very big eyes. She used to cry after me when I would leave their house. She always wanted to go to my house, and she still does. She always spends Wednesday nights with me. Monday will be Alexander's birthday, and he is adorable. He was Jon and Annette's first son, and they were so glad to have him. He is blonde, blue-eyed, and has the cutest dimples. He is very active and all boy, and he also loves to visit us. My maiden name was Alexander, so I really love his name. Well, those are all of the July birthdays in our family. July is a very special month indeed, and I'm so blessed to have each of these children in my life.

## 23 Jul 2001 - Aunt Bert

Aunt Bert was my mother's oldest sister. Her name was actually Bertie Mae, and I was partly named after her. (Daddy's sister Flora's middle name is also Mae, and she always thought I was named after her.) My middle name is Mae, so I was named after two different aunts. I was born at Aunt Bert's house while my mother was visiting there. Aunt Bert had two daughters and a wonderful Christian husband. Once when I was visiting Mamaw, I went to the church where Uncle Emory was the Sunday School Superintendent, and when he stood up to give some kind of report, I was so proud that he was my uncle. Another time I was playing on a big rock, and there was a snake on the ground near the rock. Someone ran in and told Uncle Emory and he came out and killed the snake. So he was my "hero" again. Aunt Bert was an absolutely marvelous housekeeper, and she insisted that her daughters stay clean even when they were outside playing. They couldn't sit down in the dirt or the grass. They had to squat so they wouldn't get their panties dirty. Well, I guess Aunt Bert lived a quiet but good life. I can't think of anything very interesting to tell about her. But there was one thing that was hilarious that happened when she was old and apparently had Alzheimer's Disease. She was staying with one of her daughters, and her grandson had some beer in the refrigerator. One day while her daughter was out and her grandson was staying with her, she went to the refrigerator and got a can of beer, thinking it was a soft drink, and drank it. He didn't tell her what she had drunk, but he told his mother later. Well, the next day the daughter was curious to know if her mother knew what she had drunk, and she said, "Mother, let's have us a can of beer." Aunt Bert was extremely indignant, and said, "I'll have you to know that I've never in my life drunk any beer and I'm not going to start now." In a way that was pitiful, but we all really had a big laugh anyway. I'm glad she never knew about drinking the beer.

## 27 Jul 2001 - Animal Stories

I remembered today the cutest story about a dog. Irving used to raise beagles, and one of them was named Jigger. (I don't know why.) One day we noticed her out in the front yard staggering and falling around. Obviously there was something very wrong. After trying to figure out what the problem was, Irving noticed that she had some wet food that had been sitting there for a couple of days and it had fermented so we knew then what was wrong. Jigger was drunk! After a little while, she sobered up and was fine. That's the only time I ever saw a drunk dog, but now I can imagine what it means to say that someone is "as drunk as a dog." Now I want to give an update on our little kitten which I found deserted in our church parking lot about six or seven weeks ago. I named it Rayne, because I found it in the rain, and because I liked the name of one of my favorite diarists. Well, I now know that it is a male. ( I hope his name doesn't sound too feminine but I can't change it now, because I was told as a child that if you change an animal's name, it will die.) Well, he is the cutest thing, and extremely playful, and he is sometimes even affectionate. He has learned to dodge the younger grandchildren as much as possible because they want to hold him too much. If you are interested in what he looks like, I discovered a picture in an album at Tinoz' diary which looks just like Rayne, except that it looks a good deal older. But as you may have guessed, I am enjoying my little kitten. My son told him awhile back that he hit the jackpot when I brought him home. Maybe I did too.

## 28 Jul 2001 - Aunt Edith

She was my daddy's sister, younger by maybe five or six years. Her husband, Uncle Charlie, died when their only daughter was about nine years old. They had two houses and a car and a truck, and because there was no will, Aunt Edith had to sell one of the houses and one of the vehicles and put this money in the bank for their daughter. So she had it hard financially after that, because she had to support herself and her daughter with no help. But she did a really good job, I think. She kept a nice home and they always seemed to have whatever they needed. Her daughter was able to get a good education, and turned out to be one of the nicest and most well-loved people I ever knew. Aunt Edith lived a rather uneventful life, but I know that she was so proud of her daughter and her three fine grandsons. She died nearly four years ago of Parkinson's Disease, and a little over a year ago her daughter, Mary Faye, died from cancer. But I know that Mary Faye was grateful that God allowed her to live long enough to see that her mother was always taken care of. I have only good memories of Aunt Edith.

She was always kind to me.

## 29 Jul 2001 - My Aunt Louellen

She was my daddy's youngest sister, and she had a lot of tragedy in her life. Her first marriage was not good at all. Uncle Herman joined the Army or was drafted. (I don't know which) They had a daughter and a son, but Uncle Herman never acknowledged the son as his. Uncle Herman got sick at the Army base and died. We never really knew what happened. But he had things fixed so that his daughter would receive support, but not his son. This was just awful and so unfair, because as Terry grew, he looked so much like his father, it was obvious that he was his son. Well, the daughter received a government check each month until she was grown, and Louellen always made sure to match the amount for Terry. She worked hard to support them, then she made the mistake of getting pregnant and gave birth to a son. In that day and time, this was really a disgrace. But the little boy was so sweet, all the family loved him. When he was still very small, Louellen remarried and had three more sons. When Mikey was about twelve, he and his younger brother went to a nearby creek to play in the water. They had done that so many times, but Louellen didn't know that the county or the state was dredging that creek and had made it much deeper where the boys went to play. Well, Mikey couldn't swim, and when he got into that deep area, he drowned right in front of his brother's eyes. This was so horrible for all of our family, but of course, it was just too much for Louellen. She blamed herself, because she had given him permission to go there. She had to have several shock treatments during the next year or so, and she was never quite the same as she had been before. One thing that made it seem even sadder was that she and her husband had just told Mikey a few days before that Charley was not his real father, and naturally this was hard for him. But they felt like it was right for him to know the truth. On top of all this tragedy, several years later, her first grandson was killed in a car wreck. I had spent a lot of time at her house when I was a child. I could just go there on the bus and stay as long as I wanted to. Well the last time I talked to her, I mentioned something about those days and she told me that she didn't remember much from back then, and I really felt like I lost something from my childhood, since she couldn't remember it. The shock treatments had destroyed a large portion of her memory. She died a few years ago, and I miss her. She was special to me. I believe that she is in Heaven with Mikey now, so I don't need to worry about her.

# 1 Aug 2001 - I Can't Resist Sharing This

This was actually in my local newspaper yesterday: A man who said he grew marijuana for pain relief called police to report someone had stolen his plants. Now he faces felony drug charges. The man was charged with one count of manufacturing a controlled substance and one count of maintaining a dwelling to keep a controlled substance. He had called police Friday to report that a man had taken 27 marijuana plants from his yard."He had come to my garden and was stealing my marijuana plants and breaking them off at night," he said. "I told him to stop and if he didn't he was going to get in trouble." The sheriff's deputy said the man took him to his garden and showed him the damaged marijuana plants. Authorities valued the marijuana at $1 million, but the man said the plants were not valuable until they had matured. (I left out the man's name and location, but this really was in my newspaper yesterday, and I thought it was one of the most ridiculous things I'd ever read.) Surely this could be used in the making of a sequel to "Dumb and

Dumber."

## 4 Aug 2001 - Beauty Parlor Or Jewelry Store

I've often wanted to tell about this in my diary, but it seemed like it would be hard to explain. It is really funny, so I'm going to give it a try. When I was seventeen and my boyfriend was just home from Korea, I was so hoping he would buy me an engagement ring. We had been planning to marry for a long time, but hadn't made it official. Well, this particular evening, he was coming to see me. His home was about 125 miles from mine, and I was expecting him around seven or eight o'clock. So early in the afternoon, I was bent over the sink in the bathroom washing my hair, when he arrived. (Things were pretty different then. Girls washed their hair about once a week, and usually it was at the sink. A lot of trouble, and took a lot of water changes to get it rinsed well.) Well, when he got there he stepped into the hallway to speak to me. The bathroom door was open, and when I saw him I was a little bit flustered. He said,"I brought you a surprise." But he wouldn't tell me what it was, and I so hoped it would be a ring. Here is what I said to him: " I just hate washing my hair. The next time, I think I'll just go to the jewelry store. Oh, jewelry store!! I meant to say the beauty parlor." That was one of the most embarrassing moments of my life, but he did give me a beautiful diamond engagement ring that evening.

## 7 Aug 2001 - My Aunt Sis

Her name is really Velma, but she has always been called "Sis." She is my mother's youngest sister and has always been my ideal. I always wanted to be just like her. When I was a baby, she stayed with us a good bit, and she dearly loved me. She loved to take care of me, and even begged Mother to let her wash my diapers. She was eleven years old when I was born, and she still says that I was the prettiest baby she had ever seen. Ever since I can remember she has been beautiful in my eyes. I used to watch her getting ready to go out on a date, and I just hoped I would grow up to be just like her. She would fix her hair in an upsweep, and I loved that. And she was tall and slender, and just about perfect in my view. When she met and married my uncle Jay, they both hit the jackpot. He is absolutely wonderful too. He became a Baptist preacher and Sis became an outstanding Christian. Her greatest joy was and is seeing someone receive Jesus as Savior. They had four children and really had to struggle financially. One day Sis went into a laundromat and saw a baby in a cardboard box, very dirty and poorly cared for. The lady who was tending to the laundromat was minding the baby. Sis' heart went out to this little child and she told the woman, "You tell this baby's mother that if she wants to give her away, I'll be glad to take her." Well, the next day, the mother called Sis, and told her that if she really wanted the baby, she could have her. So Sis picked her up and took her home with her. Sis and Jay and their children all love her so much and they've been such a blessing to her and she has blessed them. So after she had adopted Angela, she later adopted two of her grandsons, whose mother was not really capable of raising them. So her life has been a struggle and so busy, but so full of love. I think if she saw a child now who needed a home she would really want to adopt it, but she is seventy-eight and Jay is eighty. I don't think they could quite manage another one, but their hearts are so full of love. They are both so precious, and there is more that I could write about them, but maybe another day. Jay is still preaching and I don't know if he will ever stop until the Lord takes him home.

## 11 Aug 2001 - How To Handle Stress Or Maybe Not

I took a psychology course years ago, and yesterday when I was cleaning out a drawer I came across this paper I had written about how to handle stress. It's amusing to see how well it describes me even now. Here is what I wrote: When my life is stressful, I feel that I must deal with the situation, but at the same time I don't want to face it. I want to run away and hide and hope that the problem will resolve itself while I'm away. I feel nervous, unhappy, and alone in a sense. I may even feel resentful at having my usually peaceful and pleasant routine disrupted. Then at last I feel that I must pull myself together so that I won't let these negative feelings show. So I cover up, and in a sense I hide my head in the sand. But then it works for me.

## 12 Aug 2001 - A Mostly Good Day

I don't really have any theme in mind to write about, but thought I'd just tell about my day. I got to church at about 9:30 as usual to get ready to go over the choir songs. Everything went fine. I think the music was good, and the sermon was very good. We have a very special pastor. As soon as I got home, Jami called and asked me why I wasn't at the fish fry. I told her that I wasn't invited, and she assured me that I had been invited weeks ago. I can't imagine forgetting an invitation to eat, but her memory is better that mine. So Irving and I headed back to the church where we enjoyed a really good meal. Next comes the bad part of my day. The Braves got beat badly, and I was so disappointed. But there will be another game on Tuesday, and I will hope for a great win. After church tonight, Jamison and Jordan came home with us to spend the night, and they are now in bed. My little adopted kitten, Rayne, is doing so well. We have a lot of laughs at him. He loves to jump out and scare people. Well, I guess that's enough rambling for tonight. It's getting near 11:00, and I'm going to bed.

## 18 Aug 2001 - Phi Theta Kappa

My granddaughter visited with us last night and brought me a gift. I was delighted when I opened it and found a mug with the Phi Theta Kappa symbol. This is an honor society which I was inducted into when I was in college. I was telling Jami about the mug this morning and about how it brought back such a good feeling and such good memories, and she said I should write about it in my diary. I was middle-aged when I went to college. (I still tell Jami that I am middle-aged now, and she laughs at me.) I went part time, except for one full time year, and it was rough, since I had two children at home, housework and cooking and laundry to do, and I was directing the music at church. Many times I would be up late at night finishing an assignment, but still I loved it, and considered it a wonderful privilege. When I was invited into Phi Theta Kappa, I could hardly believe it. I can't remember what the grade requirement was, but I know it was rather high, so I felt so honored. At the next graduation, I was asked to be a marshall, and that was another thrill for me. And when I graduated, I got to wear a gold cord. I graduated cum laude. I can't say how excited I was. For a girl who had quit high school in the tenth grade, this was beyond my wildest dreams. So I got my associate degree in Church Music, and I feel so richly blessed. That was twenty-three years ago and I'm still excited. I could never have done that without Irving backing me and supporting me. When I met him, I felt so beaten down and inferior, and he has made me feel like I was someone important. He's always been proud of me. Forgive me if I seem to be bragging. I don't mean to, because I know that just in my own strength I couldn't have done this. I had wonderful support from Irving and the children. And always, there was God blessing me and helping me. So Miranda's gift of the mug really has me remembering today.

## 23 Aug 2001 - Imagination

Children today don't need to use their imaginations when they play, because their parents buy them toys to use for whatever game they may want to play. When I was small, I often played Cowboys and Indians with friends, and I didn't have any thing to use for a horse or a gun. But it was great fun to imagine that I was riding a horse just by galloping along on my own two feet, and my finger made a perfectly acceptable gun. I added sound effects by saying "pow! pow!" This probably would seem dumb to today's children, but my friends and I really enjoyed it. And I especially loved to play movie stars. My girlfriend and I would decide who we were that day and then pretend whatever we wanted. We both usually wanted to be Betty Grable, but if we couldn't be her, we'd settle for June Haver or June Allison. Our boyfriends in our imagination might be Van Johnson of Peter Lawford or Robert Taylor or Alan Ladd. When I couldn't find anyone to play with, I'd be whoever I wanted. It's a little sad to realize that my imagination has left me now. It would be fun to pretend again. I really enjoyed it when I had it. Well, I must go now. It's time for my Braves to play, and I don't need any imagination to enjoy this game.

## 24 Aug 2001 - A Nice Evening Coming Up

I'm so looking forward to this evening. We have invited a dear friend to go with us to a fish restaurant. She is a member of our church, a recent widow, somewhere in her sixties, and one of the most lovely Christians I have ever met. She is an encourager. Whenever I try to compliment her, she always turns it back toward me. She writes the most beautiful letters to people to comfort and lift them up and to encourage them. After my granddaughter Hannah sang a solo at church awhile back, Margarette sent her the sweetest letter. A long time back, she sent me one about a song I had sung and what a blessing it was to her. She is the best teacher I have ever heard, whether it be in Sunday School or a Study Course, and she isn't well educated in the eyes of the world. I truly believe she is inspired by God. You may have guessed by now that I love her dearly. When I spoke to her about going out with us tonight, she talked about how sweet we are and how much she is looking forward to this evening. But I'm pretty sure that we will be the ones who will be blessed.

## 6 Sep 2001 - Visiting Loved Ones

Last Sunday after church, my granddaughter Miranda picked me up and we headed out to visit some very special people. Our first stop was at a rest home in Statesville, where my aunt Flora is living. She is 95 years old, my daddy's last sister, and she was so glad to see me. She called me by my mother's name several times but that was fine with me. She is the cutest little lady, and has her right mind although she is forgetful. So many times she said, "I forgot." But it didn't seem to worry her, and that's all that matters. 1 really hope I can get back up there soon to visit her again. Our next stop was at Old Fort. This is a very small mountain town where my aunt Pearl is living with her daughter. They closed in their garage and made a beautiful room for Aunt Pearl. She has her own furniture in it, and it is so big that it is a bedroom and sitting room combined. Aunt Pearl is 90 and doing rather well, except that she can't see much anymore. Her mind is still good, and I'm so glad. She has always been like a second mother to me. She is my mother's sister.

We then got a room at a motel and the next morning after breakfast we went to visit my Aunt Sis and Uncle Jay. He is a Baptist preacher, 81 years old, and still preaching. He is a wonderful Christian man and I've always been so proud of him, although he is related to me through marriage. He is as dear as any of my uncles, if not more so. Sis is 78 now and has a lot of health problems, but she is still beautiful in my eyes. I always wanted to be just like her when I was growing up. She is my mother's youngest sister. I have two uncles living in that area, but didn't get to see them. Maybe next time. Miranda was such a great chauffeur and took me everywhere I wanted to go. She was the driver and I was the navigator. She is really interested in our family and I'm glad of that. Well, we got back home safe and sound, for which I'm thankful. It was a really good trip.

## 10 Sep 2001 - Remembering

Yesterday would have been my golden wedding anniversary, but the marriage failed a long time ago. I have so many memories, and I'm grateful for the good ones. I really loved him and he was so special until drinking ruined him. He was bright and kind and romantic but the alcohol changed him. Is there any wonder that I despise alcoholic beverages? Well, it ruined his health and damaged that bright mind, and he died a couple of years ago. He never really knew our wonderful grandchildren, and that was another tragedy. But I'll always remember the person he used to be. And I'll always love him. But the Bible says that "all things work together for good to them that love God, to them who are called according to His purpose," so I know that I am abundantly blessed. I have a wonderful Christian husband, a precious family, a good home, and everything I need. So I am very thankful to God. But since yesterday brought back so many memories, I feel a little blue. But I'll be fine tomorrow.

## 13 Sep 2001 - The Hideous Attack

I feel that I should make some comment about Tuesday's events, but I don't know if I can add anything to what others have said so well. I've read many really beautiful entries in Dear Diary, and my heart has been touched by them. Those evil men have done a hideous act, and my mind can't grasp such hatred that would bring them to such a thing. Thousands of people are in such pain, because they've lost loved ones, and my heart goes out to them all. I heard someone today talking about how these terrorists believe that by murdering all of these innocent people, they would be assured of Heaven. Then the question was asked, "What would they have to do to go to Hell?" What kind of religion teaches this way of life? Our God, in His Word, teaches us such a different way. We are to love others and treat them the way that we would want to be treated. One good thing that I've seen come from these awful attacks has been a rebirth of patriotism, and we've needed that for a very long time. After our prayer service last night, we all joined hands and sang "God bless America," and it was a moving experience. Those evil men caused a lot of pain, but they won't defeat our wonderful country.

## 14 Sep 2001 - A Letter To Paulette

Happy birthday. It's hard to believe that it has been 49 years since you came into my life. In a way it seems like you should still be a little girl. You were such a pretty child with the most beautiful blonde hair. And you were basically a good child with a sweet disposition. I was proud of you. When you learned to play the violin I thought you were so talented. I remember you played a solo in church once, and I was beaming. You were really jealous of your grandmother, since you were her only grandchild for your first 10 years. A lot of the children at church loved her and called her Grandmother, and you didn't like that. They always wanted to sit with her, and I remember one Sunday morning when I came into the sanctuary with the choir, I looked for you as always, expecting to see you sitting with Grandmother, but you weren't there. I finally spotted you sitting on the other side of the church looking as mad as a wet hen. But years later when you finally got a little sister, I never saw one bit of jealousy in you. It was beautiful to see the way you loved her, and you've been such a sweet big sister to Jami and to Jon. You've been an excellent mother to your two little ones, and an outstanding grandmother too. There are so many good qualities that I could talk about: your kind heart, your gentle spirit, your sweetness. You are dear to my heart and I'm thankful that God lent you to me. May He always bless you. I love you very much. Mother

## 15 Sep 2001 - A Morning With SALT

Maybe you remember my joining a group of volunteers which helps the Sheriff's Department in a lot of different areas. I had worked one afternoon at the desk which takes care of the visitors who come to the jail, but it wasn't a day when they have visitation. I just came home from working all morning at that desk during the regular visiting hours, and it was a really hectic time. My job was to receive the money they brought for the prisoners and write the receipts, and I stayed busy nearly the whole time. The language barrier makes it a little harder, because a lot of the visitors are Mexicans, and a lot of them can't speak English well at all. I felt so sorry for the people bringing money, because it was obvious that many of them couldn't really afford it. The amount ranged from five dollars to twenty dollars generally. There was one person who left fifty dollars. I realized today that our group is really badly needed, and I'm glad that I can help a little.

## 24 Sep 2001 - Alzheimer's

A friend at church is the activities director at an Alzheimer's unit, and she told us yesterday about a lady who was brought there recently by her son and dumped. He hasn't been back to visit her, and neither has anyone else. This is heartbreaking. Some of the workers there are planning to have a bake sale soon, and the money will be used to purchase some of the things this lady needs. She still has a good bit of her mind left, and probably realizes her situation. No mother should ever be so cruelly treated, nor should any person. I expect this will come back one day to haunt the son. I've observed a lot of patients over the years, mostly when my mother-in-law was in a nursing home, and a lot of them can still have some quality time if they are cared for. There was one who had this stuffed dog named Jimmy, and she was so proud of him. She always wanted everyone to notice him, and she fed him every time she ate. Sometimes his face would be in a terrible mess, but apparently someone would wash him up pretty often. A lot of things were so funny, like the lady who came to the table for lunch wearing a pair of underpants on her head. But I realized later that if that had been my mother, it would not have been funny. My aunt's mind was nearly gone the last time I visited her. She was in a nursing home and I'm not sure whether she knew me or not, but after I talked to her for just a few minutes, she said she had to go. I asked her where she was going, and she said she was going to the store. She turned her wheel chair away and left the room, so I just told her goodbye. She died not very long after that, and I felt relieved for her to be out of her troubles. I could go on and on, but I just had to tell about that poor lady who was deserted at the nursing home. I plan to visit her very soon, and see if there is anything I can do for her. If my mother were there with no one to care about her, I would sure hope that someone would visit her.

## 27 Sep 2001 - Superstitions

I have a list of ideas of things to write about in a journal which Jami sent me. This morning I was looking over it and started thinking about superstitions and luck. I was reminded of my grandmother on my daddy's side and how superstitious she was. She would really get upset if anyone opened an umbrella in the house, or if anyone rocked a rocking chair with no one sitting in it. [never could make any sense out of these things. My mother-in-law believed that it was bad luck not to come back the same way you went somewhere. For example, at my parents' house, there was a back porch with two doors into the house. One went into the kitchen, the other into the living room. When my mother-in-law and I would go there for a visit, she would always be sure that we left through the same door through which we had entered. And so many people think that black cats bring bad luck. I've always liked black cats. I just have never been a superstitious person. I don't like to hear anyone say that they were lucky when some calamity passed them by. I much prefer to give credit to God for His protection. I heard years ago that the word "luck" came from the same root word that the name Lucifer comes from. That's something to think about, isn't it? So I never say that I am lucky. I am simply blessed. And I have no problem with umbrellas being opened in the house, or with a rocking chair being rocked with no one sitting in it, or with black cats. And when I go somewhere, I often come back a different way just to see other scenery. I sure am glad I'm not superstitious, because I'd hate having to keep up with all those things. The other day when my little granddaughter, Rebecca, was visiting me, she was in the yard playing with a little neighbor girl when they saw a "writing spider." They showed it to me, and I told them how people used to say that if the spider heard your name and wrote it, you would die. I first teased them and told them to be careful not to say each other's names where the spider could hear them. They looked at me with great big eyes, and I quickly explained that this was just a silly old superstition, and that they shouldn't believe it. I'm so thankful that we don't need to be concerned about foolish things like this. Just remember that we don't have to have a spirit of fear, if we put our trust in God. He'll take care of us. And that's a promise.

## 28 Sep 2001 - Go Braves!

I have just finished watching the Braves play a game against the Mets and it was so exciting. My granddaughter, Hannah, watched it with me, and we had a great time. In case you didn't know, the Braves won the game 5 to 3. We even played card games while we watched the game. Hannah is really good at Rummy, but tonight I am the champion! She has only recently learned how to play Casino, but I am the champion of that one tonight! So this was my night and I'm exhausted now. So I'm going to bed to rest up for tomorrow's game. Go Braves!!!

## 2 Oct 2001 - Just Checking In

I'm thinking a lot about my daddy's death, after reading this morning about Honey's dad dying. I'm so sorry for her. I know she is really feeling heavy-hearted tonight. It really feels awful to lose a parent even though he is old and very sick, because he has always been there. It seems he is not supposed to leave you. And I will probably always feel a little guilty because Daddy was alone when he died. I had been at the hospital most of the days and nights, since I am an only child, and I was really tired. So Irving said that he would stay so that I could go home and get some sleep. We agreed that I would go back to the hospital at midnight, but Irving called me a little before midnight and said that there had been no change, and that I might as well sleep the rest of the night. So I went back to sleep and Irving came home and went to bed. Then the phone rang probably about two o'clock and they said I needed to come to the hospital. We got up and hurried back, and found that Daddy had died. He had been in a coma, not responsive at all, but I'll never know whether he might have awakened for a moment. I hope he never knew that he was alone. But I know that there is no need to fret over that, since I can't change it. I really wish that I had stayed at the hospital that night, anyway. Honey said that she and her sister were with her dad when he died, and I know that will always be a special memory for them.

## 6 Oct 2001 - Contrasts

We had a funeral at church yesterday. An older man died after several years of various illnesses and even though it's a sad time for his family, it is a blessing for him. Then today we had a wedding at church. It was so beautiful and such a happy occasion for that family. As I was leaving the church I pulled into the cemetery, and visited the graves of our parents. They all lived a long time. Both of my parents lived 81 years, and Irving's mother lived 83 years and his daddy lived 91 years. So these all seemed natural and right, although sad. But then I went to look at a new tombstone which was placed last week. It was for a lovely 16 year old girl, who was killed in a car wreck. Quite a contrast, but we don't have to understand everything. God knows what it is all about.

## 9 Oct 2001 - This Has Been A Good Day

I'm so thankful every time I can say that this has been a good day. This morning I delivered "meals on wheels," and this always blesses me more than it does the ones who get the food. Hannah, my granddaughter, went with me to help, and I feel like she was blessed too. She even got an opportunity to help one lady carry in some groceries from the car. The lady has really bad knees and is in a lot of pain all the time. What better thing could a child do than to help someone like that. And this particular lady has spent her life trying to help others. Afterwards, we went to the church where we have ladies' prayer every Tuesday morning. What a privilege it is to pray for those who have special needs. On the way home, we stopped and got ourselves two cups of cappuccino. That was delicious! Then after lunch, I watched my Atlanta Braves play a great game. That was fun. Then this evening, my stepdaughter and her husband visited with us awhile. Also, their daughter and her two little daughters visited. That was so nice. But the greatest thing that happened today was when I asked a dear friend whether she had ever received Jesus Christ into her heart, and she assured me that she had. That was wonderful. So I am really especially thankful for this very good day.

## 13 Oct 2001 - A Nice Day

The weather here has been just super lately. I hope it will last a while longer. Irving and I went out for a ride today. We were just looking around to see if there were any special looking houses for sale and we rode all the way down to South Carolina, because we've heard that seniors don't pay property taxes there. It may or may not be true. But it's pretty far from our church and that's not good. We really love our church. It was a pleasant ride, and Irving needed to get out for awhile. He stays at home nearly all the time. After we got home, we got ready and went out again. This time to the fish restaurant. A great supper. So now we are just sitting around watching television. What a life. I think now I'll watch the Yankees and the Oakland A's and see how that comes out. As you may know, my Braves won three games straight against Houston, so they have three days off now. I've absolutely loved watching them this season, and even if they don't win another game this year, I'm so proud of them. But I'd really be delighted if they could win the NL championship. Go Braves!

## 18 Oct 2001 - A Really Nice Short Vacation

On Monday afternoon, I went to a place called Caraway, which is owned by North Carolina Baptists, for a senior adult retreat. Three friends went with me, and we had a delightful time. The conference center is located way back off the road among the most beautiful trees which are turning colors now. It's just the most restful place, and I dearly love to go there. The people who work with senior adults are so good at it. They have a lot of activities planned for us, which include devotional times, singing hymns, and just great fellowship. We also had four different classes to choose from, and we could go to two of them. My favorite one was about understanding the Hispanics who are coming into our area. I think I gained respect for them. We had an excellent speaker who is a retired minister, and he spoke to us on four occasions. Tuesday night. we had a Fall Festival where we played bingo, darts, cake walk, fishing, and even musical chairs. Also there was a pumpkin carving competition. It really was a nice evening. And the food there is delicious. It's always such a treat when I get to go there. I came home yesterday (Wednesday) and was glad to get back. But who said getting old was all bad. Jami says she is looking forward to being old enough to do some of the things I do. I'm not sure whether she is serious. You'd be surprised to see a large group of seniors together, having fun. I really enjoy their company, even though I don't feel like a senior adult. I'm so thankful to be able to do things like that. It adds a lot of joy to my life. And before I close this entry, I just have to add that my Braves won last night. Go Braves!!!

## 19 Oct 2001 - The Lady Was Discarded

I went to a nursing home yesterday where a friend from church works as the activity director. The place is an Alzheimer's unit. My friend had told us at church about this lady and I kind of want to adopt her as a friend. I was surprised to find that she is in her fifties, a very attractive person. I expected a much older lady, but she is younger than I am and still able to have a conversation. I was told that her son had brought her there some time ago, dropped her off, and has never been back. This breaks my heart to think of anyone's mother being treated that way. It appears that she was discarded like a bag of trash. I'm convinced that her son will regret that one day. The people who work there are having a bake sale today with the intention of using all the proceeds to buy her whatever little personal items she might need. They really are a kind bunch of people. I learned that she loves chocolate, so I told her that I'll come back soon and bring her a chocolate bar. She was really pleased about that. I think she should have a candy bar every day. Her name is Eleanor.

Please pray for her.

## 22 Oct 2001 - The Braves Lost Last Night

Well, the Braves went a long way and I am delighted with them, but I had kinda gotten my hopes up that they might go farther. But I'll just have to wait now until next Spring. No use getting depressed about it, but it's always a little sad to see it end. Now I'm not sure who I'll pull for in the World Series, but if the Yankees make it, I may pull for them. My good friend, Betty, who died in June, always pulled for them, so maybe I'll do that in her memory. We always had a little rivalry about our favorite teams. Until next year, Go Braves!!!

## 23 Oct 2001 - Forgiveness

I put an entry into the Prayers' diary awhile ago, and it got me started thinking about one part of that prayer that Jesus taught. It's something all Christians must deal with, so I just decided to give you a free, short sermon. That part of the prayer says, "Forgive us our trespasses as we forgive those who trespass against us." It seems to be saying that if we fail to forgive others who hurt us, then we need not expect God to forgive us. That's really serious business. So I would like to pass along a tip I learned years ago, which has helped me forgive others. If 1 pray for God to bless the one who wronged me, then it is not hard to forgive that person. Very simple, isn't it? Try it and see if it helps you. End of sermon.

## 25 Oct 2001 - My Second Visit With Eleanor

I went back to the nursing home today to visit my new friend, Eleanor. I wrote about her last week. She has Alzheimer's Disease and no one to visit her from her family. I went into her room and had to reintroduce myself, and she seemed glad to have a visitor. I gave her a Hershey bar, and she was so pleased to get it, it did my heart good. I sat and talked with her for a good long while, and asked her questions. I learned that she had an older brother and two younger sisters who were twins. I asked her what the twins' names were, and she said Tootsie and Tommie. But then she said she couldn't remember her brother's name. She said she doesn't know where any of them are. She realizes that her mind is failing, and I can't even imagine how awful that must be. She said she doesn't have anything at all. No home, no car, and not even a penny. Then I asked her if she had any children. She paused and thought for a moment or two, then said that she doesn't remember. I know that she at least has one son, the one who brought her there to the nursing home and left her and hasn't been back since. It may be a blessing that she doesn't remember him. Well, she may not remember me next week, but I fully intend to go back and take her another candy bar, and at least let her know that she has a friend. I can reintroduce myself. I don't mind. My heart aches for her. And I have so much to be thankful for. I really want to share with her.

## 27 Oct 2001 - I'm So Thankful

I got a great sort of an essay from someone on the internet recently and I copied it because it is full of things to think about. It talks about many different things to be thankful for. I can't give credit to the author, because I have no idea who originally wrote it. But I want to write about different parts of it in this journal. The first one I want to share is: "I am thankful I can see the beauty all around me; there are those whose world is always dark" . I've thought so often of Helen Keller, who was blind and deaf. And of Fanny Crosby who was blind. And I'm amazed at the way they were able to deal with their situations and live a happy and fulfilled life. It seems that they did more with their lives than most of us who can see, doesn't it? It makes me ashamed that I haven't fully appreciated the gift of sight. But I'm going to try to be more thankful from now on. I've been allowed to look at the sweet faces of my babies, and at all of the precious grandchildren they gave me. How wonderful and how good God has been to me.

## 29 Oct 2001 - I Am Thankful I Can Walk

Another quote from the essay: "I am thankful I can walk; there are those who have never taken their first step." How often do we even give a thought to being able to walk? We take this gift for granted instead of thanking God every day for it. What a wonderful freedom it adds to our lives. My children were all blessed by this gift, and I so enjoyed watching each one taking their first unsteady steps. When I see someone who is crippled in some way or in a wheelchair, I'm reminded to be thankful, and to have more compassion for others. I certainly don't deserve to walk any more than anyone else. It's just a special gift that God chose to give me, and I really am so grateful.

## 30 Oct 2001 - Erma Bombeck

She was a well-known television personality a good many years ago. She had a quick wit, a great sense of humor. I was reading this article that she wrote titled "If I had my life to live over," It really started me to thinking about my priorities. She said that she would have talked less, and listened more. She would have invited friends over to dinner even if the carpet was stained and the sofa faded. She would have sat on the lawn with her children and not worried about the grass stains. She would have eaten popcorn in the 'good' living room, and worried much less about the dirt when someone wanted to light a fire in the fireplace. She said there would have been more "I love you" more "I'm sorrys" and there were several other things she would have changed if she could go back. But of course she couldn't go back and live her life over, and neither can we, but our lives are not over yet. So we can start now doing some things differently, and we can start to realize what things are really important, so that when our time comes to leave this earth, we'll have less regrets. When my children were little, I spent a lot of time with them, but if I could go back, I'd spend more time doing things with them. We don't have those dear little people with us for very long, so we need to give them all the time and attention we can. And Paulette, if I could go back, I'd fix you a lot more French Toast.

## 1 Nov 2001 - I Can Hear Music

I am thankful I can hear music playing; there are those whose entire life has been spent in silence. I so often take the gift of hearing for granted, but when I think about it, I think how awful it must be to be unable to listen to music and unable to sing. Singing has been a major part of my life for as long as I can remember and the thought of losing that gift is horrible to me. I'm amazed at how Beethoven was able to compose music even when he was deaf. What a wonderful gift God gave him, and what a wonderful gift his music has been to the world. Even more sweet than hearing music is to be able to hear my loved ones' voices. I'm so blessed and truly thankful. Before I close this, I wanted to tell you that I visited Eleanor today and took her some M and M's. She was so glad to get them, but she didn't remember me visiting her last week. Bless her heart, she can't remember hardly anything. Not her brother's name or her own birthday or even whether she ever had a job. I keep asking her questions, hoping she will be able to remember something, but so far it hasn't worked. But she does seem to enjoy having company and that pleases me. That brings me right back to the gift of hearing. If I were deaf, I couldn't visit with her.

## 3 Nov 2001 - S.A.L.T

I worked at the Sheriff's Office again this morning from 8:00 til 12:00. It was really busy and a little frazzling. I took care of people signing in to visit, and watched the line to keep people getting their rightful turn. That is not as easy as it sounds, because whenever I turned my back on the line, it seemed that some folks got into it that weren't there before. Then I'd have to get the book and check their names and numbers to get it straightened out. And so many of the people can't speak English that it's hard to explain to them. But I learned a new phrase in Spanish. I needed to tell a young woman that I was sorry I got her place mixed up, so I asked who could tell me how to say "I'm sorry" in Spanish, and a man spoke up and said "lo siento." So I'll try to remember that phrase the next time. I feel so sorry for those who can't speak English. They must feel a little scared and a little helpless. I really wish I could speak more Spanish. I know a lot of words but not nearly enough to carry on a conversation. I just said Adios to one person and he looked so pleased at that simple word. He grinned and said, "Yes." I don't know when I'll work next. We have our next meeting next Monday.

## 7 Nov 2001 - Thankful For Freedom

I am thankful I can move about freely and express my beliefs; there are those who live in constant fear. When I think about what people in other countries are going through it makes me shudder. Especially the women in those places where women are treated like they are worthless. And they are beaten or killed for such small! offenses. How horrible. They can't even let a small bit of skin on their arm show in public. Some of our females show too much skin, and J am sometimes appalled at this. I saw a very pretty young women at one of the World Series games, who sang The Star Spangled Banner, wearing what I thought was a most unbecoming outfit, with her navel showing. That might have been acceptable at the beach or at a party with other young people, but not standing in front of the whole country, singing what I consider a sacred song. You may or may not agree with me on this, because this is indeed a free country. And that young lady will not be beaten or persecuted, because she has the freedom to wear what she likes. I am so thankful for the freedom we have here in America, the freedom to do whatever we wish as long as we don't hurt anyone else, and the freedom of speech. And I'm really thankful to be a woman in America. Here we are treated like we are special, with respect and consideration. What more could we ask?

We are truly blessed to be Americans.

## 9 Nov 2001 - Lost In The Country

Irving and I had an adventure today. We headed way out in the country to buy some pecans from a lady. She gave us directions on the phone, but she forgot to mention a detour. So when we came to the detour, we followed the signs for miles and miles. We finally found her and bought 20 pounds of pecans, then we tried to find a shorter way home. Well, we drove until we were in the next county, then Irving decided we must be on the wrong road. We turned back and tried a different way, and after awhile we were in another county, but we did finally find the highway which we knew would bring us back home. It was all kind of funny, and it was a beautiful day. Actually, we enjoyed seeing places we hadn't been to before. I told Irving that at least gas prices are down now, so that it didn't cost much. We got so hungry on the way back home, we stopped at Kentucky Fried Chicken and bought ourselves a great meal to bring home. So, all in all, we had a right nice day. And we have a lot of pecans to crack and shell for the freezer.

## 12 Nov 2001 - Another Reason To Be Thankful

I am thankful I can work; there are those who have to depend on others for even their most basic needs. A lot of times I don't want to do anything, certainly not work, but when I think of how it would be if I couldn't do anything, I realize I need to be more thankful. I remember a time years ago when I was in the hospital for about two weeks and wasn't able to do any work. I'd look around my room and think how pleasant it would be to clean it and tidy everything. I know a lady who is on our "meals on wheels" route, who has so much pain in her back and her knees that she can hardly do anything. She wants to get her house in order, but can't stand long enough to get much done. I know she would dearly love to be able to work. We are taking another lady into our route in a day or two who lives with her niece who is also disabled and is not able to take care of her. So I was told today that they have been eating mostly cereal, and they are losing weight. I can't stand the thought of that. So now the lady will be able to have a hot meal each weekday. Of course, that's not enough but it will help. She is 77 years old, and I guess she doesn't have any children to look after her. I'm sure she would so love to be able to work and do things for herself. So I'm reminded of how thankful I should be, because I'm able to get around and fix food for my husband and myself. God is so good to me, and I'm truly grateful.

## 16 Nov 2001 - Lauren Is Twelve

We just got back from Jami's house. She invited us over for dessert to help celebrate my granddaughter Lauren's twelfth birthday. Lauren is spending the night with Hannah, and I think they are having a nice time together. Irving and Calvin sat in the den watching a Clint Eastwood movie, while Jami and I visited with the girls in the kitchen. We enjoyed singing and talking and looking at some things Jami has learned to do on the computer. Our brownie sundaes were delicious. So it was an altogether pleasant visit. Tomorrow, I am due to work at the jail in the afternoon from 12 til 4, during visitation time. Then at 5, we are having a barbeque and a gospel singing at the church. I'm looking forward to that. I'm always so thankful to have something to look forward to. This has been a good day.

## 18 Nov 2001 - A Big Day

Yesterday I worked at the jail again during the afternoon visiting hours, and once again I am wishing that I knew enough Spanish to communicate with the Mexicans who come to visit. I feel so sorry for them when they are trying to explain something. I wrote the receipts for all the money that was left for the inmates and I feel that it is a hardship for most of these people to leave ten, twenty, or thirty dollars. And one or two people left two dollars. That seemed to say that they didn't have hardly any money. It's really a sad situation, but as long as folks keep on breaking the law, this type of thing will go on. Now for something happy to tell about. When I left the jail, I went to the church for the barbecue/gospel sing and had a really nice evening. The food was so good, and the group who came to sing did an outstanding job. And I'm so proud of my daughter, who organized the whole thing. When I got home, I was very tired, but I did want to watch "Rocky V" which came on at ten o'clock. L love the last part of that movie, but I fell asleep about eleven and missed the best part. Oh well, maybe next time.

## 23 Nov 2001 - A Good Thanksgiving

Yesterday was a really nice day for us. We went to Jami's house for lunch and it was so enjoyable. The food was delicious, but the good visit was even better. Then I spent the night with Jami's children while she and Calvin went to visit Calvin's sister. This morning I went to have my eyes examined and I'm getting new glasses about next Wednesday. My stepdaughter, Vicki's husband is an optometrist and they are giving me the glasses for my Christmas gift. I think that's outstanding. So sweet of them. This afternoon I took the children to a movie. We saw "Hearts in Atlantis" and it was good, although a little over Jamison's head. He liked it anyway. We all like Anthony Hopkins. Well, I've talked a lot lately about things I'm thankful for. Here is one that means so much: I am thankful that I have been loved; there are those for whom no one has ever cared. I've always known I was loved, from the time I was very small, when my mother loved me more than anyone else in the world. I knew that my grandmothers loved me too. My husband shows his love to me every day in his actions and in his looking after me. My children love me and all those wonderful little grandchildren do too. I'm so very thankful I don't have the words to express it. I know two ladies in nursing homes for whom no one really cares, and I cannot imagine how awful that would be. I pray that God will give me the grace to share my love with others. There's a song that starts with these words: Because I have been given much I too will give. Thanks be to God for his gifts to me.

## 27 Nov 2001 - A Busy Day, But A Good One

My first job was to deliver Meals on Wheels, then on to the church for ladies' prayer meeting. Hannah helped me with the deliveries, and that shortened my time a lot, then she practiced her music during the prayer time. After I came home and fixed lunch, Hannah and I headed out again. We went to the nursing home to visit Eleanor. We had missed our visit last week, so I took her two Hershey bars. She is always so glad to get chocolate. We noticed that today she stuttered a good bit and had more trouble talking. That may be a sign that she is getting worse. What a terrible thing it must be to not be able to remember hardly anything. When we left there, we went to Wal-Mart for some Christmas shopping. While we were there, we saw Jami's good friend,

Kathy, who has been dreadfully sick for a long time. She has had both feet and one hand and all the fingers on the other hand amputated, but here she was in a wheel chair, doing some shopping with her mother-in-law. I had not seen her since before she got so sick, but as we talked I soon became aware of her beautiful spirit. She told me that she teaches music to a class of handicapped children at her church. She said that she used to play piano. Now my piano playing is not very good but I dearly love it, and think it would be awful to lose it. So I asked her if she missed it terribly, and she said she did, but that she had a choice about how she would deal with it. She said that she could either be bitter about the fact that she had lost it, or she could be thankful that she had had the gift for so long. She chose to be thankful. She said she had a friend who was born without arms from her elbows down, and this friend had never had a chance to learn to play piano. I was so blessed by this young woman. I didn't see the first hint of self-pity or depression in her. I could only see that Jesus Christ lives in her. How wonderful. She made my day a bright one.

## 29 Nov 2001 - This And That

Yesterday my Aunt Pearl turned 91. I always call her on her birthday, so I enjoyed our conversation. She has always been special to me. She is hard-headed and opinionated but when she loves you, she'll fight for you if necessary. Her daughter and son-in-law took her out to eat for her birthday and she said she really ate a lot and enjoyed it. I delivered Meals on Wheels this morning, then ate lunch at Wendy's. Afterwards, I bought groceries. Later on, Irving and I went to look at some floor coverings to get an idea of what we might want for our den. The nice stuff is really expensive, but then I guess everything is. Then we went by to see our newest great-grandson, Drew, and he gets sweeter every time we see him. He's 5 months old. We came home and I fixed supper. Now I have dishes to wash, but not enough to run the dishwasher. Boy, I didn't realize what a full day I've had until I started writing. No wonder I'm tired. Well, I guess I'll go and clean up the kitchen. And then I may just go on to bed. Pardon my rambling, but it's been kind of a rambling day.

## 1 Dec 2001 - Can It Really Be December?

Well, here we go again. Christmas carols, shopping, crowds, laughing, excited children, cantatas, nativity scenes, parties, gifts, decorations. I'm never quite ready, but that doesn't matter. This year, I'm really kind of slow getting started; running out of time for our Christmas music preparations with both the adult choir and the children's program, and only a few presents bought. I must stop and take the time to remember what this season is really all about, and put Jesus Christ first in my heart. He came into this world as a baby, the Son of God, to be our Savior. And that's what is important. I must focus on Him and then all of these other things will fall into place. I must be sure my priorities are in order. I know that the best gift I can give at Christmas is to share the love of Jesus with others. This is my desire.

## 3 Dec 2001 - SALT Christmas Party

Our Christmas party was really enjoyable. I think nearly every member was there. It was held at a Baptist church fellowship hall. The food was delicious. We had a lot of door prizes that had been donated by local businesses, and I got three prizes, all food. Yay for me! I know I'll enjoy them. You may suspect that I really like to eat out. Irving is thin and has never cared much about eating out. He prefers my cooking. But he does like to go to a fish restaurant maybe once a month. Well, that's about all for this time. But I do want to include this very special reminder: Jesus is the reason for the season. He is the Way, the Truth, and the Life.

## 6 Dec 2001 - Working At The Jail

I went to the jail yesterday to work the afternoon hours of visitation. It seemed kind of hard to go because I had choir practice on my mind. We are getting near the time to do our Christmas music, and I always get a little worried about this time. So I sat there at the desk with one eye on the clock, when I noticed a very attractive woman coming in. She was crying, and my heart went out to her. I learned that she had a daughter in jail and she was trying to arrange to get her out on bail. We talked a good deal. She told me that she had never felt so ashamed in her life as when she walked into that area. And she was so angry with her daughter who apparently has been wayward for some time. She has custody of her two young grandchildren. As a mother, I felt such compassion for her, and when my time was up I told her that I wished her the best, and she told me that I had made it better. Those words meant so much to me, and certainly made my time at the jail worthwhile. There was nowhere that I would rather have been at that time. And after my worry about choir practice, it went so well I now have hope that we just might make it. I should learn to trust God more. He always helps us. And before I close this, I just want to say "Thanks be to God for His Unspeakable Gift." You know on that first Christmas, He gave His only begotten Son. Let's not forget.

## 8 Dec 2001 - A Very Nice Trip

I took a trip to Myrtle Beach on a tour bus with our preacher and 40-something others, and it was so nice. We left yesterday morning. When we arrived at Myrtle Beach, we spent about 3 hours at a place called Broadway at the Beach, where we looked in many different shops and ate lunch. Then we went to our hotel and checked in. We left the hotel around 5:15 and went to eat at the greatest seafood buffet that I know of. They have just about every kind of seafood plus a lot of other food and great desserts. Naturally I ate too much. No will power, I guess. When we left there, we went to the Alabama Theater for a show called "Christmas in Dixie," which was really good. Today, we shopped at a mall for awhile, had lunch there, then went to see my favorite show, "Carolina Opry." It was simply wonderful from start to finish. What talented people! Great singing, dancing, comedy, beautiful costumes. Near the end, one of the men who is a great comedian, became quite serious and sang a song called "Unto us a Son is Born." It was excellent. And the show always ends with a song called "He's Alive!" The woman who sings it does a wonderful job. It is a very touching spiritual experience to see and hear this. And the audience always gives a standing ovation. Someone said as we boarded the bus, "If that doesn't ring your bell, your clapper must be broken." Well, it was a really good trip, with such outstanding entertainment, and such good fellowship with fellow travelers. Three of them were among our oldest members; one is about 87, one is soon going to be 86, and one is about 85. They had a great time, and I'm so glad they were able to make this trip. I hope all of you who read this are aware each day of what Christmas really means, that God loved us so much that He sent His only begotten Son. I can't think of any other gift quite so marvelous as this. Thanks be to God for His Unspeakable Gift.

## 13 Dec 2001 - Thoughts About Christmas

I just read a little book by John Gresham titled "Skipping Christmas" which told about a man and his wife who decided to skip Christmas and everything connected with it, and to spend the money on a cruise for themselves. Started me thinking. Sometimes I would like to skip all the trappings of Christmas, just celebrate the birth of Christ. We never go into debt to pay for gifts, but I know a lot of people do, and that really starts off the New Year in a bad way. People often feel that they have to spend the same amount that others spend on them, even though they can't afford it. And often children get hurt because they didn't get as much as their friends did. Years ago, when our church had its Christmas party, gifts would be brought to the church and handed out near the end of the party. Some children would get many packages from their large extended family, while other children whose family didn't attend church would get one small gift from their Sunday School teacher. This really hurt me, and I'm so glad that the practice was stopped years ago. I sure was a bad idea. But when I think about things like that, I think it would be best to leave off some aspects of our celebrations. And Christmas has always been a little sad for me because of some bad memories. I could really get depressed if I would let myself. I suspect a lot of people have some sad feelings during this season. But I really wouldn't skip Christmas, because it would hurt and disappoint a lot of dear people. And there are some very nice things about it. It's fun to see a child's face brighten when he or she receives a present. The Christmas music is beautiful. And being with our precious family is wonderful. And of course the true meaning of Christmas is something well worth celebrating, so I won't be skipping Christmas. The little book just started me thinking. But I'm going to think positively and do all I can to make this a happy Christmas for those I come in contact with. After all, the first and most wonderful gift came down from heaven on that first Christmas Day. Who wouldn't rejoice and be thankful for Him?

## 15 Dec 2001 - Counting My Blessings

I worked at the jail again this afternoon from 12 til 4, and I've been sitting here just now counting my blessings. My children are safe and sound so far as I know, they have shelter and food to eat. Those poor people who come to visit their loved ones at the jail must have broken hearts. It makes me realize again how thankful I should be for my blessings. I have a good place to live, pretty good health, enough money to meet our needs, a really fine husband, a good church family, precious children and grandchildren and great-grandchildren, a good many friends. And so much of the time, I take all of this for granted. I am no better than those folks who visit the jail and I don't deserve all the blessings I have. So this evening I feel so grateful to my Father in Heaven for all of His kindness to me, and I want to somehow, someday, be worthy of His care. And you know He even sent His Only Begotten Son into the world to pay for my sins. I can't fathom such love as that, can you?

## 17 Dec 2001 - Yesterday Was Busy But Great

Always when it's nearly time for our Christmas program at church, I get a little stressed. I'm afraid we won't know our music well enough or that some major thing will go wrong. But God always blesses us and helps us and everything works out. Last night was a special night for us, because our program was good, I think. To start it out, Jami sang " O Holy Night" from the balcony. (The church was dark except for some lights among the greenery.) Then, as the choir sang "Who will come to Bethlehem?" we had little children portray the Nativity Scene. That was precious. Then the children sang "Away in the Manger" Next the congregation sang "Joy to the world." Then a little boy who is 6

## 20 Dec 2001 - Lost In The City

Jami, Hannah, and I decided to go shopping on Tuesday. We wanted to do some Christmas shopping at the Christian bookstore (formerly the Baptist Bookstore) which is close to Charlotte. But before going there, Jami and Hannah wanted to treat me to lunch at a really nice place in Charlotte. They said it would be an early present. Well, I did the driving and we finally found the restaurant. We had a really good lunch, then we set out to go to the book store. Jami had no clue how to get there, and J got all turned around. J found the road J was looking for, but I went in the wrong direction. We went a long way until that road ended, and I realized I had chosen the wrong direction. I told Jami and Hannah that we weren't lost, that I knew where we were, I just had to figure out how to get where we wanted to go. We came to a street that I knew would take us to the highway that would take us to the book store. Well, we finally got there, but we sure did take the long way. But it was funny to me, a kind of adventure. We bought several things, including a Thomas Kinkade picture that I had been wanting. It was priced at 199.00, but I had a coupon for 25

## 22 Dec 2001 - I Think I'm Ready

I wrapped my last present a little while ago. I seemed to be so far behind with my shopping, but it all somehow got done, and I'm so glad. And I"m relieved. I don't like to be this late getting ready for Christmas. My mother had this routine of getting off from work at noon on Christmas Eve, then doing all of her shopping, and coming home after dark to do the wrapping. I wonder how she stood it, but she really didn't have a lot of choice in those days. She had to use that last payday to pay for gifts. She lived under such a strain for so many years, with never enough money to make ends meet. I'm so thankful that during her last years, she had enough. She was really grateful too. She often talked about how God had blessed her. Back to getting ready for Christmas, I didn't spend much money, mostly bought small things, but I think everyone will like theirs. We are still waiting to sell our other house, so we are being pretty thrifty these days. At this point, we have a closing date for January 2. If that works out, then we can finish paying for this one, and get our finances back in better order. But I'm sure not complaining, because we are well, and we have everything we need. And we have a precious family. I look forward to spending time with all of them in the next few days. Isn't it wonderful that God sent His Son into the world for us. We don't know the exact date of His birth, but we can still celebrate and be thankful that He came.

## 24 Dec 2001 - Christmas Eve

Well, I've made dressing and cranberry sauce, and my turkey is in the oven. My grandson, Alex, is visiting with us, but he's out playing with friends in the neighborhood. This evening we are going to my granddaughter's house, and that should be nice. So for now, things are quiet and peaceful, even though I do have some more cleaning up to do. Yesterday was so nice at church. Our dear young friend, Amber, who had surgery on Wednesday, was there and looking so pretty. That was a wonderful answer to prayer. Thanks be to God. And Jami sang "Heaven's Child," which is so meaningful. That little baby in the manger truly was heaven's child, sent down by the Father to be our Savior. How can we ever thank Him?

## 27 Dec 2001 - I Can't Sleep For Some Reason

I slept a short nap, then woke up and can't get back to sleep. So now at 2:35, I'm up and writing. Before I decided to get up, I thought about a saying that my daughter cross-stitched a long time ago; when you can't sleep, don't count sheep, talk to the Shepherd. So that's what I did. Then I decided to write an entry, because I often think I'd like to write something but feel like I don't have the time. Well, I sure do have time now. My Christmas Day was a good one. We went to Jami's house for breakfast and enjoyed that a Jot. Then after I spent a little time at home, I went to visit two friends at nursing homes. I've talked about both of these a good many times. One was Lola. I've made it a tradition to visit her on Christmas Day for several years now. She is 93, and has no one. (Except for a nephew, and she doesn't even know where he is.) We had a good laugh when she told me what happened to her teeth. She had put her upper denture under her pillow, then the next morning after she got up, someone took the linens off her bed to wash them. That was the last of her teeth. But she said they are making her some new ones. The other lady I visited was Eleanor. I sat with her in the dining room while she was waiting for lunch. She often talks about wanting to go back to the town where she spent a lot of years. She says her family is there. But she can't decide what to do, because the nursing home where she stays is so nice. She said, "It doesn't even cost me anything to stay here." Her mind is so bad that she can hardly remember anything, and she said she might just get me to start deciding things for her. These two ladies always cause me to stop and count my blessings. I have loved ones who care about me. Who could ask for anything more? But there is more, so much more. I'm able to go places and do things. I have a good place to live. I'm a long way from being rich, but I have everything I need. My car is 10 years old but I think it still looks good, and it really is dependable. And Irving has a van that is 8 years old, and we really enjoy it. We have a good church and dear friends there. I could go on and on, but I just wanted say how thankful I am. Life is good in so many ways.

## 28 Dec 2001 - Getting Back To Normal

Well, the rush and busyness of Christmas is past now. It always seems good to me to put away the cards and decorations, although I don't do much decorating. And as far as New Years is concerned, we don't do anything special. When Mother was living, she always cooked black eyed peas and collard greens, plus some extra dishes, and she would have all of us come to her house for dinner. It really was good, and tradition says that if you eat the peas and greens, you'll have money all year. As far as the food we had for Christmas is concerned, I'm about to get rid of it. I made turkey soup today, and that used up most of my leftover turkey, but now tomorrow I'll have leftover turkey soup. We still have cake, but I put two containers of cake in the freezer so we wouldn't lose it. But now things will get back to normal, and that's a lot easier for me. Jami and Hannah and I went to the movies this afternoon and saw "The Majestic." We enjoyed it. I've never seen Jim Carrey act serious before. Winter time has finally arrived here, and it's a little hard to take. But I heard today that Buffalo, NY, had almost seven feet of snow. That makes our cold weather seem like nothing. I'm glad we have milder weather than a lot of other states. Well, that's all for this time. I'm beginning to ramble.

## 30 Dec 2001 - A Family Affair

My daughter, Paulette, has finally started a diary here. I'm glad and looking forward to reading what she might have to say. She has three little grandsons who light up her life, so I expect we'll be reading about them. That's fine by me. They are adorable and very nice children, even if I do say so. Do you suppose I might be slightly prejudiced? And I wanted to share with all of you that we have another great-grandchild, born this morning. A little girl. She was born on her brother's second birthday. I think that's neat. I haven't learned her name yet, but she weighs a little over 8 pounds and is 20 inches long. Maybe we'll get to see her tomorrow. Well, this has been a nice peaceful day, and I've enjoyed it.

## 31 Dec 2001 - New Year's Eve, And All's Well

Well, it's 9:50, and I'm getting sleepy. We don't plan to do any celebrating. Jami and Calvin have gone out with friends, and Jon and Annette have gone to a party at the home of some friends. Jon's son, Alexander, is spending the night with us and is already asleep. So it is a very quiet night at our house. So peaceful. 2001 was a good year for us, in most ways. But we all are aware that September 11th totally ruined the year for so many people. It's so hard to realize that there are people in this world who would deliberately murder so many innocent and unsuspecting people. God said, "Vengeance is mine. I will repay." So I know for sure that the guilty ones will be severely punished. We all hope so earnestly that 2002 won't bring any bad things to us, and that there will be peace very soon. Also, we would all love to see all of our military men come back home soon.

I know this has been so hard for them and their families. I'm praying for wisdom for our President and his advisors, that they might be able to make good decisions for America. On a happier note, the new little great-granddaughter is doing fine, but when I talked to her mother earlier today, she still hadn't made up her mind what the name will be. But she is leaning toward Alexandra. I'll let you know when I find out. But for now, I wish all of you a healthy, happy, prosperous, and blessed New Year.

## 1 Jan 2002 - Beginning A New Year

Well, it's 2002 and it's hard to believe. Where have all those years gone? They say that time flies when you're having fun. It seems to me that it flies even if you're not having fun. We've had a very quiet day today. Alex stayed with us until around 1:00, and he was a pleasure. He just had to go outside a few times, even though it was so cold, but he had brought his new bicycle and our neighborhood is perfect for bike riding. So who could blame him? Irving and I had our collard greens and blackeyed peas and cornbread, so we should have money all this year. One of our granddaughters dropped by and brought us some banana nut bread that she had made, and it really is good. And now I can announce our new great-granddaughter's name. It's Alexandra Christina. Quite a mouthful. The baby has an aunt named Christina, so that's the reason for the middle name. Well, that's about all the news from our house. I have just about quit making resolutions, because I don't seem able to stick to them, so for 2002, I'll just resolve to do the best I can to make this year a good one. I think that's all God requires of us, that we do our best. Sometimes we fall, but we can just get back up and try again.

## 2 Jan 2002 - All Set For Snow

We are getting a pretty snow here. I always enjoy seeing it, but I feel bad for those who have to get out in it to go to work. I went to the store this morning, and made sure we have everything we need in case the streets get slippery. I expect school will be out tomorrow, and that won't hurt any child's feelings. I kind of doubt if we will go to church tonight. I made sure to get all the stuff to make snow cream. I love that. I was always told not to make snow from the first snowfall, but I don't much think I can resist it. I'll just make sure I don't use any yellow snow.

## 3 Jan 2002 - Such A Pretty Day

This title may seem strange, but it's true. This day so far has been beautiful. Early this morning, I looked out and saw the blanket of snow which covered my yard and driveway. Then I saw a lot of little birds at our bird feeder, and they were really enjoying the seeds. After breakfast, I made more snow cream, (we'd already had some last night) and we enjoyed that. Hannah always spends Wednesday nights with us, so she got her daddy to drive her over last night even though the streets were slippery. She just couldn't miss her Wednesday night visit. So we are enjoying having her today. A little while ago, she looked out a window and said,"There's a man out there in your driveway shoveling snow." We looked out and Chris, who lives next door, was out there working so hard for us. He had already cleared our sidewalk and nearly had our path to the mailbox all done. I stuck my head out the door and thanked him. He just said, "No problem. I grew up doing this." He is from New Jersey, I believe. Then he cautioned me about walking where he had shoveled, because it might be pretty slick. I was so impressed with his thoughtfulness. What a sweet neighbor, and how blessed we are to have him. Right now, it is only snowing a little bit, so maybe we are through, but it may take a while for it to melt. I know this day hasn't been a pretty one for a lot of people, and I'm sorry about that, but for us it has been a very pretty day.

## 4 Jan 2002 - A Good Samaritan

This evening when Irving and I rode out to our other house to check on the electricity, I was reminded of the last time I drove on a snowy day. It was probably a little over 20 years ago. I had two or three classes at college, and when it started to snow, I still had one to go and I really didn't want to miss it. So I convinced myself that it probably wouldn't matter if I stayed just one more hour. Well, the school is about 12 miles from our house, and each mile I drove got more and more slippery. It was nightmarish for me. Each time I came to a stoplight, my car would slide a little. By the time I drove about half way home, I was at a place where there were embankments, although not large ones, but scary nonetheless. Every time I would put on my brakes, I slid toward the bank. I was scared to death and my nerves were at the breaking point. So when I got stopped, I decided I could not go any further, I would sit there in my car. I didn't know what else to do. About that time, a fellow church member was heading to town along with his son-in-law to pick up his daughter from work. When he saw me, he got out of his car and came to my car and asked me what was wrong. I told him I just couldn't drive any further, that 1 was too upset. Well, he just had me to slide over and he got in and drove me home, while his son-in-law followed. I couldn't look at the road, I just sat looking at my lap. But he got me home with no problem and I'll never forget what a hero he was to me that day. He died a few years later, but he left behind a special memory. And I decided that day that I would never try to drive in the snow or ice again.

## 5 Jan 2002 - Finally Able To Drive Again

I had not been out of the house since it snowed Wednesday, except to ride with Irving once to our other house yesterday. So today the streets are clear, mostly, and I was able to go to the grocery store. Then we went to see our newest great- grandchild, Alexandra. She is so pretty, with dark hair and a sweet little face. She weighed nearly nine pounds at birth, so she is not wrinkled or red. She looks older than newborn. She is our seventh great-grandchild and our twenty-second grandchild, counting regulars and greats together. Her brother is two years old, and maybe a little jealous, but that's so understandable. I'm so glad we finally got to visit them today. I hope our roads will stay clear tomorrow, so we can get to church safely.

## 8 Jan 2002 - Mixed Emotions

We sold our other house today, and I hardly know what to feel. It took months to get it all worked out, so we had gotten to the point of not knowing what to expect. We lived in that house for 21 years, and loved it, and now it isn't ours anymore. Hard to believe. But now we can pay this one off, and not have house payments, and that's a real plus. When we moved into the other house it was a gift from God. We had lived in a trailer for 13 years and I wanted a house so bad. And after we started building it, the money was always there as we needed it, so that when we moved into it, it was totally paid for. Irving said today at the closing that the house had never had a mortgage on it. I'm still so grateful that God gave it to us, and it was a wonderful blessing to us. But now I need to put that into my sweet memories and get on with life. But I do feel homesick. I hope that passes soon.

## 9 Jan 2002 - It's A Boy!!!

Thirty-seven years ago today, my third child was born. I had two daughters and was hoping the third child would be another girl. I knew that little girls were so cute and sweet, and I knew nothing about little boys. Also, I was in a terrible spot financially. I had nothing. My first husband had left me two months before, and we had no idea where he was, and we never had any financial support from him. So if I had another girl, at least I could make use of hand-me-downs, and three little girls could always share a room. But oh how wrong I was! If I had known how adorable a little boy could be, I would have been so hoping for a boy. But God knew exactly what I needed, and He very kindly gave me a son. I wish I could tell you how precious that son was then and is today. He was always a good baby, and he continued to be a joy to me. His stepfather had always wanted a son, and was so proud when Jon became his. Jon gave us almost no trouble when he was growing up, except for climbing into the barn, or disappearing into the woods and scaring me nearly to death. He grew into a big boy, but he was always gentle. He would never hit anybody or use his strength in a bad way. When he was old enough to drive, he worked and bought his own car and paid his own way. Whenever he could not get home by 11:00, he would call me so I wouldn't worry. He grew into a fine Christian man, and I'm so proud of him. I guess I'm allowed to brag on him on his birthday, right? Dear Jon, I love you very much. Happy Birthday!!!

## 12 Jan 2002 - Ladies' Jubilee

I went to a meeting at another church last night and today called Ladies' Jubilee. I've been to two or three of them before and they are just wonderful. This is the first one I've been to that included Friday night. Last night, there was a good deal of singing, including a group of girls from a home for girls. I was told that the girls at that home may be orphans or just have a need for a place to live. Or they might be wayward girls. I understood that most any girl who needed a place would be welcome there. Anyway, it was beautiful to see them standing before the church singing. And I was told that the church who started this home for girls is planning to start a place for boys soon. My granddaughter, Lauren, went with me last night, and I was glad she went, because I felt like something like that would benefit a young person. We heard two speakers and they both had good testimonies. I went back alone today, heard more good singing, and two more good speakers. One of them was the wife of Alvin Dark, who was a famous baseball player years ago. I had heard of him, and I asked his wife which team he had played with. She said he had played for the Braves before they were in Atlanta, and also for the Giants. She said he had been the Rookie of the Year in 1949, and later had even been a manager. I was really interested in that, since I am the number one Braves fan. At the Jubilee, they always give away a lot of door prizes. Last year, I won a bird house, and today I won a Tupperware snack keeper. And they always have a great lunch which is free. There is always barbeque, marinated turkey, fried chicken, beans, slaw, potatoes, and delicious desserts. All of the door prizes and food is donated by different businesses and individuals. It really is so special and uplifting to be with a large group of women and girls with like minds, all praising the Lord. I guess you can tell that I had a wonderful day. And to top it off, when I got home a little after three, Irving asked me if I'd like to go out and eat fish. I told him we'd have to wait awhile because I was stuffed. So we went later than we usually do and the fish was especially good. I really shouldn't eat anything tomorrow, but I probably will. Maybe I can keep it light. Tomorrow is Sunday, and I am tentatively planning on singing a solo titled "Whiter than snow." I pray that my voice will be in good shape, but lately it is sometimes kind of rough sounding, and feels kind of like I always need to clear my throat or like I need to cough. I hope it doesn't mean that my singing days are coming to an end. That would be hard for me, but God has allowed me to sing for a long, long time, so if it should end soon I shouldn't complain. And God has given a lot of talent to my children and their children, so one day they can just take up the torch and carry on.

## 13 Jan 2002 - Our Preacher Resigned Today

Our church was so shocked this morning when, after the sermon, our preacher read his resignation. He has been with us for about 14 years and we dearly love him. He has been such a good pastor, always there if you need him. And he is one of the best preachers I've ever heard. I feel like he will be hard to replace. I know he probably has very good reasons for his decision, but we will miss him and his sweet wife so much. We started working on our Easter music tonight at choir practice. We just sight read through the book, and it is going to be pretty easy, I think. The title of it is "Amen." So now we have a little over eight weeks to get it ready. I have two little grandsons spending the night, and they just went to bed, so now I think I'll turn in too.

## 15 Jan 2002 - Choose To Be Happy

This is one of my favorite philosophies of life, and since Jami brought it up in her diary, I'd like to talk about it a little further. Now I realize that there are times when we can't possibly be happy; when death takes a loved one, or when sickness strikes, when we find ourselves in any major kind of trouble. But normally, when things are going fairly smoothly,

I think we can choose either to be happy or to be down. I believe that some folks actually enjoy being sad or depressed, and they bring others down. I have never liked to be around anyone who was perpetually in a bad or depressed mood. Here again, I don't mean anyone who has a real reason to be that way. I'll always be glad to stay and listen to problems. But I prefer to stay in a good mood and be cheerful as much as I possibly can, even if I must sometimes "put on a happy face." I decided many years ago that I don't want people to feel sorry for me, so I often cover up my feelings. I would never want to cause another person to become depressed or troubled. So I choose to be happy, and it's usually not hard to do. When I take the time to count my blessings, I have to feel cheerful about that. And I love that verse in Proverbs that says, "A merry heart doeth good like a medicine." It's really true.

## 16 Jan 2002 - A Special Visitor

This morning our pastor came to visit us, and it was so good to have him. Even though we had just seen him at church on Sunday, we are already missing him, because he submitted his resignation. He will preach two more sermons. Those will be on the last two Sundays in February. He told us that he wanted us to know how much he appreciated us, and the way we've always supported him. He said he was not resigning his friendships. Of course we knew that he would always be our friend and brother, but it was so sweet that he came and told us that. He has been so special in our lives. Anytime we had sickness or death in our family, he was always there to help and comfort. He has always been an encourager to me with the music. We won't forget him.

## 21 Jan 2002 - Changing Carpet

Boy, is my house upside down tonight. A friend is coming in the morning to put down our new carpet in the den. Calvin and Jordan came this evening to move the heavy furniture and take up the old carpet. My sofa is crowded into the little dining area, and various other pieces are crowded in here and there. It's awful, but maybe it will be worth it tomorrow after everything is back in place. My cat, Rayne, is even upset. He can't understand all these changes. He likes to nap on the sofa, and tonight he didn't know what to do. He was acting so strange, I just put him out in the garage where he sleeps a little earlier that usual. At least I won't be here much while all of this is being done. I have to leave about ten to take meals on wheels, then there's ladies' prayer at eleven, then I have a dentist appointment at twelve-thirty. Our friend is due here at ten, so he may be all finished before I get back.

We had a nice weekend. Our little grandson, Alex, spent most of it with us. He brought his bike and had a great time riding all over our neighborhood. It really is a good place for children here.

Well, that's all I have on my mind tonight, and it's getting late for old folks, so I'll close this for this time.

## 22 Jan 2002 - The Carpet Looks Great

Our new carpet is all finished in the den, and it really looks good. We still have two pieces of furniture to put back, but we will wait for Calvin to come. We just can't manage anything heavy.

My daughters have given me a couple of good laughs lately with their entries, better than jokes. Paulette wrote about what Austin said about a piece of clay. And today

Jami wrote about going to the store in her pajama bottoms. I loved both of those stories. And Paulette reminded me of how we got so tickled at Miranda's baptism. I'm enjoying reading their entries.

## 24 Jan 2002 - A Few Of My Favorite Things

Some things I can hardly resist are pretty dishes, clocks, and mugs. I used to buy dishes at the grocery store every time they would sell them. You could buy a place setting for three or four dollars, for every time you spent a certain amount of money for groceries. I can't even guess how many sets I've bought, then I've given them away later to make room for more. I have finally decided that I just mustn't buy them anymore, that it doesn't make sense. But the last time they offered a set at Bilo, I just had to buy two of the mugs. But later I decided that I didn't really like them and I gave them to Jami, who had collected probably a whole set. I guess she has inherited one of my weaknesses. I also love pretty clocks, but seldom buy one, because they are a little bit expensive. I remember buying a beautiful one when I was very young. I loved it. Then my future mother- in-law admired it and I gave it to her. I've never quite gotten over that. We realized recently that my grandson, Jamison, loves clocks too. I wonder if he has inherited that quality. It's interesting to me. Now lately, I have begun to love mugs. I don't know how many I have, but I would guess at least a dozen, so I certainly don't need one. But today I went into a shop in the mall and noticed a sale table. And there was the most beautiful mug. It was just the kind I like best, large and thin. Seems to be fine china, and was marked down from $20.00 to $5.00. So I simply had to buy it, couldn't pass up a deal like that. On the way home, I stopped by Jami's and showed it to her. She offered me a cup of coffee, and I wanted to try out my new mug, so she washed it and poured coffee in it and set it before me along with some real cream. Now that was great coffee. I think the beautiful mug was part of the reason it was so good. I must be simple-minded in some ways, because it doesn't take very much to please me. I'm looking forward to having coffee in the morning.

## 28 Jan 2002 - I Heard A Funny Joke

My granddaughter told me a joke this evening that was so funny, and when I called Jami and told it to her, she said I should put it in my diary. So here goes: Three men were doing construction work away up high on a building, and when they stopped to eat their lunch, the first man said, "It's a sausage sandwich again. I'm sick of it. If I ever see another sausage sandwich I'll jump." The second man looked at his lunch and said, It's another burrito. If I ever see another burrito I'll jump." The third man, who happened to be a blonde, looked at his lunch and said, "It's a ham sandwich. If I ever see another ham sandwich, I'll jump too." So the next day at lunch time, they sat down on the scaffold to eat. The first man opened his lunch- box, and when he saw another sausage sandwich he jumped. The second man opened his and there was a burrito, so he also jumped. The third man, who just happened to be blonde, saw that he had another ham sandwich, so he jumped too. Well, after the three funerals, the three wives were talking, and the first wife said, "If I'd had any idea how he felt about sausages sandwiches, I would have been glad to fix him something else." The second wife said, "And if I had known that my husband was so tired of burritos, I could have fixed him a taco for lunch." The blonde man's wife then said, "Don't look at me. My husband always fixed his own lunch."

## 29 Jan 2002 - Mrs. G.

When I was delivering "Meals on wheels" today, I stopped at the first lady's house, and for the first time she really wanted to talk. Her niece, with whom she lives, is in the hospital so Mrs. G. was really lonely. She always has the plastic oxygen tubes in her nose with the connecting tube in the floor following her. I don't know what her physical problems are but I assume that either her heart or her lungs must be bad. She asked me to come in and see the new bedroom suite that her niece's husband had bought for her while she was in the hospital. She was to come home today, and Mrs. G. said she would be so thrilled to see the new furniture. It really is beautiful. Mrs. G. told me that she had lost both of her children in a period of three years; the son had cancer and the daughter had some kind of stomach problem. Mrs. G. had been living at the beach, and just could not live alone, so her niece brought her here to live with her. She said she had a granddaughter who lived near her at the beach but didn't seem to care anything about her. She only cared about getting as much of her money as she could. I felt so sorry for this lady, and I was reminded again of how blessed I am. My children are all well and I believe that my grandchildren all love me. And on top of all that, I have a perfectly great husband who loves me. I feel so grateful that I can go to Mrs. G's house and take her a lunch and maybe another time I can stay a little longer, if she seems to be lonely.

## 1 Feb 2002 - A New Member's First Impression

A little over fifteen years ago, a man came to our county to get work and start over, because there just wasn't work to be found in his home state. He started coming to our church and really liked it, so when he had gotten settled, he sent for his wife and two sons to join him. Well, the first time he brought Nancy to our church we were having a celebration of some kind. I think it was the Fourth of July. A lot of folks were sitting outside in lawn chairs, so Nancy sat down to wait while Sam went inside for something. Soon Nancy was joined by some very friendly people, but they acted a little strange, almost retarded. She wondered what kind of group she was getting involved with and was very uncomfortable. It turned out that these were some residents from a local rest home who had been brought to our church to enjoy our celebration. It really was funny when Sam came back out and discovered Nancy's plight. He explained the situation to her and we have enjoyed this story over the years. Nancy is very intelligent and well-educated, and I'm sure she was wondering how she would get along in such a church. But she soon found out that we were mostly just ordinary people who were very glad to have her and her family with us. And by the way, they have prospered and everything seems to have gone extremely well for them.

## 2 Feb 2002 - Barry

Our son-in-law, Barry, had open heart surgery this morning. It was a triple bypass. We are so thankful that he came through it. He has always been special to us, willing to help us anytime we need him. He is a very hard worker, and a fair and honest man, a real Christian. He has gone to Brazil at his own expense several times to help the people there. I think it has been mostly to help build churches or to repair them. He is dedicated to his church, teaches Sunday School, sings in the choir, serves as a deacon. We are so proud of him. Well, on a lighter note, we have our little grandson, Alex, spending the night with us. He's already asleep. He had to go with us to the hospital today and that really didn't fit in with his plans, but he was good anyway. And after we got back, he had a good bit of time to play in the neighborhood. So I guess all's well that ends well.

## 7 Feb 2002 - Cruising

Our weather here has been so miserable yesterday and today, and Jami has posted the accounts she wrote about her wonderful cruise, and now I'm just itching to take a cruise in the Caribbean. Maybe take one day in several different ports. I took one cruise in my lifetime when I came home from Puerto Rico, but it was on a military ship, not very luxurious. Paulette was two years old at the time and I think she enjoyed the trip, except for the one time she threw up in our stateroom. That was doubly bad because my husband was feeling sick and taking Alka-seltzers, and I didn't feel very well. But we managed to get it cleaned up. One good thing happened: Paulette liked the walk down the hallway to the bathroom because we swayed a lot from side to side. And because she liked that walk, she became potty-trained at last. We made a stop at Guantanamo Bay, Cuba, for just a few hours. I don't remember why, but at least I can say that I've been to Cuba. Then we went on to New York City. I saw the Statue of Liberty for the first time. That was awesome! We spent one night in New York, and the next morning we took a train home to Charlotte. That was my only lengthy train ride, and it was so pleasant. But the best part was getting home after being gone for about a year and seeing my parents again. Well that trip was one of my big adventures. What a memory!

## 10 Feb 2002 - Another Tragic Suicide

My friend's son committed suicide yesterday morning. He was almost 43 years old. He was her third child and he came to her house to visit. He told her some of his problems, including the fact that he wanted to die. He said he hadn't slept for three days and he was like a zombie and so totally depressed. His mother offered to fix him something to eat, but he said that food was the last thing on his mind. He went to the bathroom a little later and shot himself in the chest. Surely he couldn't have been in his right mind, or he wouldn't have done that to his mother. He dearly loved her. Now she says that she can't live in that house anymore. This is such a sad situation. I just pray that after a few days she will begin to heal. I think she is still in shock now. I just can't imagine anything worse in this world that could happen to a mother. And of course his sisters and brothers are all broken-hearted too. It's awful to realize that there are people who are so depressed or so troubled that they can't bear to live. We've had two suicides in our family, so we know how painful this can be. I just wish I knew some way to help this family. I know that God can help more than any mortal can, so I'll be praying a lot about this.

## 15 Feb 2002 - A Sad Anniversary

I debated with myself a lot before deciding to write this entry, because the memories are still so painful. But maybe I can say something that will help someone else. Four years ago today my mother left us. It was not of her choosing. She wanted to live so that she could be with her family. But it was God's time to call her, and certainly He knows best, and

I have no doubt about where she is now. I know that she is safe and at peace and that I will see her again one day. She was definitely a Christian, and I am so thankful to know that. She was in the hospital for thirteen days and during that time she sang her last song which was Amazing Grace, she heard her last scripture which I recited to her while she was dying. It was the 23rd Psalm. I don't think I will say anymore this time. I've tried these four years to stay in control and I don't want to lose it today. But I must say that she dearly loved me, her only child, and she adored her three grandchildren and her great-grandchildren. She also loved my husband like a son. Maybe sometime later I'llI talk more about the way she helped me during the hard times. But here is my advice to you who still have your mother: Show her that you love her, and not just with words. Make her life a little happier. You'll never regret it. I have no regrets about how I treated Mother, but I'm sure I could have done more. But she knew beyond any doubt that she was very special to me and all our family and words can't express how much we all miss her.

## 19 Feb 2002 - Aaron, A Real Cutie

My grandson Aaron had his fifth birthday last Wednesday. He is one of the happiest children I've ever seen. But this morning was a little rough for him. He had to have three shots in order to get ready for kindergarten this Fall. I went by to console him afterwards, and he had three band-aids on his little arms. He said he cried, and I told him I didn't blame him. I feel so sorry for little ones when they have to go through something like that. But he seemed to be pretty much over it when I saw him, and I took him some cookies which I think will help him to recuperate.

We have two new people on our "Meals on Wheels" route. It's a couple, and I was told that they really were in need of this service. I understand that the wife is in very bad health. I noticed this morning that there were several small items of clothing hanging on the clothes line, and I wondered if the husband had washed them and hung them out. It was just a small thing but it seemed touching to me. I'm glad we can help them a little with lunch.

Well this has been a good day, and that's something I'm always thankful for. And tonight I'm looking forward to watching the ladies' short programs in figure skating. I love to see that. It's such a beautiful and graceful art.

## 22 Feb 2002 - Giving Credit For A Kindness

Back in January, We had new carpet put down in our den and it is so nice. I wrote about this, but I didn't share the story of our friend who did the work for us. He told Irving to start with that he wouldn't charge us anything for doing it. But we felt like we wanted to do something for him in return for his long hard day of work. He's a fine young man who is a member of our church. He has a great wife who is a stay-at-home mother to their two children. We surely didn't expect him to do all that much for us for nothing. When he was finished, Irving got him to accept a very small amount of money, but we still weren't satisfied that we had treated him right. So I called and told his wife that we wanted to take them out to eat as a way of saying thank you. Well, when he called me back, he asked me why we wanted to take them out to eat, and when I told him, he said that we had already thanked him. He then asked me, "Am I your friend?" Of course, I said yes. Then he asked me, "Why do you want to make me your hired hand?" He said he just wanted to help us out since we needed something done, and he was able to do that. So I dropped trying to pay him. I thought it was a beautiful gesture, and I'll be looking for a chance to do something for him sometime. This should be a great reminder to all of us that there are people who are not looking for anything for themselves. Thanks, Eric, for reminding us.

## 24 Feb 2002 - Our Preacher's Last Day

Today our preacher preached his last sermon as our pastor. We are really so sad to lose him, but he feels that it is time. He was with us for over fourteen years, and he has been such a blessing to us. He really is an excellent preacher and he has been such a faithful pastor. He has accepted a part-time job with our county Baptist Association and will be the Church Development Consultant, so he will be working with all the churches in our Association. I'm thankful that he will still reside in the community, so we can still stay in touch. His wife has done a tremendous job with our nursery. She is wonderful with babies. Their son is our pianist and he and his family will still be with us. Their son's little boy, Joshua, sang a song this morning called "I am a Promise," and he did a very good job. After church, we had a covered dish lunch in honor of the preacher and his wife. He told me afterward how much my husband has meant to him all of these years. Irving was always willing to go with him anywhere to visit, and he said that Irving has brought him through some hard times. That was special for me to hear. They will always have a place in my heart. They got a lot of nice gifts, including a painting that Hannah gave them. They seemed to really love that. Well, the day at church was bittersweet, but we'll all be fine.

## 5 Mar 2002 - I Need To Vent

I've been hearing on the news for the last day or two about old people in rest homes being abused. There have been reports of patients being dragged down the hall, of them being beaten in their beds, of some being sexually abused. I don't have the words to adequately express how I feel when

I hear things like this. It makes me sick and furious to think that anyone could possibly be so cruel to someone who is helpless. 1 know that some old people can be worrisome and irritating, but they should still be treated decently, because they can't help themselves anymore. And often their minds are nearly gone, so that they say things they would never have said when they were in good health. To me, it's just as awful to mistreat an old person as it is to mistreat a baby. I am not a violent person by any means and I avoid confrontations at all costs, but if I should ever see someone treating an old person cruelly, I really believe I would attack them. I think about my own parents who became helpless before their deaths and the thought of anyone hurting them, even with unkind words, is more than I can bear. Well, I don't know what good this venting will do anyone, but I just needed to get it off my chest. And if any of you have a loved one in a nursing home, please visit them often and be sure that no one is mistreating them. They would never have allowed anyone to mistreat you when you were helpless.

## 7 Mar 2002 - Dustin

There was a boy in our church named Dustin who was truly unique. To start with, he wasn't supposed to be born, because his mother had her tubes tied after his sister was born. So Dustin was a big surprise for everyone. He was such a cute, happy little boy, and everyone loved him. When he was around seven or eight years old, his daddy died. He was doubly precious to his mother during that hard time, and when his grandfather died some time later, he was a great blessing to his grandmother. He spent a lot of nights with her. He loved life and he loved the church. Well, about two years ago, he and his sister had a wreck coming home from school and Dustin died. I think he was fourteen years old. This was such a shock to his family and to our whole church. During his funeral, there was a hail storm such as I've never known. We couldn't hear half of what the preacher said for the noise of hail stones hitting the roof. As we were starting out of the church a little later, someone said that they wondered if Dustin had requested that hail storm as a joke on us. This brought a smile to his mother, because she knew what a sense of humor Dustin had. We later realized that the storm was just over the church area, not widespread. I don't know whether God would allow something like this, but if He would, then it may be that Dustin was responsible for it. We will always remember Dustin and his happy personality.

## 8 Mar 2002 - Grandparents Day

Today was Grandparents Day for grades K-2 at my great-granddaughter's school, and since Sophie's grandmother couldn't go today, I got a call to go. It really was a sweet program. All the children sang three songs. Then after the program, we were directed to go to the classrooms and pick up our little one for a tour of the school. It is a Christian school at a church about 8 or 10 miles from here, and it really is nice. Sophie took me to the gym for refreshments, then she showed me the computer room, the Spanish room, the library. She is in the first grade, little for her age, and so cute, with blonde hair and blue eyes. She gave me a bookmark that she had made, and before I left, she went to her desk and got another bookmark, and asked me to give it to Granddaddy. I thought she did a really good job, and I enjoyed spending time with her.

## 9 Mar 2002 - A Visit From Four Boys

My grandson, Andrew, brought his three boys to visit this evening, and it was a joy. The two big boys, Colton and Austin, went around my neighborhood selling candy for their school, and they sold all they had brought. Quite the little businessmen, aren't they? While they were out, I held little Drew, and he was so sweet. After a little while, he went to sleep on my lap, with never any fussing at all. I really goofed today. I was thinking all week that I was scheduled to work at the jail from twelve to four today. When I got there, I learned that next Saturday is my day to work. A senior moment, I guess.

## 12 Mar 2002 - What Might The Neighbors Think?

I've written before about my cat, Rayne. I'm very fond of him. Lately, he has started staying out at night, and in the morning, I'm always eager to get him in the house and fed. Then he will usually lie around and sleep the biggest part of the day. Well, when he is not waiting at the door, I go to the back door and call him. If he doesn't come, I go to the front door and call him. This morning, it was raining, and I stuck my head out the back door and called out, "Rayne, Rayne." Then I went to the front door and did the same thing. It dawned on me a little later that if any neighbor heard me, they may have thought I was a little bit crazy. Rayne came in early this afternoon, all wet, ate his fill, and has been sleeping nearly the whole time since. I think the next time it rains in the morning, I should probably just say, "Here, Kitty."

## 16 Mar 2002 - Working At The Jail

I worked at the jail today from twelve til four, and I never got up from my chair the whole time. I took the money the visitors were leaving for the inmates and wrote the receipts for them. Every time I accept money from one of them, I feel so sorry for them, because I feel sure it is a hardship for them. One young woman was telling me that she couldn't afford to leave more because she had her own expenses to take care of. She said that, due to some kind of mix-up, her paycheck was not right this week, and that caused her to write a bad check. So she had that to straighten out. I asked her if the man was her husband, and she told me he was a friend of hers. Another woman, who was a Mexican, told us that she had three babies by the man she was visiting. I asked if he was her husband, and she sort of giggled and said that he was her boyfriend. Call me old- fashioned, but I think that marriage should come before three babies arrive. But this whole situation is tragic, seeing family members and friends coming to visit under those circumstances. One mother came out feeling so pleased that her daughter was looking good. She told us that her daughter had been taking some kind of prescription cough medicine, and got hooked on it. So when she couldn't get any more from her doctor, she resorted to trying to steal it, and she got caught. I don't know how long her sentence was, but her mother said she will be there until the middle of April. And the mother is taking care of the three grandchildren while their mother is in jail. How sad.

## 18 Mar 2002 - Dear Diary

I'm kind of amazed at how DD can become so important. It has become like a hobby in such a short time. I look forward to reading my special favorites every morning or afternoon. I consider several people on DD to be my friends, even though we've never met. I'm concerned about their problems, I share in their joys, I laugh with them over funny things that happen. And they feel the same about me. That's neat, isn't it? And I think that writing here has really been good for me, making me use my brain and my grammar skills. You know, whatever skills you have and don't use can soon become rusty, and I don't want that to happen to me any sooner than it has to. And I just have to mention that my journal has been in the top ten for a few days, and that pleases me so much. If it never happens again, that will be fine, but I've really enjoyed this little while.

## 19 Mar 2002 - Learning To Appreciate

I had the devotional at our ladies' prayer meeting this morning, and I chose to read a short article by Dr. James Dobson, in which he talked about his father's prayer the last time they were together. Dr. Dobson, his wife, and children had spent a week with his parents, and when they were about to say goodbye at the airport, Dr. Dobson asked his dad to pray for them. They gathered together and his dad prayed a beautiful prayer, thanking God for the joy they had experienced and for all the blessings He had given them. He acknowledged that these good times might never come again, but he was grateful for God's gifts no matter how long or how short the time might be. I'm probably not expressing this very clearly, but the point I got from it is this: We haven't been promised that our family will always be together, or that we will always have good health or prosperity. Dr. Dobson's father died suddenly a short time after this prayer, and his mother soon followed him. I hope that I will not take my loved ones or my other blessings for granted any more, but I hope to be careful to appreciate every good gift as it comes. I want to have a more grateful and loving heart, because I owe my Heavenly Father so much.

## 25 Mar 2002 - Bits And Pieces

I just wanted to write an entry, but I don't have any particular topic in mind. So I'll ramble a little. I stayed with Jami's children Thursday night and Friday night, and we got along fine. The only problem was that I stayed cold the first day or so. The children are used to a cold house, so they didn't mind, but I finally turned up the thermostat. I've decided that if I ever have to move in with Jami and Calvin, they will have to fix me a room with a separate thermostat. I'm warning them now that I'll be cranky if I get cold. We learned about the house burning down, and feel so bad for that family. (Jami wrote about it in her diary.) I hope to visit the young woman tomorrow, and see what we can do for her. Her parents and her sister and brother are faithful members of our church. I also learned yesterday of the death of a lady in the community. She didn't go to our church, but she and her husband operated a store nearby and she was very friendly, most enjoyable to talk to, a "people person." She left four grown children, three daughters and one son. My heart goes out to them. I know how hard it is to lose a mother. Tonight was the third time I have visited the funeral home in about two weeks. Maybe there won't be any more deaths for a long time. Well, we had a good day at church yesterday. Jami sang a beautiful song called "The Via Dolorosa." I'm not sure if I spelled that right, but it talks about Jesus walking along that way toward Calvary. She did a very good job, as always. I think our choir is ready now for our Easter musical. They'd better be, because we will perform it next Sunday. It is titled simply "Amen." Well, I guess that's all for tonight. Until next time.

## 26 Mar 2002 - A Good Morning

This morning, I delivered "meals on wheels," then went to ladies' prayer meeting at church. When I left there, I stopped by to visit the young woman whose house burned recently. Her son was home from school sick and I gave him the bag of gifts Jami had sent him. He was pleased with it, especially the socks. He said he hadn't been able to find his socks this morning, so he needed some. It was so sad knowing that they had lost everything they had, but she told me that a lot of people had come to see her or called, and that she had really gotten a lot of help. That will always mean a lot to her and her family. I told her that sometimes we can see good things come out of things that seem so bad, and I think she is already beginning to see that. I'm so glad that she has her parents to help her, and that she and her son can stay with them until she is able to get another place.

## 29 Mar 2002 - Eleanor Seems Worse

Hannah and I went to see Eleanor today at the nursing home, and she was needing a visit. We found her coming from a sitting area, and she was tearful. I think it was because someone had mistreated one of the cats who stays there. But she took us to her room and we sat with her for maybe 15 minutes, and she seemed to feel better. But I believe her condition is getting worse. It was really hard to understand her speech. Today was the first time that she seemed to remember me, although she can't remember my name. I told her that if it made her glad for me to visit her, then I was glad too. I gave her a chocolate bar, as usual, and she was really pleased with it. She loves chocolate candy. When we started out of her room, there was one of the cats lying by her door, and she let it go into her room, so I expect she is having a nice visit now with her little furry friend.

## 4 Apr 2002 - The Braves Won!!!

The Braves just finished their third game of the season. They won the first one and this one tonight, so they've gotten a good start. I love it. The final score was 11 to 2. Tomorrow they play the Mets and I'm looking forward to watching it. I must surely be the number one fan. I have a fantasy that one day I can sit in the dugout during a game. That would be great fun.

Well, today was a full one. I went to see my little great-grandson, Drew, and that was a treat. He is growing fast and getting sweeter all the time. Then I had a taco salad at Taco Bell. It was so good. I bought groceries, then came home. Later we went to Lowe's and bought a weed-eater. We tried it out and it seems to be fine. It's lightweight, so we'll be able to manage it. Next I fixed supper, cleaned up, then watched the game. So obviously I've had a very good day, and I'm so thankful for it. Now I'm looking forward to tomorrow. Hey, I just discovered that I have another person on my notify list. I'm glad.

## 8 Apr 2002 - A New Job

I started today keeping a little 7 week old boy. If all goes well, I will be doing this until the end of July, when his grandmother retires. The parents really didn't want to put him in a daycare, so they seem very grateful that I decided to keep him. Today was rough, even though he was picked up early. He loves to be held nearly all the time, and I'm hoping he will start taking naps on my bed soon. He is a precious little boy, and I'm sure to get attached to him, almost like another grandchild. I've known his mother since she was in grade school, when I worked in the library there. She and my granddaughter, Miranda, have remained friends all this time. She is a lawyer now, and I hope she will be really successful. Maybe she will defend me if I ever run afoul of the law. Well, I'm off to watch my Braves play ball now. I surely do hope they will win.

## 10 Apr 2002 - April 10th, A Special Day

Happy birthday, Jami. It was a special day for sure when God sent you to me. I didn't realize at the time how much I would need you in the days to come. But God knew, and I'm grateful to Him. You've been, and still are, a wonderful daughter and a great friend. Words can't express what I'd like to say, but I think you know how I feel. So I wish you much happiness today and every day in the future. You've always trusted me and respected me, and I want you to know that that means a whole lot to me. Thanks. And again Happy Birthday!!!

## 11 Apr 2002 - Little Joey

Today was my last day this week to keep little Joey. His mother will keep him on Fridays. He is so cute and so sweet. He has cried a lot this week. We think it may just be a lot of gas on his stomach, but his mother is taking him for shots on Monday and will see if the doctor can find out what is wrong. Today was his best day this week. He smiled a good bit and slept more than usual. Hannah helped a lot this morning. She changed every diaper and held him a lot. She is really good with babies. Tomorrow, I am scheduled to work at the jail from 12 til 4. It should be very easy because there is no visitation on Fridays. I'll probably just take in some money for the inmates and give receipts and answer a few questions. I just finished watching the Braves game, and was so glad that they won. They're not doing so well yet, but I hope they'll get better soon. I sure do love them.

## 25 Apr 2002 - Another Routine Day

1 don't have any very interesting things to write about tonight, just wanted to keep in touch. Some time back, I mentioned something about times like this meant that at least no calamity had happened, and Diane commented that we should thank God for days like this. I think she is right. When I think about it, I realize that days when nothing very big happens are often extremely peaceful days. And Irving and I do mostly have peaceful days. I thank God with all my heart. Irving has been more active lately than he has been for several years. He has been trimming our hedges and has even

been going fishing now and then. A few days ago, he picked up our grandson, Alex, and took him along. Well, Jon had bought him a new spinning rod, and it got tangled up and, while he was trying to fix it, it fell into the pond. I felt so sorry for him, but I think Jon will probably get him another one soon. I hope he'll get to fish again with Granddad. Well, little Joey had a really good day. He smiled a lot and is trying to talk now. I think it is so precious when babies do that. I won't see him again til Monday, and I told his mother not to spoil my baby over the weekend. My Braves lost badly tonight, and that's always so disappointing, but there's always tomorrow.

## 28 Apr 2002 - Sundays Are Pretty Full

I've just about finished another full Sunday. I got up early, did several small routine things, had breakfast, then got ready for church. I practiced with the choir, then went to my Sunday School class for a little while, then it was time to get ready for the worship service. I think our music was really good today, and I really enjoyed preaching. A longtime friend of ours is in his last semester of studying at a Bible college, and he came to preach for us. I'm so proud of him. He's not a young man, but when he believed that God wanted him to preach he started preparing and studying. Then after church, we had lunch and a Braves ballgame. (They lost but I still love them.) When the game was over, there was time to eat a snack and get ready to go back to church for choir practice, then to Training Union. We came home, ate our usual popcorn, and now it is nearly time for bed. Jami's boys always spend Sunday nights with us, and Jamison and I played two games of Crazy Eights. I won one game and Jamison won one. Then the boys went to bed. So I'll be going soon. I'm exhausted, and tomorrow little Joey will be with us again. We've missed the little sweet thing. Don't think for one minute that I'm complaining when I talk about my day being so full. I wouldn't trade places with anyone. It's been a great day.

## 2 May 2002 - Calvin's Dad Died Today

I feel sure that Jami will write a good deal about this when she gets a chance. Calvin's dad died this afternoon, and I'm so sorry for the family. I just wanted to let all of our friends at DD know, because I know a lot of you care. Irving and I always liked Ray, and he was so nice and friendly to us. He had a hard life in many ways, what with losing his leg in the war, but I never saw a bit of self-pity in him. He was a highly intelligent man, and very talented. He even designed the house they've lived in for a while now, and it is beautiful. Irving and I went to see him in the hospital awhile back and he assured us that everything was right between him and God, and that's the most important thing in the world. He loved his family so much, and I know they will all miss him for a long time. Please pray for all of them

## 4 May 2002 - The Graveside Service Was Today

The weather was absolutely terrible with light rain and cold that caught everyone by surprise. I feel like it made the occasion even sadder. My heart goes out to Calvin and Diane and their mother and the whole family. It has been a hard time for them all. There was a 21 gun salute, taps, and a beautiful flag on his casket. He certainly deserved that honor for his service to our country. Jami and Hannah sang "Haven of Rest," and I'm sure he would have liked that. He was a good man, well-respected, and a lot of folks will miss him, including Irving and me.

## 5 May 2002 - A Happy Birthday

Yesterday was Irving's birthday, and today was mine. Birthdays just don't hold the same thrill anymore. When you turn 68, it isn't very exciting. But this evening Jon and Annette invited us to Shoney's after church, and I really had a nice time. The children were so sweet, and they seemed to enjoy our get-together. They had made cards for us, and they sang some new version of "Happy Birthday." They helped to make it a happy birthday. Jami called when they got home this evening to see if they could take us out to breakfast or lunch tomorrow, but I can't do it because I'll have little Joey. So I asked for a

rain-check. I'll have that to look forward to. Miranda came to see us yesterday, and brought us a pound cake she had made. It is a delicious cake. And my stepdaughter came and brought us two pretty little round jars of strawberry jam that her husband had made. I had some on toast this morning and it is very good. Seems like everybody wants to feed us, but that's okay with me. I have a very healthy appetite, for which I'm thankful. So it has been a good day

## 11 May 2002 - The Fishing Trip

Irving, Calvin, Jon, and the five little boys went to Cane Creek for their first fishing trip together, and I think it turned out great. Irving said that all of the boys caught some fish, although they were small. He said that he and Jon and Calvin stayed busy helping the boys untangle their lines and bait their hooks and things like that. I started the day by making a bunch of sandwiches. I put the bologna and the peanut butter and jelly ones in a Tupperware container, and put it in the refrigerator. Then I made four egg salad sandwiches, cut them in half, wrapped them in aluminum foil, and put them in the box in which I had packed some other snacks. Well, when they were loading things in the van, I took the box out to the van, along with a small cooler of drinks. Then when they drove away, I looked in the refrigerator for something, and there was the Tupperware container with most of the sandwiches in it. I felt terrible, but there was nothing I could do, because I was due to leave for my volunteer shift at the jail. Irving said it turned out okay, because the boys were so busy they hardly had time to eat anyway. They were just thirsty. They really enjoyed being together, and I hope they can do more things like that much more often. They gave their bucket of fish to a fellow who was fishing nearby, and I think he was glad to get them, even though they were all small. Maybe one day we can have a fish fry after one of these trips.

## 12 May 2002 - Mother's Day 2002

I've had a good day. First, church, then a snack, then rested and watched the Brave's game. (They lost.) Then Irving took me to Western Sizzlin' for supper. I had a great steak. Afterwards, my sweet granddaughter, Miranda, came by and brought me a beautiful card. After her visit, we went to Jami's house for dessert. Jon and his family were there, and so was Paulette with two of her grandsons. I really enjoyed being with all of them, and they had a good time. I think being a mother is a good thing. I love it. I've thought about a song about mothers a lot today. I don't have any music for it, wish I did. The only place I ever heard it was on a radio program in Charlotte when I was a child. Here are the words: You are a wonderful Mother, dear old mother of mine. You'll hold a spot down deep in my heart til the stars no longer shine. Your love will live on forever, down through the fields of time. For there will never be another to me like that wonderful mother of mine. I really like what this song says, especially the last line. I had a wonderful mother, and in my heart she will always live. I treasure the memory of her.

## 16 May 2002 - Rayne Has A Mind Of His Own

My cat, Rayne, is a year old now and Irving and I had to take him to get his rabies vaccination. I've been dreading that trip for awhile now, not knowing how I would manage to get him there without getting clawed or losing him. Well, I borrowed a cat carrier from my stepdaughter, and thought that might solve the problem, but do you think he was willing to be put into that carrier? Absolutely not! We tried and tried to force him in, but he braced himself and spread his feet out, and there was no way we two adults could manage that cat. So I decided we'd just have to wrap him up in a towel and carry him. It took two towels to secure him with just his head sticking out. We got into the van and away we went. He didn't really struggle much after that, but he was tense and watchful. Well, at the clinic, which was held outdoors, Irving held Rayne in the van while I stood in line to get the paperwork done and to wait for our turn. I had turned the radio on in the van so that he wouldn't hear all the dogs barking, then Irving turned on the air conditioner because he knew Rayne must be mighty warm wrapped in two towels. I so hoped that the vet would go to the van window to administer the shot, and when our turn came, he just asked where our animal was. I pointed out our van and he just went right over and gave Rayne the shot through the open window. What a relief. Then we brought the little rascal back home and he was none the worse for his ordeal. Now we have this to look forward to next year. Yay for us. Boy, Rayne is one hard-headed cat, but I sure do like him anyway.

## 18 May 2002 - A Wonderful Rain

This morning when I got up, it was raining, and it continued for hours. A steady, gentle rain that really soaked in, my favorite kind. But since we had a wedding at church at 3:00, we hoped the rain would stop by that time, and it did. A special blessing. The wedding was beautiful, and so was the reception. Jami sang two songs and did such a good job. Hannah was hired to be the photographer's assistant, and that really kept her busy. She said she should have worn more comfortable shoes. Well, we learned this morning that a friend died last night. It had been expected for a good while now, but I'm sure his wife will miss him for a long time. It was brain cancer, and he had no pain. I was so surprised by that, but so thankful for his sake. One thing that makes the whole thing sadder is that their first grandchild is due in July. I had hoped that he might get to see it. But the most important thing is that Bob was prepared to die. That fact will be a comfort to his wife and son, but he will be missed greatly.

## 22 May 2002 - A New Mower

My grandson, Alex, has wanted for so long to drive our lawn mower, but we didn't feel that he was old enough. But today he came here after school, and Granddad let him do some mowing. He did a good job, and was so excited. He said he loved it. I heard him ask Granddad if he could drive it fast around the yard after he finished mowing, but we couldn't let him do that. It seemed too dangerous. We are so proud that he made the A B honor roll at school. Congratulations, Alexander. And his younger sister, Rebecca got the Math Award today. She's finishing the second grade, and was tested to be in the class next year for the Academically and Intellectually Gifted. That's AIG, for short. And she made it. So congratulations to you too, Rebecca. Do I sound like a proud grandmother or what? All of our grandchildren are bright and they are all special in different ways. I'll probably be bragging on all of them, but that is a grandmother's prerogative.

## 26 May 2002 - Home Again

We came home a day earlier than we had planned from the Myrick reunion and it seems good to be home. We are both tired, but we did enjoy it a lot. It was held at a beautiful place, Lake Junaluska, in the mountains. This was the second year of the reunions. Irving wasn't able to go last year, but he did well this year, thanks to God. We really enjoyed spending time with so many of his cousins. I heard so many stories about their childhood days. I hope I can remember several of these stories to write about another day. One of the sweetest things for me happened last night after supper. I was sitting at a table with Aunt Eva, whom I dearly love. She's 86, and so sweet. Out of the blue she asked me if I could sing without music. I told her that I could, but it wouldn't sound as good. She then asked me to sing Amazing Grace for her. I felt a little self-conscious, but I could not refuse her, so I told her that I would sing it. She took hold of my hand and looked at me so intently the whole time I was singing. She seemed so happy to hear it, and that was such a blessing to me. Well, that started about an hour of singing. Three others joined me and we harmonized, and every time we finished a song someone would ask if we knew this one or that one. It ended up being a great time of fellowship, and this morning after breakfast at the last gathering, they wanted our little makeshift group to sing again, so we sang Amazing Grace and The Old Rugged Cross. I would have preferred to have a songbook and time to practice the different parts, but everyone seemed to really enjoy our efforts. So that is one story of the reunion. I hope to share more very soon.

## 31 May 2002 - Shopping At Wal-mart

We went to Wal-mart this evening to look at the patio furniture, and decided to get a set which included a table with an umbrella and six chairs. We've been wanting to fix our deck up to look better, and we wanted a place to eat outside when the weather is just right. Calvin and Jami and their children came over when they heard about it and helped put it together. Then we enjoyed sitting around outside and visiting. I always enjoy having something new. So maybe I'll be out on the deck early tomorrow having my coffee. Well the Braves started their game tonight, then it started to rain. So now I'm waiting for the rain delay to end. I hope they win.

## 8 Jun 2002 - More From The Reunion

One of the most interesting things about the family reunion we attended two weeks ago was hearing more about the new member who was there with us. His father was a Myrick, but grew up with another last name. His parents had divorced when he was very small, and his mother married again and raised her son as a Broadway. This boy's name was Gaither, and his stepfather was mean to him, and I believe his mother was cruel, too. She had other children by this second husband and preferred them over Gaither. Once when Gaither was very young, his father managed to see him secretly, and gave him ten dollars. (That was a good deal of money in those days.) But when the stepfather learned about that, he made Gaither go and give it back to his natural father. I don't know all the details, but Gaither grew up and raised a family by the name of Broadway. I think all of them knew there was some kind of mystery in the family, but no one would tell them anything. Anyway, Gaither died a year or so ago, and in going through his papers, his son Donald learned a little of the mystery, then he went to courthouses looking for marriage licenses and death certificates. On the marriage certificate for Gaither's mother and stepfather, which I believe was among the personal papers, the mother's name before the marriage was marked out. But on the marriage certificate at the courthouse, it showed her previous married name as Myrick. As a result of a lot of searching, Donald located a cousin of his father and contacted her. And he eventually learned the facts about Gaither's real name. Donald is so proud to know a lot of his real Myrick cousins. He came to the reunion and was so enthusiastic about his new-found family. We really like him, and are proud of him. His grandfather was a brother to Irving's father. He remarried after the divorce, but never had any children by that marriage, so Gaither was his only offspring.

## 11 Jun 2002 - June 11th Is A Special Day

Today is the anniversary of mine and Irving's marriage. Thirty-six years together, and I still wouldn't trade him for anyone I know of. He took on quite a load of responsibility, marrying a woman with three children, and he has done a terrific job supporting us. He has worked very hard and has been successful in his business. He is a great manager, and that is the reason we have what we need today, now that he is not able to work. He has always been faithful and trustworthy. I have never known of him telling a lie. He never uses bad language. He is devoted to our Savior and to our church, and has always been more than willing and ready to go to help anyone who needs counseling or spiritual help. He has quietly helped so many who needed him through the years, in many different ways. Because of his love and trust and encouragement, I have become a stronger person with self-esteem that I never had before. I could go on and on, but I guess this is enough to show how proud I am of my husband. I think I'll keep him.

## 16 Jun 2002 - Father's Day

My daddy was not really a good father, he never knew how to be. I really think he never grew up, and then after he left home he started drinking. That ruined so much of my childhood, and we never had the things we needed because his money was wasted on alcohol. But there were some good things about him, and since this is Father's Day, I just wanted to remember them. I think Daddy always loved me, but didn't show it often. When I got badly burned as a toddler, Daddy was at work at a nearby mill. A neighbor boy ran there and told him what happened. Instead of going to the door, he jumped out the nearest window and ran all the way home. He often talked about how scared he was. He taught me a lot of things, including how to hitchhike, (I'd put my thumb over my shoulder and say, "Going my way, Mister?) I don't think we ever actually hitched a ride. He taught me how to perform in a stage play with him, and I loved that. He was so proud of me whenever I sang in contests. Mother taught me to sing, but I think it was Daddy who was behind all of my opportunities. Daddy should have been in show business. Well, he was, for a short time, before he and Mother married. He toured with a traveling show, and did some skits, and some comedy things. He could always entertain a group of children. He would go out of the room, and make noises that sounded just like a cat fight. And I remember him taking me and my guests for a good walk in the woods at my seventh birthday party. While I was growing up, he taught me to play Rummy, and he and Mother and I spent a lot of time playing cards together. One day I was walking home from town, and when I got to the train depot, a man stepped up to me and made a very ugly proposition. I was probably about thirteen, and didn't now much about sex, but I sensed that what he wanted me to do was very wrong and very ugly. He offered me money, and I just took off running. We lived in the first house past the depot, and I hurried in the door sobbing. Daddy happened to be there and he asked me what was wrong. I told him that I couldn't say what the man had said to me. I was too embarrassed. But Daddy insisted that it would be alright to tell him, and when I did, he was furious. He asked me to describe the man, and he asked what he was wearing. After I told him, he rushed out the door in a rage. He was back in about five minutes or so, and his knuckles were all skinned on his right hand. He said he spotted the man right away, and just grabbed him, and knocked him down, then ran home. I always felt good about Daddy defending me like that, and I've often wondered if the man connected that with what he had said to me. I expect he did. Well, there were a good many things about Daddy that I could write about. He really was a character. When I had children, he loved them dearly, and did a lot for them. I believe he was trying to make up for the things he didn't do for me. When he was old, he had something like a stroke that put him into a coma for a long time, and during the many hours I sat at the hospital and stood over his bed, I was able to forgive him. And when he finally woke up, I told him that I loved him. He said, "I love you the mostest." That meant so much to me. I don't remember us ever saying "I love you" any other time. But I really am so glad that I told him that, and that I could forgive him for the bad things. He died at the age of 81, just a short time before Hurricane Hugo came through. It will be 13 years in August. I so hope that he's in Heaven.

## 22 Jun 2002 - Two Birthday Parties

This day was a full one. My grandson, Jordan, had his birthday celebration at the bowling alley, and I really enjoyed watching the games. Jamison had to bow! with his left hand because of the cast on his arm, but he still did pretty well. After I left the bowling alley, I went home for a little while, then Miranda picked me up, and we went to my great-grandson's party. Little Andrew Reed will be one on Tuesday, and he really had a big party. He got so many new clothes, he'll never be able to wear all of them, and he got so many nice toys, it looked like Christmas morning. I hope his mother will put some of them up for later. I know he is overwhelmed with all those new things. By the way, since Jordan turned 12 today, we now have three 12-year-olds in the family: Hannah, Lauren, and Jordan. But that will end on July 21, when Hannah turns 13. Well, this has been a very good day. Two birthday celebrations, a little bit of much needed rain, then a great big win tonight for the Atlanta Braves.

## 5 Jul 2002 - Allegiance

I've been thoroughly offended by the person who raised a fuss about our Pledge of Allegiance having a phrase in it which says that our nation is "under God." Well, of course it is under God. It was founded that way, and even though the majority of folks don't seem to really respect Him anymore, that doesn't change the truth. Ever since people have been trying to put Him out of our schools and out of our country, it seems that the moral fiber of our wonderful America has been going downhill. I still have a great love for my country, and I'm so grateful to have been born here where I am free to believe and to live the way I choose. Even with her faults,

America is by far the greatest place in the world, in my opinion. And now, on a lighter note. My little grandson, Aaron, spent the day with me today. He is five years old, and so precious. We've had so little time to be with him alone since he was a baby. We had a good day with him. I took him to see a movie, along with Jami's boys, and all three boys enjoyed it a lot. We saw Scooby Doo, and while I was glad that the boys had a good time, I can't say that I enjoyed the movie at all. But I guess it wasn't made with grandmothers in mind. Aaron was a really good boy for me today, and I'm glad we had this time together.

## 12 Jul 2002 - Rebecca Had A Birthday

Rebecca had her eighth birthday on this past Wednesday. Since I was tied up that day I picked her up this morning so that we could do something together to celebrate. I let her choose where we would have lunch, and she chose KFC. Then we went to the Dollar Tree where she chose several items. Children always enjoy going to the Dollar Tree, and I do too. Maybe I'm still a child at heart. We went from there to the grocery store, then back to my house. It was a good visit with her. She really is a sweet and beautiful child. Her mother picked her up after work and took her to get her ears pierced. I haven't heard how that turned out. I hope it didn't hurt much. And speaking of piercing, I learned recently that a very special young man at our church had his tongue pierced. I am dumbfounded over this and can't understand it for the life of me. Well, on to a brighter subject: The Braves won again a little while ago. It was awesome!!! I so hope they can keep it up. I'm having a great time watching them.

## 14 Jul 2002 - A Proud Grandmother

We had the most wonderful program at church tonight. Jami and our pianist, Neil, have worked all week with a group of children to prepare their concert called "God is Love in any language." I was amazed at how all the children knew all their parts so well, and they had memorized all the songs so quickly. There were sixteen boys and girls in the group and eight of them were my grandchildren and great-grandchildren. I have to admit that I was so proud of them all. All except one sang special parts, and the one who didn't has a very good voice. He is just at an age where he just doesn't want to sing alone. 1 hope he will change his mind later. I look forward to the next special program like this one. I loved it.

## 20 Jul 2002 - My First Cruise

Jami and I have been talking a lot lately about taking a cruise, and it is so exciting just thinking about it. Jami took a wonderful cruise a couple of years ago. Well, I started thinking about my one and only cruise, and I decided to write about it. It was about 47 years ago, and my first husband was in the Marines. We had been stationed in Puerto Rico for two years. When it was time to come back home, we had the opportunity to travel back on a Navy ship. The saddest part was when we were standing on the deck waving goodbye to several friends, a couple of whom were crying. But then we were on our way, and I was so glad to be coming back home. Paulette was about sixteen months old, and she did fine on the trip, except for throwing up in our stateroom once. She was not potty trained until we were at sea, but she really liked that trip down that narrow hallway to the bathroom, so we went often. And she was thoroughly trained by the time we left the ship. We had such good meals, but sometimes the plates would slide around on the table. We had to be careful about that. And once our waiter vanished for a little while, and when we asked someone about him, we were told that waiters have stomachs too. My husband took Alka-Seltzer often, and I stayed slightly nauseated. They had movies on the ship, and some other activities, but I don't remember taking advantage of them, probably because of Paulette. She needed her naps, and was accustomed to going to bed early. We had one stop at Cuba, and spent just a few hours at Guantanamo Bay. That was exciting. Then when we arrived at New York harbor, I soon got my first look at the Statue of Liberty. Now that was awesome. We spent one night in New York City, then took a train to North Carolina. Arrived in Charlotte late that night, and it was so good to be home. But I've often enjoyed remembering that big adventure at sea. I expect that my next cruise will be much more pleasant. I can hardly wait!!!!

## 1 Aug 2002 - Perilous Times For Children

I don't know when I have heard of so many children being abducted and killed or molested in some way. What a terrible time we are living in. It seems we have to make our children afraid of all strangers in order to protect them. I wonder how this is going to affect their personalities in the future. Can they ever be comfortable when they are meeting new people? Will they always be tense and fearful when beginning a new job, or starting any new situation where they will have to meet new people? I don't know what the best solution is, but I do wish we could somehow protect them and still allow them the freedom of trusting others. I know that we can never go back to the way it used to be, and that is so sad. When I was out walking early this morning, I saw an adorable little boy in his yard. He was all dressed and ready for the school bus, and his dad was standing nearby. I said hello to the child and asked him if he was going to school, and he just looked at me. His dad quickly said to him, "She's speaking to you." The little boy very slightly nodded his head, and I told him that I hoped he enjoyed it. I kept thinking about that and wondering if the child was really confused. No doubt he had been told never to speak to strangers, then he was told to speak to me. I just hope the child realized that there are some strangers who are okay, and that his dad could be trusted to help him recognize them. As I said before, I don't know what the answer is, but certainly our little ones must be protected somehow.

## 3 Aug 2002 - A SALT Day

I worked at the jail last Saturday and again this morning. We were very busy. The morning visiting hours are from 9 til 11, and we had 72 visitors. So many of them are Mexicans, and they can speak very little English, so it is very hard to explain things to them. They try to understand, but some things are too complicated. It really is sad, but we managed the best way we could. There was one couple who were there last week for their first visit with their son. These were Americans, they'd never visited a jail before, and they really felt bad about their son's situation. Today they were back, and the dad told me that I had been helpful to them. That meant so much to me. One man that I remembered from last week was there again to visit his wife. I learned that he walks to the jail, which is about 7 miles from where he lives. But he said that she is worth it, that she had made a mistake, but that she would be alright. I was impressed with his devotion, and I told him that she was blessed to have him. It seems to me that she couldn't be all bad if he loves her that much. Another lady was there to visit her son. She told me that she has three sons, and that the other two are very stable and settled. Only this one can't seem to stay out of trouble. But you know, a mother's heart always goes out to the one who is troubled. It makes me think of the parable in the Bible about the Prodigal Son. You know the one son stayed home and did everything he was supposed to do, but the younger son was wild and wasteful and broke his father's heart. But the father didn't ever give up on him, and one day he came home and was warmly welcomed. So the mother I was talking about earlier won't give up hoping that her son will be alright someday. I hope he will too.

## 16 Aug 2002 - Too Busy To Think

What a week this has been!! I stayed at Jami's house during the days on Monday, Tuesday, and Wednesday taking care of little Joey. She has just recently started keeping him, but had to go to Asheville to testify for Suzy. Then yesterday and today I kept our little great-granddaughter, Alexandra. She will soon be 8 months old. Yesterday was really rough because she was so unhappy at being left here. But today she did just fine, took 2 good naps, and played in the floor, crawling all around exploring the place. I haven't had time to do much of anything else but babysit. But I was eager to just write a few words so no one would forget me. Now I have to go and watch the Braves. I'll be back later.

## 22 Aug 2002 - Lots Of Sad Things

My friend's 37-year-old daughter, who had been needing a heart and lung transplant for a long time, finally had the lung transplant a couple of weeks ago, but things didn't turn out well and she died a few days later. She left behind a husband, a son, and a daughter who gave birth to a baby a few days ago. She also left parents who dearly loved her and two brothers. I feel so bad for them, but there is one bright spot: Not long before she died, she told her pastor that however things turned out, whether she lived or died, she would win. And I'm convinced that's true.

Another sad thing was hearing that my cousin's husband died suddenly of a heart attack. Irving and I attended the memorial service for him in Statesville yesterday. His three sons were so shocked and will miss him for a long time. Their mother (who was my cousin, Mary Faye) had died about three years ago, so they've had to face a lot in a short time. One thing that I thought was beautiful was that about 15 highway patrol officers came in to show their respects to the youngest son, who is an officer with the highway patrol. There had been a large group of them who attended the mother's funeral. I know this must give comfort to that son.

Our interim pastor's wife had a tumor removed from her breast on Tuesday, and the news so far is very good. The doctor thinks they got all of it. And the dear lady was at church the next night. I'll be praying that the pathology report will be good, but I'm sure that God will bless her.

I visited Paulette at her new/old house tonight. Boy, do they have a lot of work to do, but Paulette is delighted to have it, so I'm glad for her.

We'll be having Homecoming at church this coming Sunday. I hope the church will be full. It's always a special day. One of our former pastors will be our speaker.

Well, it's getting late, and I'll be keeping little Alexandra again tomorrow, so I need some rest. We had a very good day with her today

I'm sorry to report that my Braves have lost two games in a row, but maybe tomorrow they'll win again.

## 25 Aug 2002 - An Enjoyable Day, Full Of Blessings

Today, we had "Homecoming Day" at church, and there was a good crowd there. One of our former pastors was our speaker, and it was so good to hear him again. I think our music was very good. Our choir sang a round consisting of 3 songs and I think everyone enjoyed it. Then the anthem was "When God's Trumpet Sounds." Afterwards, our meal was really good, and a gracious plenty of it. My son and his family were there, and I always enjoy having them there with us. And my granddaughter, Miranda, came too. It was good to see her there.

After we got home and rested awhile, we had a wonderful rain. It has been so dry here for a long time, so we are really grateful to God for sending us a good shower. I sat out on the porch and watched it for awhile. How wonderful!!!

It is now about 6:30pm, and we have nothing else to do but rest and be lazy for the rest of the evening. Of course, I do have a Braves game at 8:00. They have lost a few games lately, but I'm hoping tonight will be a good game. And I'm hoping that there won't be a strike. That would really upset me. Well, we'll see.

I expect Jordan and Jamison will be here to spend the night soon. They will watch the game with me, and Jamison will be full of questions and conversation about baseball. He really is a cute little fellow, as are all of my grandchildren. I am truly blessed. Rebecca spent the night with us on Friday night, and she was a joy. She is 8 going on 15, I think, and a beautiful child. Well, enough for now. Thanks be to God for so many blessings.

## 3 Sep 2002 - September Already?

It's amazing how time flies, after one gets older. (Notice that I didn't say old.) I was talking about this to Jami's boys this morning, and Jamison says that it seems like it takes two years to get to his birthday or Christmas. I remember when it used to seem that way to me. Well, Jami and her family are at the beach for a few days. I really hope they have a wonderful time, but I so wished I could have gone too. But

I'm keeping little Joey while Jami's away. I sure wouldn't want him to have to stay with strangers. He was so happy to be here today, and that warmed my heart. He's wonderful.

Our grandson Alex called yesterday to see if we had any work for him to do. He's ten years old and a great little worker. He mowed our yard and did some weed eating. Irving said that he had never in his life seen a child who loved to work like Alex does.

Well that's about all for now. My Braves lost tonight, but I guess they can't win them all. Maybe they will win tomorrow.

My daughter, Paulette, is still not online at her new home, and she is chomping at the bits to get back to Dear Diary. Maybe it won't be long.

## 6 Sep 2002 - Farther Along

Jami wrote in her diary about a terrible tragedy that happened to a beautiful young woman. She lost custody of her three young children, and we simply cannot understand it. I know her, and she is a wonderful mother. I've always heard about persecution of Christians, and this must be a prime example of that. But we will definitely continue to pray and hope for the day that this will be made right. I thought awhile ago about an old song which says, "Farther along we'll know more about it. Farther along we'll understand why." For now, we will be praying for protection of the innocent children. My heart is hurting for all of them. I'm glad that Susie has a strong Christian husband who will stand with her.

## 8 Sep 2002 - A Mostly Very Good Day

We had such a great service at church today, in memory of the attacks on September 11th, 2001. The music was inspiring. There was even a young man in the balcony who played Taps on the bugle. We had several "heroes" as our special guests. And after all these special features, even though there was little time left, our preacher gave such a good sermon which fit in so well with our theme. He talked about the terrible things that happened to Job: He lost his riches and his ten children and, finally, even his health. But he never gave up his faith in God. He said, "The Lord giveth and the Lord taketh away. Blessed be the Name of the Lord." The Lord blessed him in a mighty way after that. I kind of needed to be reminded that, even when our world seems to be crashing around us, God is still there, and He is still able to put things in order again. Sometimes it may seem that He hasn't answered our prayers, but He never fails us. He always knows what is best for us. If He could heal Job, give him another big family and more riches that he had before, surely He can solve any problems I might have.

## 13 Sep 2002 - What A Week This Has Been!

This week has been super-busy. I've wanted to write every day, but just didn't have time. Let me tell you about it. On Monday, I went to the monthly SALT meeting at the sheriff's department, after which we got a tour of the jail. This was most interesting. Then I hurried home for supper. Next I went to our precinct voting place to help set up everything we could for our primary election. (Our primaries are always held in May, but this year there was some disagreement about redistricting which caused our primary to be put off until September 10th.) On Tuesday, I arrived at the precinct at about 5:45, and that was the start of a very busy and exhausting day. I love working in the elections, but it really is hard the last few hours. I got home about 8:45 that night.

Wednesday and Thursday, I took care of our great-granddaughter, who is eight months old. She is beautiful and precious, but very busy. She crawls and finds so much to get into. It keeps me on my toes keeping her out of danger.

This morning I will be delivering "meals on wheels," then the rest of the day is mine. I need to get groceries, but I'll probably do some fun shopping, maybe eat lunch out. I'm looking forward to today.

Tomorrow I'm scheduled to work at the jail from 8:00 til 12:00 noon.

I hope to spend some special time with my firstborn, Paulette, tomorrow. It's her birthday, and I hope it will be a happy one.

This is Friday the 13th, but that doesn't mean anything to me, because "This is the day the day which the Lord has made. I will rejoice and be glad in it."

## 14 Sep 2002 - Isn't It Nifty?

Today is Paulette's birthday, and she might not want me to broadcast her age, but since I am 68, and was 18 when she was born, one might be able to do the math. It's one of those hard birthdays, and I really do sympathize with her. She is very tiny and very cute, so she will probably always seem much younger. We are going over to her new/old house for a cookout to celebrate. Maybe I won't tease her. One of the ladies on my "meals on wheels" route had a birthday this month. She is 102. Isn't that amazing? I mentioned her birthday yesterday, and she said, "Yes, I'm 200 years old. That's getting on up there, ain't it?" I thought that was too cute to correct her.

We've had some more wonderful rain today, and I'm so thankful for it. Our grandson, Alex, came and mowed for us yesterday, and our yard looks so good.

I worked at the jail this morning, and all went smoothly. I always feel especially sympathetic towards parents who are visiting their children. I can't imagine the pain that must cause.

That's about all for this time, except that our revival at church starts tomorrow morning and goes through Wednesday night. I hope we'll see a lot of blessings.

## 17 Sep 2002 - A Visit With A Friend

On Sunday after church I stopped by a friend's house for a brief visit. She recently lost her daughter, who had finally received a double-lung transplant, after waiting too long for it. She was 37 years old, and she suffered for two or three years or more. I've forgotten just how long she was sick. My heart hurts for the parents. Naturally, their hearts are broken. But I can't possibly know how they feel, and I hope I never do. This was a reminder to me that I am so very blessed to still have all of my children. I don't ever want to forget to be thankful. So often I take God's love for granted, but 1 don't want to do this anymore. He is so kind and good, He is worthy of praise and adoration and gratitude. Thank you so much, Father.

## 20 Sep 2002 - The Blind Can Lead Sometimes

I heard the cutest true story about Irving's cousin "Clip" recently. His two sisters went to the cemetery to visit another brother's grave, and they couldn't locate it. The cemetery is a rather large one. They told Clip about this, and he said, "I can take you to it." So he went with with them, and directed them to turn left right after they entered the cemetery. Then he told them to look for the big oak tree, and to park right before getting to it. Then he said to walk to their left just a few feet and there they would find the grave. Well, sure enough, it happened just as he said, and the sisters were amazed because Clip was totally blind. I guess he was very observant before he lost his sight, and he must have had a great memory

## 10 Oct 2002 - First One Thing, Then Another

I've been wanting to write here for a long while, but either was too busy or couldn't think of anything interesting to tell. So since I find myself with a little bit of time, (Alexandra's asleep) I'll write about a few things . First of all, maybe most of you know that the Atlanta Braves lost the last game of their playoff series against the Giants. I love the Braves so much that this is hard for me. Irving said that it's really hard to be a baseball fan, and it is so hard when they lose. But they had a remarkable year, and I thoroughly enjoyed it up until the end. So now I'll just be looking forward to next Spring Training time. In the meantime, I don't know who to pull for in the National League playoffs . I went to a retreat for seniors on Monday with four other women from our church, and we really had a nice time. The place is kind of in the edge of the mountains, and way back in the woods, among the most beautiful trees. We were hoping the leaves would be changing colors, but it's not quite time. We enjoyed all the meetings, the fun, the fellowship, the food. We came home yesterday, and even though I really enjoyed the trip, I'm very glad to be home, and back to my routine. Well, I hear little Alexandra making sounds, so I guess I should sign off, so that I'll be ready to get her up while she's happy . By the way, did you know why it's hard to make a blond snowman? You have to hollow out the head. My granddaughter sent me a bunch of these today, and I always enjoy them.

## 15 Oct 2002 - Number 300. Wow!!!!

I believe this is my 300th entry. I've tried to think of something outstanding to write about on such an auspicious occasion, but I just can't. Everything in my life has been going along at an even keel, so I'll just have to write a rather ho-hum entry. One thing that is just wonderful is that God has been sending us the rain we have been pleading for. Our thirsty land has really gotten soaked. Awesome news. But I was wondering this morning how long it will take us to start complaining about the rain.

Our choir had a dinner Sunday after church to honor our interim pastor, and I think everyone enjoyed it. We have learned to love Rev. Crain. He is the sweetest, most humble man, and he really has been a blessing to us while we wait for a full-time pastor.

Hannah went with me this morning to deliver "meals on wheels," then we went to ladies' prayer at church, so it has been a rather full day so far, but still a good one.

I'm feeling very, very blessed.

## 19 Oct 2002 - Missing The Braves

I've always enjoyed the World Series, even before I got so interested in the Atlanta Braves. So I've been sitting here for almost two hours trying to decide which team to pull for. I am still not sure, but I'm kind of leaning toward the Giants. But it is so sad that the Braves aren't playing . Oh well, next Spring will be here before long, and I so look forward to Spring Training.

This has been a long day, not a good one, not a bad one. So this evening Irving suggested that we go for a ride just to get out for a little while. We continue to be interested in houses that are for sale, so we like to look around now and then. But buying a house can be such a hassle and so stressful, I expect we will probably stay here.

Well, I guess I'll get back to the ballgame, and see who wins, but I can't get very excited about it.

## 24 Oct 2002 - Just A Little Talk About Memories

I was watching a show on TV a while ago about the life of Frank Sinatra and started thinking about how important celebrities have been in my life. I loved to hear Sinatra sing, and I loved to watch Astaire and Kelly dance. I loved Cagney in Yankee Doodle Dandy. Now all of these are gone, along with so many others. I was kind of partial to musicals, but [ also thoroughly enjoyed many of the dramatic actors and actresses like James Stewart, Henry Fonda, Tyrone Power, Robert Taylor, Rita Hayworth. And all of these are gone. One of my favorite actresses was Betty Grable. I often pretended that I was Betty Grable, but sometimes my friend Alice would insist on being her, and then I would have to be June Haver. I think of those days a lot, and sometimes wish that I could pretend again, but we seem to lose that ability when we grow up. But we can still have our memories to enjoy.

Today we kept our little Alexandra, and she was so sweet. She finally has her second tooth.

My granddaughter, Miranda, had a birthday today, but couldn't really celebrate because she had a class this evening after work. But she and I are planning a big day this Saturday. We hope to go to the mountains and visit several of my mother's relatives. And I think my son's daughter, Lauren, will go with us. This will be so good because she really doesn't remember Mother's family very well. She was devoted to my mother, and I think she will enjoy seeing some of her great-great aunts and uncles.

My great-grandson, Colton, also had a birthday today. I can hardly believe that he is eleven today. He is a really great little boy. I was planning to take him and his brother out this evening for a little shopping and a milkshake, but something came up and he couldn't go. So we'll have to do it another day. Maybe tomorrow.

Well, I plan to watch the fifth game of the World Series in a little while. Both the Giants and the Angels are really battling fiercely, and the games have been good. But I still miss the Braves.

## 29 Oct 2002 - Super Saturday

Two of my granddaughters and I took a trip Saturday and had such a nice time. We left at 7:00 and went first to visit Aunt Flora, who is in a nursing home. She is my daddy's only surviving sibling, and she is 96 years old. She always calls me by my mother's name when she first sees me. We had a good but rather short visit with her. Next we headed towards the mountains, where we visited my Aunt Pearl. She is my mother's sister, and she will be 92 next month. She has always been a favorite of mine. I spent many happy days visiting her house when I was a child. Our next stop was to see My Uncle Golly and Aunt Lizzie. (Real names: Clifford and Elizabeth.) It's been a while since I saw them. My aunt has emphysema and looks so bad, but she seemed to enjoy our visit. Our last visit was to my Uncle Jay and Aunt Sis' house. These are among the most precious people in the world. Sis was 11 years old when I was born, and she always says that I was the prettiest baby she has ever seen. She wanted to take care of me, and even begged Mother to let her wash my diapers. We've always been so close. I wanted to be just like her when I grew up. Her husband, Jay, has been a preacher for 50 something years now, and when I asked him if he was ever going to retire, he said he would die if he quit preaching. So we headed back home. I think it was a little after 8:00 when we got here. I'm especially glad that Lauren was able to go with us and meet some relatives she didn't quite remember. Everyone was taken with her. She has grieved for a long time for my mother, and I felt like it would be good for her to be around some of Mother's family. I think maybe she was able to see a little of her beloved great-grandmother in them. It was really a wonderful day, and Miranda even brought back a new sweet companion. Jay and Sis gave her their little dog, Oscar. They had wished they could find a good home for him, because it was getting a little hard for them to take care of him. Miranda will be very good to him, and I think he will be good for her. I told Paulette that she now has a grand-dog.

## 1 Nov 2002 - Bedtime At Last

I love Eastern Standard Time, but it always takes awhile to adjust back to it, so the evenings have been very long this week. My son and his wife are at the beach for the weekend, and we have two of the children until Sunday afternoon. They have just gone to bed, and I plan to go very soon. I'm planning to take them to the Renaissance Festival tomorrow. I hope it will be both educational and fun for them. Jami and her family are going too, but we can't all ride together so we will meet there. Alex and Rebecca will love being with Jordan and Jamison. And I do want them to have a good time while they are with me. Fortunately, the two of them get along really well.

I delivered Meals on Wheels this morning, and that is always a blessing to me. But today I found one of our dear ladies in terrible pain. She said her knees, legs, and feet all felt like they were going to burst. I told her she should probably lie down, but she had hoped to be able to get a little bit of work done. But I hope she did lie down. She's a precious lady, one of our church members who has always helped others in every way she could. And she comes to church every Sunday that she can possibly make it. I surely do hope that she is feeling better by now.

Well, I guess that will be all for this time. It's almost 10:30, but it feels like much later than that.

## 3 Nov 2002 - A Full Weekend

My grandchildren, Alex and Rebecca, were here with us from Friday after school until this evening. I took them to the Renaissance Festival yesterday, and I think they mostly enjoyed it, partly because they got to be with Jami's children. But it just about wiped me out, with all the walking I had to do. When I left, I felt like I might not make it back to my car. I was so tired that when I came in the door, I headed straight to my bed to rest awhile. This was my second time to go to the Festival, and I'm almost sure it was my last.

We had a pretty good choir practice tonight. We're getting ready for our Christmas music, and it's already coming together. It's mostly simple, and that's the way I like it.

Well, Jami's boys came home with me tonight after church, which is our usual habit. They'll probably go to bed about 10:00, and I won't be far behind.

I need to get all rested up, because I'll be working at the polls on Tuesday, and that always wears me out. But I really like doing it. I sure do hope the election goes my way, which I naturally think is the best way. But we'll soon find out.

I love blonde jokes. Here's one that I have really enjoyed: Why is it harder to build a blonde snowman? Because you have to hollow out the head.

## 6 Nov 2002 - Election Day

I generally always work at the polls, and yesterday was no exception. As usual, I slept very little the night before, so when I got up about 4:45, I was so tired. Then I arrived at my precinct at 6:00, and that was the beginning of an extremely busy, hectic day. We workers didn't dream we'd have such a large turnout; we all brought books to read, and plenty of food for the day, then didn't have time to even open a book or to eat a meal. We had to just grab a minute or two to gobble a few bites for lunch, then the same thing at suppertime. The voters came in steadily all day long, and near the end there was a rather big crowd waiting. Afterwards, there is always a lot to do before we can go home, so I got home a little after 10:00 last night, totally exhausted but glad that I had the opportunity to work again. And the election went nearly all as I had wanted. We are glad to know that there are so many people in our state who came out and elected good candidates. (At least, we consider them to be good candidates.) Time will tell.

Today I don't plan to do much. I'll just do a minimum of housework, then go to church tonight for about an hour. Mostly I'll just be lazy.

## 12 Nov 2002 - If I Should Ever Get Old

This morning as I delivered "meals on wheels," I was talking to two of my grandsons, Jordan and Jamison, who nearly always help me. We talked about Mrs. Alma, who is now 102 years old. I said that I feel that she should have anything she wants to eat, whether it contains fat or sugar or whatever. The boys agreed. I said that if I should get old, I hoped there would be people like them around to see that I had whatever I wanted. Jamison assured me that I would always have candy bars, and both boys said they would see to it that I was looked after. Jamison thinks Jordan will be a rich cartoonist, so I can expect to have a really nice little apartment near him. The only problem is that the boys might marry women who won't care that much about me. I'll have to really pay attention when they start dating. The other problem is that I would have to admit that I was old in order to qualify for all that attention. I really have reservations about that part of it.

## 16 Nov 2002 - My Aunt Is Probably Dying

Her name is Elizabeth, but we've always called her Lizzie. She is my mother's brother's wife. I learned a couple of days ago that she has cancer, and that she is too weak for surgery. It's very advanced; her family has tried for a long time to get her to go to a doctor, but couldn't convince her until now. I learned yesterday that she is now in a coma, and it sounds like her time is nearly up. She told one of her daughters that she is ready to go, and that she is worn out. I keep thinking of how she has always been so good to me. One small incident happened when I was seven years old. My mother and I were staying with her and my uncle "Golly." Their first child was a young baby, and I was carrying her around when I fell with her out the back door. I was so horrified I can still feel it. 1 just knew that Lizzie would hate me for hurting her baby. (Fortunately, Janice wasn't hurt at all.) I must have hit the ground first. But Lizzie was so understanding and so kind, she wasn't mad at me at all, and I have never forgotten how much that meant to me. I know it sounds so small, but it was huge to me. Sixty-one years later, I am still so grateful to her. She has been a faithful wife to my uncle for almost sixty-three years. His mind seems to be getting weaker, and he cries a lot, wondering what he is going to do. My heart breaks for them both. I think it was two weeks ago that two of my granddaughters and I went to the mountains to visit relatives, and Lizzie and Golly were two that we visited. I'm so thankful we went. Her daughter, Janice, told me today that her mother was so excited about that visit that she talked about it all the following week. I'll always be so grateful for that time with her.

## 19 Nov 2002 - Lizzie Died

My aunt died Sunday night. She left a husband and three children and several grandchildren. She will be sorely missed. It seems like she went so quickly, but she had known that something was bad wrong for quite some time. I knew that she had emphysema, but had no idea that she had cancer. Her husband prayed for her Sunday night and asked God to take her because she obviously couldn't get any better. Then he kissed her and told her that they wouldn't be parted for long. Of course, she was in a coma, but I've always heard that people can hear what we say even though they aren't conscious. So it seems that we can sometimes give them a release to let go and pass away. I think I did that when my mother was dying. I knew she probably wouldn't last more that a few hours, and I talked to her and told her that this was going to be a wonderful day for her, and that her mother was waiting for her. Well, I think it was about ten or fifteen minutes until she just quietly stopped breathing. I want to believe that I gave her my blessing to leave. Well, there is a visitation for Lizzie's family tonight, and Paulette and her daughter, Miranda, are on their way to the mountains for that. Then tomorrow Irving and I will go there for the funeral. I plan to sing, but I'm really uneasy about it. I want with all my heart to be a blessing to her family, but I must have God's help.

## 21 Nov 2002 - Lizzie's Funeral

Irving and I went to the mountains yesterday to attend the funeral for my aunt Lizzie. It's hard to say goodbye to one we love, but we fully believe that Lizzie was prepared to meet God, and is now in Heaven with Him. So we mustn't feel sad for her, but we are sad for ourselves. I spoke to her oldest daughter this evening, and I can identify so well with all she is feeling, since I went through the same thing when my mother died. I think maybe it helped Janice to know that I understood so well. Lizzie was special! to me, and Janice told me that I was always special to her mother. I think I already knew that, but I'm glad Janice told me. It was good yesterday to see so many cousins and aunts and uncles that I seldom get to see. Usually it is only when someone in the family dies that we get together. Such a pity.

## 25 Nov 2002 - A Very Easy Day

Yesterday was so busy, as Sundays usually are, and last night I was tired out. But today was just mine, to use however I wanted. I love that. This morning I fixed Jordan and Jamison their usual Monday breakfast. (Peanut butter toast and hot chocolate. They love it.) Then they were ready to go home, so I drove them. I got to visit awhile with Jami and Hannah and Joey, then came home and just piddled most of the day. Irving and I took a ride this afternoon, looking at some lots we had heard about. Later, I fixed supper, washed the dishes, and now I'm just sitting around again. Sounds boring I guess, but I've enjoyed it. Now tomorrow promises to be a different story, a very full day, but that's okay. I think it will be a good one.

## 28 Nov 2002 - A Happy Thanksgiving Day

This has been such a good day. It started out very, very busy, but when we went to Jami's house at one o'clock, it became a really happy day. We enjoyed a delicious dinner. Paulette and Steve were there, too, and we all just had a great time. Then to top it all off, Jon and his family stopped in and joined us. It's always such a blessing to have all of my children together and to watch them having fun and laughing. Jon and Annette usually go to her mother's for Thanksgiving dinner, then visit us later. I was so glad they stopped at Jami's house. Jami had some kind of laughing spell on, and she was hilarious, and had us laughing nearly the whole time. Of course, Paulette and Jon can really be clowns too. So it was a very good afternoon, and I am truly thankful for my family. The only thing missing was Jamison. He's at his aunt Susie's for the week and he is having a ball. It will be good to see him Sunday evening. I hope that everyone who reads this entry has had a wonderful day. God is so very good to us that we should have a Thanksgiving Day every day.

## 1 Dec 2002 - The Wedding Trip

I just got back this afternoon from our grandniece's wedding in South Carolina. It was so pretty, and I really enjoyed seeing some of our dear family that we seldom see. My granddaughters, Hannah and Lauren, who are both 13, went with me. We had such a good time together except for while we were lost in Summerville. Even though I had a map showing exactly where the church is, I couldn't find it for ever so long, and time was running out. It began to look like we would miss the wedding, but we finally found the place. So we were seated about 10 minutes before the bride came down the aisle. Talk about being stressed out. But after that, everything was great. The reception was elegant, the food awesome. When the bride and groom arrived, they looked so sweet and so happy. It was a joy to be there. Yesterday evening, we rode around over Charleston for a long time. I was so glad for the girls to get to see the beautiful old houses there. I love that city. Well, there was a lot more I could tell, but I think that will do for now. We had a very safe and fun trip home, and I am so thankful to be here.

## 5 Dec 2002 - Traveling Again

Last week I went down near Charleston to a family wedding. Now I plan to head out early in the morning on a bus trip to Myrtle Beach. Our former pastor takes tour groups to different places during the year, and I especially love this one. We always stop at a place called "Broadway at the Beach" for shopping and lunch. Later, we check in at our hotel, rest awhile, then go out to supper at a fabulous seafood buffet. Afterwards we go to see a show. This time, we plan to see "Legends." which I haven't seen before, but I expect it will be good. Then Friday after breakfast, we check out and usually go to a big mall to shop. After lunch, we go to see the show "Carolina Opry," which I think is really great. It's my favorite by far. Then we will head back toward home. We will probably get back around 7:30 or 8:00. So I'm excited about my Friday and Saturday this week.

## 8 Dec 2002 - The Myrtle Beach Trip

1 thoroughly enjoyed my trip. There was plenty of visiting time with friends who went along, and plenty of shopping time at two different malls. The food was so good at the seafood buffet, but the place was awfully crowded. The show "Legends" was a little disappointing, but some parts were good. The person imitating Liza Minelli did a pretty good job, Louis Armstrong was good, and the best part was the Blues Brothers. They really seemed like the real thing. We saw Carolina Opry yesterday afternoon, and their Christmas show is always fabulous. I'm always amazed at all that talent. The music is excellent, the comedy is hilarious, the dancing and singing outstanding. I wish everybody could see it at least once. Well, I got home about eight last night, tired but

so glad I got to go. Now I'm hoping to go again next year.

## 15 Dec 2002 - Another Good Sunday

Our music was really good today at church. One of our teenage girls sang "Breath of Heaven," and our choir sang "No wonder the Angels sang" and "Christmas is a time for singing." We had a guest preacher who preached a most interesting sermon. He brought out the simple fact that we must all make a decision about Jesus Christ, whether to receive Him or not. In my heart, He is the most wonderful Gift I have ever received, and I am so thankful that He came . Tonight we had our children's program, and it was very well done. I thoroughly enjoyed it. Afterwards, we had a time of fellowship, with great snacks. Jon and Annette and their precious children came to the program, and it's always a joy to have them with us at church. Their little Aaron sat with me and I loved it. They sat with Jami, Calvin, Irving and me, and Hannah at our fellowship time. The food was so delicious, but the visit was much better. I said that we just needed Paulette there and we'd really have a ball. She always adds a little spice to our gatherings, kinda like paprika. That's from one of our silly little family jokes, which she should really write about sometime. Well, it has been another fine day for me, and I feel totally blessed.

## 22 Dec 2002 - A Very Blessed Day

Today has been so good. First, our Christmas music at church turned out really well. Everyone seemed to enjoy it a lot. So it was surely worth all of the time and effort we put into it. Jami and Hannah both sang solos, and they did great i This evening, Irving and I went to another church where my son and his family are members. Their childrens' choir was doing a special Christmas program, and two of my grandchildren were doing speaking parts and solos. Well, it was wonderful! Alex is ten years old, and he played Sam the Samaritan, and we were so proud of him. He sings well. And his sister Rebecca was a shepherd. She has a really pretty voice, and we were so proud of her too. She's eight years old. Their little brother, Aaron, is five, and he was in the choir. He kept his parents in such suspense, wondering what he would do next. It was hilarious watching him, with all his funny faces and gestures. He may not have had a solo part, but he really performed for us. I thoroughly enjoyed it.

Well, Jami's boys always spend Sunday nights with us, and they are now all settled in bed, so I think I'll call it a day. (A very blessed day.)

## 25 Dec 2002 - Visits With Friends

This morning, Irving and I went to Jami's house for breakfast. We had such a nice time. Yesterday evening we went to Miranda's house for a Christmas family get-together. Had a great time there too. But I feel that what I did after all of our family festivities was more in the real spirit of Christmas. I picked up Jamison and we went to visit at two different nursing homes. First we visited a lady named Lola, who is a member of our church. Lola is a widow who never had children. She is 94 years old, nearly deaf, and so pitiful. I think she really enjoyed the visit. Then we went to another nursing home to visit my friend, Eleanor, whom I have really neglected lately. She has been moved to a different place, and I just hadn't gotten around to going there. Eleanor's mind is worse than it was before, and it's hard to understand her when she speaks, but she seems to still be strong in her body. The people who work there say that she hasn't had any company until today, but that was no surprise, because she never had any company before except for my visits. It's a horrible thing when people are dumped out at a nursing home and promptly forgotten. Eleanor loves chocolate candy, and I took her some, but she didn't seem to know what to do with it. At first she tried to give it back to me, but I finally got her to put it in her pocket and keep it. I don't think she will get any better, but I'm asking God to help her through the rest of her days. The things I saw today reminded me of how much I have to be thankful for. I hope I won't be neglecting Eleanor so much anymore, because even though she can't even remember my name, maybe she can sense that someone cares about her.

## 26 Dec 2002 - Shopping And Loving It

I really enjoyed my morning. I got up early and left the house at 6:30 to go check out the after-Christmas sales. I kind of expected a mob scene, but there was none. People were polite and pleasant. And I found several things to buy, including candy which was half-price. My first stop was at Wal-Mart, then I went to Belk's at the Mall. I found a beautiful porcelain nativity set at 60

## 31 Dec 2002 - Another Year Ending

I don't really care for New Year's Eve or New Year's Day. They are just like any other days to me. But I still sometimes like to take stock and see whether the year just passed was a good one. And I've decided that it was basically good. One son-in- law had a heart attack and open-heart surgery, but he has recovered well and seems to be just fine. Other that that, we haven't had any major sickness, and I think that is outstanding. I lost an aunt, but that wasn't what I would call a tragedy, because she was old and very sick and ready to die. I believe she is in Heaven with Jesus and I'm happy for her. Of course, her husband and children will miss her for a long time, but I believe they all realize that she is much better off now. So I would say that 2002 has been a very good year for us. I usually think about resolutions too, but that's about as far as I get. It seems to me that nearly everyone makes almost the same resolutions, and most folks forget about them after a week or so. Most people want to be better than they were last year, and that's certainly good. I feel that way too. Most people want to look better than they did last year, and I have that same wish. I guess most people want to be more prosperous, and there's nothing wrong with that in itself. But I hope that folks will be very thankful to God for all He has given them this past year. And if one has relatively good health, enough food to eat, a good place to stay, enough clothes to wear, a decent mode of transportation, and maybe a little money left over, what more could we ask for? I guess if you have all those blessings, you're as prosperous as you need to be. I know that we are.

## 6 Jan 2003 - Darla's House Burned Today

We had a call from my step-daughter this afternoon telling us that her daughter's house was on fire. She said that Darla was on the way home so we went straight over there. She only lives less than a mile from us. It was horrible to see the house with broken windows and smoke pouring from the roof. It had been so pretty since Darla and her husband moved in and fixed it up so nicely. When Darla arrived, she seemed to be in a state of shock. She just stood there crying. My heart went out to her. One fireman told her that there might be some things that could be salvaged after everything cooled, but Irving said that it looked like all of the furniture was ruined. Fortunately, she said she does have insurance to cover the contents of the house, but I'm sure there are many things that can't be replaced. We don't know what caused the fire yet. We just know that Darla's heart is broken, and that she'll never forget this day. How tragic.

## 7 Jan 2003 - Quite A Mixture Of Emotions Today

I was so touched yesterday evening when a family from our church came to check on us. Ronny's mother had seen me on TV watching a house burning, and she was concerned that it might be my house. She told Ronny about it, and they tried to call us. We weren't at home and they couldn't find out what was going on. So after a while they just got in the car and drove to town to see about us. They stayed a good while with us, and were so glad that it wasn't our house that burned. I know that if they had found us in trouble, they would have gladly taken us home with them and looked after us. That meant so much to me. I called that visit "the church in action."

Another precious thing that happened was that when I went to deliver meals on wheels this morning, I told a woman about Darla's house burning yesterday, and she was so sympathetic and kind that she sent a check with me to give to Darla. It was for $100.00. She said she just couldn't stand to think of such a thing happening. I was blessed to see such compassion.

We went to Darla's house late this afternoon and went inside to see the damage. It was horrible, so black and ugly and wet and smelly. She plans to go back tomorrow to see what might be salvaged. That will be terribly hard for her.

Well, in spite of the sad things that happen, there are still some very nice things happening that bring us a smile. Today, my little granddaughter Rebecca came in second in the school spelling bee. She is only in the third grade and a fifth grade boy won. I am so proud of her. I told her that she might win first place next year.

One other thing that we are excited about is that another granddaughter is expecting her third child. She has two little girls, ages nearly ten and seven. I'd love it if she could have a little boy this time. Her daddy needs the experience of loving a grandson.

Well, it has been a long and full day, and I'm going to go to bed and look forward to tomorrow.

## 9 Jan 2003 - It's Jon's Birthday

On this day back in 1965 the dearest son, (except for Jesus) was born. He has always been special to me, always a good son. Do I sound like a doting mother? Maybe I am, but I really believe I have three of the greatest children ever. Who could ask for more? Happy Birthday, dearest Jon.

## 16 Jan 2003 - It's Beautiful Outside

I love to see the snow falling and settling in the yards. I think we have about two inches, but it seems to have stopped now. I was a little bit concerned about driving in the morning to deliver meals on wheels, but I got a call telling me that there won't be any meals on wheels tomorrow. So now I'll need to call all of our people and let them know about this, but I suspect they won't be looking for me. I'm only concerned about one of our ladies, afraid she might not have food in the house. I'll need to check on that.

I really dislike chain letters and that sort of thing. They may say something like "Send a copy of this letter to several people within three days, and you will have good luck, but if you break this chain, you'll have a tragic thing to happen in your family." Now I am occasionally receiving things like this in my email, and it irritates me. One of my friends, whom I consider to be a Christian, sent me a thing yesterday which, briefly stated, said that I could make a wish, then send the email on to my friends. The number of friends I sent it to would determine how soon I would get my wish. Then it said that if I deleted it, and didn't pass it on, I would have a year of bad luck. Well, I simply had to reply to that. I said, "Surely you don't believe that. Tell me that it was a joke. I sure do hope I won't have a year of bad luck, but then I don't believe in bad luck." I like this person a lot, and I hope he isn't mad at me, but I couldn't just let that pass without saying anything. He hasn't answered my email yet. As soon as I wrote him the reply, I promptly deleted the message. Luck, bad or good, is just not a part of my thinking or my vocabulary. I'm convinced that my life is totally in God's hands, and that whatever He chooses for me will be for my good. There have been a lot of hard things which I believe have made me stronger, and a lot of great things, for which I am so very thankful. I intend to continue to trust Him with my life; therefore, I have no need of luck, whatever that is. So now I have gotten that off my chest, and maybe I can just put it away now. But please don't send me anything about how I might have good luck. Be nice, okay?

## 21 Jan 2003 - Mrs. Alma

That's what we call her. She is one that we take meals on wheels to, and she is 102 years old. Well, on Sunday she had a stroke. Now she is in the hospital, and the doctor says there is nothing they can do for her. They don't expect her to regain consciousness. In a way it seems sad, but mostly it seems right and good. She has had so much trouble in recent years. She has probably always been poor, and for several years her health has been really bad. She lives in a small rented house which is really old and run down, and I'm sure her income is extremely small. I don't think she has been well-cared for. In fact, I know she hasn't. I have often considered calling DSS to see if something could be done, but I was never sure if that would be the right thing to do. But now it seems that God is going to solve the problem. He knows the best thing to do for her.

## 23 Jan 2003 - Great To Feel Better

I was sick for a night and a day, and I am so grateful to feel better today. I'm spoiled because I am so seldom sick that I can hardly take it.

We awoke this morning to the most beautiful snow. I love it but if I had to go anywhere, that would be a different story. I made snow cream for Irving and me, but I put too much sugar in it, but I still enjoyed it. Jon called me to find out how to make it. I hope his turned out good.

I called a special friend this evening to find out how a recent test turned out. She had cancer surgery awhile back, and this test would show if there was any cancer in her body. She appears to be totally free of cancer, and I am so very happy for her. We were talking about writing in journals, and she told me she writes in a journal each night, and she writes down three things that she is thankful for. (1 think she said the idea came from Oprah's show.) That sounds like a really neat idea. So I thought that I would write three things I am thankful for tonight: I am thankful that God loves me. (He really truly does.) I'm thankful to have such a precious family. And I am thankful for a box of special cards that I looked through today. All the warm, loving thoughts that were expressed to me have really blessed my day and made me feel so special. Paulette and Jami and Jon, after I die, you three read through that box of cards and you will be reminded of how special I was. It will make you proud. I'm just being a little silly now, but I really do love all those cards.

## 4 Feb 2003 - My Mother's Birthday

Mother was born on February 4th, 1917, so today she would have been 86 years old. She left this world on February 15, 1998, and she has been terribly missed by all of her family. I was reading an article this morning by a man who had lost a special loved one, and one thing he said really spoke to me. He said, "She lives within me, like a stark, relentless unpresence, a reminder of what my life is missing." I'm certainly reminded every day of what my life is missing. I long to hear her voice, and I so want to share with her every little thing that happens in our family. She and I always enjoyed talking about the little grandchildren. We often laughed at the cute and funny things they would say and do. Well, those days are past, but I do have a strong hope of seeing her in Heaven, and that makes Heaven seem even sweeter to me.

## 9 Feb 2003 - Just Got Home From Church

We are having the most beautiful day. Church was good today, as usual, and all the music went well.

Now I have a pizza in the oven, and it's beginning to smell good. I kind of wanted to go out for lunch, but this will be the next best thing. I really don't like to cook often anymore, after so many years of preparing so many meals.

Well Jami is out of town for the weekend with Calvin's sister, and I know she is having a very nice time but I will be glad to see her when she gets back tomorrow. Jon's out of town too, doing some work. I don't know if he's due back today or tomorrow.

I kept little Joey Saturday in Jami's place, and I'll be keeping him again tomorrow. I can't wait to see him in the morning, because he was to get his first haircut yesterday.

His hair has a beautiful curl to it, and it's very blond, and I can't imagine how he will look, but he will still be one of the most adorable babies I've ever seen. His daddy doesn't want him to look like a girl. Actually, he has never looked like a girl, even with his hair a little long . Well, I guess it's obvious by now that I didn't have anything really interesting to write about, but I don't like to be away from Dear Diary for too long. So I'm just staying in touch.

## 11 Feb 2003 - Two Deaths Today

I heard this morning that our friend Mrs. Alma died last night. She had been in a coma for two or three weeks after a stroke. She was 102 years old, and she was one of the ladies on our "meals on wheels" route. She had a lot of heartaches in her life, and was sick for years, so I'm glad that is over for her.

Later in the evening, a friend called to tell me that a friend and former neighbor of my parents had died today. He lived a rough life, drinking a lot, with many faults, but he was always a good neighbor. And I believe in giving credit where credit is due. He was so good to my children, very big-hearted, so I was always fond of him. But in the last several years, he had become verbally abusive to his wife, whom I dearly love, and had been so hard to get along with that he had caused his four sons to stay away from him and his wife. It was a real tragedy. But since he has been in a rest home for the last year or two, his sons have shown him a lot of care and kindness. I'm glad of that. His wife is in a different rest home with a very weak heart. I don't know how she will react to this, because I think she continued to love him in spite of his bad behavior. How sad.

There is a superstition that when one hears of one death, there will soon be two others. Now I wonder if I will hear of another one soon. Don't misunderstand me. I'm not in the least superstitious, but just kind of curious. It sometimes does seem to happen that way, but I don't think it means anything. Well, we will see.

## 12 Feb 2003 - The Third Death

Last night I wrote about learning of two deaths in the last couple of days. I mentioned that the old tale says that when one hears of a death one will hear of three deaths. Well, guess what. Today a lady from our church died. It seems kind of strange, but it's true. The lady was in her nineties and had been in a nursing home for several years, so it seems natural and a blessing that she dies.

We had a really interesting speaker at church tonight. She told about her daughter being born deaf, and about what that meant for the family. They had to learn sign language so they could communicate with her, and they had to make a lot of sacrifices to provide her with all she needed. She grew up to be a lovely young woman, married a fine man, who was also deaf, then gave birth to a daughter. Not much later, she died at the age of 21. But in her short life she was a great blessing to many and left behind beautiful memories for her family. We were made aware of some of the difficulties that deaf people have to deal with, and there are many. I'm reminded to be thankful for my hearing, and for the gift of sight. I often take a lot of things for granted, but maybe our program tonight will help me to be more aware of how thankful I should be, and how I need to be more caring toward others.

## 16 Feb 2003 - Brrr, An Icy Day

This morning it was raining, and it was about 34 or 35 degrees, I think. But the temperature kept going down, and the rain got heavier, so that things began to get icy while we were at church. I expect there will be power outages before morning. I think it is now about 26 degrees, or near that, and a lot of school systems will be closed tomorrow. Our county schools are due to open two hours late, but I wouldn't be surprised if that doesn't change by morning. This afternoon, Irving discovered that our furnace had cut off, but we are fairly comfortable with our gas logs. So tomorrow, we will try to get someone to work on it.

My two grandsons who usually spend every Sunday night with us couldn't come tonight because of the weather so we've just been sitting around watching TV most of the afternoon and evening. It has been a rather long day, but now it is a little after ten, so I think we'll just be going to bed soon. I'm ready to call it a day, a very cold icy day.

## 21 Feb 2003 - My New Cell Phone

I'm always behind everyone else when it comes to new things. I remember when I first started hearing about microwaves, I had no idea why everyone wanted one. I didn't feel that I needed one. I think I thought they might even be a little dangerous. And I didn't have a remote control until just about everyone else had them. I was just late realizing how great they are. Now, for a long time I've been wanting a cell phone, but was not willing to pay a big monthly fee. My stepdaughter loaned me hers when I drove down to Charleston a couple of months ago, and it was great. Although it did startle me once when it rang while I was driving. I learned about a deal where you just buy the minutes ahead of time, and it's not expensive, and I went to WalMart today and bought myself one. Irving and I both looked at the instructions, and we are a little overwhelmed, so I'm going to get Jami to go online and get it activated for me. Then she can show me how to use it. Then I will really be in the modern world, but you won't find me walking around chatting, or driving with it stuck to my ear. I only plan to use it when it's important to make a call, and I'll be really stingy with my minutes. I'm excited about it.

## 25 Feb 2003 - Calvin's Mother Died

My son-in-law's mother died at about 5:30 yesterday evening, and it seems so sad and hard to believe even though she had not been expected to live for awhile now. I really feel bad for Calvin, but he realizes that she is much better off, and that there will be no more pain for her. She will be missed.

One happy thing that happened this week is that two of my grandchildren were baptized on Sunday. evening. That's always a very special event. Several years ago, little Rebecca told her mother that she had to get a new heart. When her mother asked her why, she said, "Because I gave my heart to Jesus." I thought that was precious. And that little girl is on the A honor roll at her school.

I kept little Joey this afternoon for Jami, and I'll be keeping him tomorrow. He is such a cute little boy and we all love him so much. But I will be exhausted when he leaves tomorrow . I'm due to keep little Alexandra on Thursday, so I have two busy days ahead.

SS I have my reservations now for my trip to Florida. I'm due to leave Charlotte at 6:00 on the morning of March 5th, and I'll be due back on the following Monday the 10th. I always dread flying. It really makes me nervous. My friend is so eager to have me come down to visit her, and that makes me really feel honored. I guess that's about it for tonight. It's time for bed, and I will need a lot of rest to be ready for Joey early in the morning.

## 3 Mar 2003 - Our Variety Hour

We had such a good program at church last night. I always worry a little about these things, but I shouldn't, because our people always come through and do a good job.

The performances were all good and the fellowship was too.

Se I'm planning to fly out of Charlotte at 6:00 Wednesday morning for Tampa, and I really dread the terrible hour, because they want me there at 4:00. Jami is driving me there and I feel bad for her having to do it, but it's a little hard to get to our airport sometimes without getting lost, especially in the middle of the night. And I feel a little afraid of the airport now with all the security checks. I told Jami today that things seem to get more complicated as I get older. But I guess someone can help me if I get lost or confused. And maybe it will all turn out fine. I expect it will be a relief to get back home the following Monday.

## 14 Mar 2003 - My Florida Trip

I flew to Tampa very early in the morning on Wednesday, March 5th. I had a good visit with a very old friend (50 years) and her husband. They treated me like a queen, and fed me too well. Mary had just one daughter, and she died nearly five years ago, never having had any children. So Mary has no child and can never have a grandchild. She is 85 years old, and her heart is broken over her daughter's loss. She can't seem to cope with it. I wanted so badly to help her, and she said I did, but she is still so terribly depressed. She said over and over again that she didn't want me to come home, but of course she knew I had to. I got back home on Monday evening, March 10, and I was so glad to be here. I was also exhausted from the long day. But I keep thinking of Mary and how lonely she is. Her husband is so good to her, but he is very quiet, and she really needs a woman friend to talk to. I'm more aware than ever of how much I have. I have my precious children who love me, and all these beautiful grandchildren. We now also have two more on the way, which will make 24. Wow!! I don't want to leave out my husband when I count blessings, because without him I don't know where I would be today. And because of my greatest blessing, Jesus Christ, I have hope of even more wonderful days. How can I ever thank Him?

## 20 Mar 2003 - A Few Jumbled Thoughts

I don't know what to expect about the war in Iraq. It's frightening, but it seems to be necessary. But I feel so sorry for all the ordinary people there. I just pray that it won't last long, and that the people there will be much better off.

We are about to sell our house, I think. We've been thinking about the possibility for some time now. We really like our house, but we would like to get out of the city to avoid city taxes. There is a house just a couple of miles from here that we think we want, if the people will accept our offer. It has a big kitchen with lots of cabinets and counter space. We will see what happens. A young man has made us a good offer for our house.

We've had so much rain lately, but maybe it will bring us a beautiful springtime. I look forward to a sunny day.

## 22 Mar 2003 - What A Beautiful Day

We've had the most wonderful day, lots of sunshine. What a contrast from the rainy weather we've had lately. Yesterday was pretty too, and our grandson, Alex, was so eager to come and mow our yard. He helped Irving put a new battery into the mower, then he did a good job mowing. He spent the night with us, and it was good to have him. Last night his mother called to tell him that they had bought a riding lawn mower, and he was so excited. I suspect that he has mowed their whole property today.

I worked at the jail this morning, and everything went along smoothly, except for one lady who couldn't speak any English at all, and we couldn't understand what she was there for. But after awhile, another lady came to visit, and she had her young daughter with her. I remembered that the girl spoke pretty fluent English, and she was able to help the first lady. So that worked out fine. It's really rough for the Hispanics here who can't speak any english.

This afternoon, my Granddaughter, Miranda, came by for a visit and asked me if I wanted to go with her to a book swap shop that she had heard about. So I went with her and we went to WalMart after the book shop. I always enjoy her company. So this has been a beautiful day in every way.

## 31 Mar 2003 - The Braves Are Back!!!

I am so excited. In about ten minutes, the Braves will begin their new season. I'm so ready. And today, Greg Maddux is scheduled to pitch. I so hope they can win it all this year. They don't know it, but I'm their number one fan.

We believe we have sold our house. So we will probably begin building one as soon as we get our money out of this one. While we are building, we will probably move into the house we built for my mother. It is empty right now. I dread to move twice, but at least 1 would get to see a lot of my son and his family. They live just two doors away. Well, we shall see . I have to go now. It's almost time for the game to start.

## 10 Apr 2003 - A Very Special Day

On this day in 1963, my second child was born. She was due on the 9th, so she was a few hours late, but very close to the target. And she has always been very prompt to be where she is supposed to be. She weighed 5 Lbs. 9 oz, but there was a lot packed into that tiny bundle. One of the nurses at the hospital called her a "feisty little thing," and that may have been prophecy, because she is still somewhat feisty. She was born as the answer to her sister's prayer. Paulette so wanted a little sister, and I doubt if there has ever been a sister more devoted than Paulette. It was precious to see them together. Well,Happy Birthday, Dear Jami. You have brought so much to my life and I thank God for you. What a great daughter you are.

## 15 Apr 2003 - I Have To Brag

I had such a nice surprise this evening. I learned that my little granddaughter, Rebecca, won the Academic Achievement Award for the third grade at her school. I feel so proud of her. Her sister, Lauren, won that same award when she was in the fourth grade, (I think it was the fourth grade.) I think that is something worth bragging about, even though I had nothing to do with it. After all, they do belong partly to me, and grandmothers do have bragging rights, don't they? So I just want to say to Rebecca, You go, Girl!!!

## 20 Apr 2003 - Easter Sunday, 2003

What a nice day we are having. I'm not referring to the weather; it has been damp and chilly all day. We started out with a sunrise service at church at 7:00, during which our choir sang an Easter musical entitled Man of Sorrows, King of Glory. I thought it turned out so well, after our many weeks of work. Then we had a great breakfast together. The men always cook it and they do such a good job. After that, we had Sunday School and came home. Irving and I had a nice little nap, then we went to my stepdaughter's house for lunch. All of that side of the family were there, and the food was excellent and plentiful. Both of our granddaughters who are expecting this year were there, and it is always good to see them. After we came home, I watched the last inning of the ballgame, and the Braves won. I'm so glad. Such a good day and it's not over yet. I think Irving and I will take a walk next. So that's all for today.

## 3 May 2003 - Such A Pleasant Day

1 went to a tea party this afternoon. I don't remember ever going to one before. My friend, Melvie, gave it to honor her mother, who is around 85 years old. There were 20 of us there and we had a most enjoyable time. Melvie had about six tables set up under her carport, and she served ice tea and lemonade, along with several delicious homemade treats, including very small ham biscuits. We played four games, laughed a lot and just visited with each other. I thought it was such a good idea. Irving is just about all set to start on our new house as soon as we close on the lot. It looks almost sure that we will get the lot we wanted to start with. And we have our plans which a friend drew up for us. I think it's going to be a very special house. In the meantime, we are just about all settled in the house my mother lived in for several years before she died. I love it here, except that it's a little small for us. I've gotten accustomed to having two baths and a guestroom and a garage, so I'm missing those things. But I'm very comfortable and feel more at home than I ever felt at our last house. I just have too much "stuff" and don't want to part with it. I'm a pack rat and don't know how to change, so I'll probably carry all of my "stuff" to our new house. But I am really trying to get rid of a few things. Jami is giving me a hard time about it. I tease her about what a good time she'll have when I die. She'll come in and start throwing my stuff out the first thing. Well, I'm hearing some thunder and don't want to get cut off before I can finish this entry. That happened to me last night and I hated it. But I do want to say that I'm thankful for a very pleasant

day and for a good place to stay.

## 11 May 2003 - Mother's Day, 2003

It has been a good day. I spent time with each of my children, and that always makes for a special day. Church was fine, but it's a little hard on Mother's Day to hear all the sentimental things that are said since my mother is gone. Not that I don't agree with it all, and I think it is wonderful to honor the mothers that are still here. But, even though my mother has been gone for over five years, it still seems so fresh at times when I realize how much I want to talk to her and spend time with her. But somehow staying here in the house where she lived for several years has made me feel a little closer to her, almost like I'm visiting her. And I certainly can't feel sorry for myself, because I was blessed to have her for so many years, and because we had such a wonderful relationship. And I have no regrets about the way I treated her and cared for her. She always knew that I loved her dearly, and would always stand by her.

## 19 May 2003 - Obsessed?

My daughter, Jami, received a comment in her diary today which has troubled me a little. The person who left it said that Jami is obsessed with her children. Well, what mother isn't, if that's what you call Jami's attitude? I feel exactly the same way about my children. I've always been interested in what they do, and in how they are, and I expect I'll always be that way. I've never called that obsession, I prefer to call it LOVE. We had a sweet visitor awhile ago. Rebecca, who is eight years old, came to tell us that her team won their ballgame. She said they beat the number one team. She looked so cute in her little ball uniform, with her ponytail sticking through the back of her cap. We went to K &

W cafeteria for lunch today, and it was delicious. That's one of my favorite places to eat. Well, we are still waiting to see whether we will get the lot we are trying to buy for our house to be built on. Maybe we will find out tomorrow. In the meantime, it feels comfortable here in the house that I still think of as my mother's house. She loved it so much and so do I. But I am eager to get our new house built, if it is God's will for us to have it. I'd just love to feel really settled down and "at home."

## 2 Jun 2003 - Monday Morning

I have always loved Mondays, except when I was working at public work. Mondays are all mine, with no extra responsibilities or obligations. My Sunday School class has started meeting at Quincy's for breakfast on the first Mondays of each month, so I'm looking forward to that in a little while... Our Vacation Bible School started at church last night. I had eight of my grandchildren there. Amazing. And I expect nine tonight. We have a class for adults which Irving and I are attending. Our teacher is the most outstanding one I've ever heard. We are so blessed to have her. She quotes Bible verses, and tells about people in the Bible without any notes. She is totally dedicated to the service of God. It's obvious that she loves Him. She has been a widow for about two years, and she said last night that she misses her husband and thinks about him every day, but that she never feels lonely, because God is always with her. We had a young guest preacher at church yesterday. I loved hearing him. He is still attending Bible college. I believe he is about 19 years old. One thing he said which really gave me something to think about was this: Troubles are inevitable. Misery is optional.

## 9 Jun 2003 - Our Vacation Bible School Was Great

I loved it. And we had the most students enrolled that we've ever had in the history of our church. Our former pastor's son, who is also our pianist, was the Director, along with his wife. They are both highly intelligent and very organized, and I'm so proud of them. There were, I believe, twelve children who received Christ as their Savior. One of them was my own little great-grandchild. We heard yesterday that our new pastor will be with us beginning on the first Sunday in July. I think all of us are really looking forward to having him. He is only 34 years old, so young that I told him that I will have to boss a Irving is getting things all lined up to begin our new house. I just hope everyone who has a part will get their jobs done quickly, because it dawned on me this morning that I may not have many years to enjoy living in it, but I pity the child who tries to drag me out of it to take me to a nursing home. They'll just have to figure out a way that I can stay there. Don't take me seriously, because I have the three best children in the world. They won't mistreat me. And if they ever tried, my grandchildren wouldn't let them, because I have the greatest grandchildren in the world. (Honey, I know you have great ones, too.) Aren't we blessed?

## 13 Jun 2003 - I Have Clay's CD.

Jami bought it for me and I really like it. I realize that Ruben is a very good singer, but I prefer Clay's style. He reminds me of the great singers of the 40's. I would especially love to hear him sing some Christian songs. Se This evening Irving and I went to the Mayfair Fish Restaurant, and it was so good. We both had flounder. We were celebrating our 37th anniversary, which was on the 11th. I'm so thankful for Irving. He has always been so totally honest, hard working, and dependable. I've never had to worry about where my grocery money was coming from. I'm convinced that he has always been completely truthful and faithful...

Well, the Atlanta Braves are doing so very well this year, after a rocky start. I am loving watching their games, except when they play on the West coast and the games begin at 10:00. I'll at least see two hours of it tonight, but if I see more, I'll feel bad tomorrow. I sure do hope they keep Winning. Well, I guess that is enough rambling for this time.

## 25 Jun 2003 - A Little Progress

The foundation is finished on our house now, and it has been filled in with dirt. Now we wait for the plumber to do part of his job, and for the heating people to do theirs, then the cement floor can be poured. The septic tank is finished. I asked Paulette this evening if she could see our new toilet. (We have a Porta-Jon there for workers.) We went looking for gas logs today, but didn't find what we want. I guess we'll need to make some phone calls tomorrow. And Irving is ready for us to start looking at cabinets. I dread making decisions like that, because if we make a mistake, we'll have to live with it. Well, I guess we'll just do the best we can. We went to our little great-grandson's second birthday party this evening. He really is precious, and I think he had a very happy birthday. Jamison called this evening. He has been in Maryland visiting his aunt since Saturday, and he won't be back until a week from Monday. He sounded a little subdued to me, but I hope he is just tired. He said they had done a lot of yard work today. We're beginning to miss him pretty much. It will be just two more weeks after this Sunday til our new pastor will begin at our church. We're really looking forward to having back. The Braves lost their game tonight,

I'm sorry to say. I always hate to see them lose, but maybe they will win tomorrow night. Well, this has been a good day, but the air quality has been bad. Something about the ozone. I am so thankful that I don't have to be outside much when it's like this. Well, it is time to quit for now and get ready for bed. I'm hoping for another good day tomorrow. God is so kind to us, always blessing us and loving us. I'm truly grateful.

## 1 Jul 2003 - Daddy's Birthday

Today would have been Daddy's 95th birthday. He always enjoyed his birthday and he made sure that it wouldn't be forgotten. He started mentioning it about two weeks ahead of time. When he was 80, we had a little party for him, but on his. 81st birthday we didn't have one, and I'll always regret that, because he told me that he didn't enjoy the day as much as he did the last one. Then he died about five weeks later. If I had known, I would have given him a big party. He was somewhat childish for the last several years of his life, and I should have realized that he would be expecting a party. He has one sister who is still living. She will be 97 on Thursday. I won't be able to visit her, because I will be keeping little Joey on Wednesday and Thursday this week. But I hope I can go see her one day really soon. I delivered meals on wheels this morning, and my granddaughter, Rebecca, went with me. She was a big help. She'll be nine years old in a few days, but seems very mature for her age.

The Braves lost again last night, and I sure was sorry to see it happen. The losing pitcher was Greg Maddux, and he has been so excellent for several years, but I'm afraid his best days may be past. I don't really want to think that, so I'll keep hoping for him to get it back. I have so loved watching him 1 Well, we have had more rain, and I just hope it won't delay our house building much. We'll see.

## 23 Jul 2003 - More Birthdays

July is our biggest month for birthdays. I already wrote about Rebecca turning nine a couple of weeks ago. Well, this past Saturday Andrew turned 33. He's my first grandson and has always had a special place in my heart. Irving has always called him Skip, because of the way he tried to skip when he was very small. Whenever he was naughty as a little boy, he never wanted me to know about it. He was always very good around me. Then on Monday this week Hannah turned 14. That's hard to imagine. The time has flown so quickly. Her brother mentioned yesterday that it wouldn't be long before she could get a learner's permit to drive. Today is Alex's 11th birthday. He's our busy one. He loves to work more than anyone I've ever seen. He's always asking if Granddad has a job he can do. (And this is without any pay. I think it's amazing.) I have a small harmonica which Alex has always loved, and he has been wanting one so badly. So yesterday I went to the music store and found him one about like mine. He was delighted with it. I told him he would probably get thrown out of his house pretty soon if he played it much. I hope he can soon learn to play some tunes.

We are enjoying our new pastor and his family so much. He's only 34 years old, the youngest pastor I've ever had. But he seems very mature in his faith and his preaching.

Our house is really coming along slowly, and all the rain we've had is making things worse. But we hope eventually it will get dome.

Irving's back is causing him a lot of pain for a month now. He has an appointment tomorrow for an MRI to see if the doctor can tell what's wrong. We are hoping and praying he can help Irving.

Well, I must stop now. I have supper dishes to do, then I must get ready for church. After I get home, I have a Braves game to watch. There's no rest for the weary.

## 26 Jul 2003 - Cara's Wedding

I just came home from a beautiful wedding at our church. The bride has been coming to our church since she was about two years old, so her family is special to us. Her daddy operates the sound system and serves in many ways, and her mother teaches Sunday School and sings in the choir. I hope the newlyweds will always be as happy as they are today. It was a really nice wedding.

Irving got the results yesterday from his MRI, and they found that he has a fractured vertebrae. So we have to be at the hospital at 6:00 on Monday morning, and hopefully the doctor will repair it. When Irving had this same trouble a little over two years ago, this doctor in radiology told us about this relatively new procedure that he thought would correct the problem. So he put a needle on each side of the fracture, and inserted some kind of cement around it, and the results were immediate and miraculous. So we have high hopes that he can help us again.

The Braves lost their game last night, but that's okay. They will have another chance tonight, and I plan to be cheering them on. They have had a fantastic season so far. I've loved it.

## 28 Jul 2003 - Another Blessing

Irving and I went into Charlotte this morning to the hospital for his appointment to get his back treated. We got there at 5:40. then there was paper work to do, and blood work to do, and lots of questions. The doctor did the procedure, which consisted of injecting cement into the fractured vertebra. (Or should that be vertebrae?) I must check on that. The procedure worked wonderfully again, and we are so thankful to God, and to the very special doctor. After lying still for two hours, when Irving sat up to get dressed, the pain was gone. What a blessing, and what a relief.

Our house is finally ready for the cement to be poured. That should happen this week, then the framing can be done. I'm really so eager to see that done. Someone asked me about pictures, but I'll have to see if Jami can go with her digital camera and get a picture and put it in my diary.

The Braves won tonight. What a great game it was. So that was the topping to a very good day. I'm exhausted now, so I guess that's all for today.

## 4 Aug 2003 - Sleepless in Carolina

I woke up a little after two, and have tossed and turned ever since, so now it's almost five, and I have given up. Maybe I'll get a nap later. I don't know what caused me to have a night like this, unless Cheerwine has caffeine in it, but that was at lunchtime. In case any of you are not familiar with Cheerwine, it is not alcoholic, just a soft drink.

So My little great grandson, Colton, had a major disappointment this past Friday. He had been so excited because he was going to be playing football for the middle school this year. I think Friday was their third time to practice, and he somehow broke his arm. I think he will be in a cast for eight weeks. There was a meeting on Saturday morning, and the coach talked about Colton and what had happened to him, and they have decided to dedicate this season to him. They want him to sit with the team during the games, and he will have a jersey to wear. I hope that will be some consolation for him. I just think it's so pitiful, but he can look forward to next year.

We had a good day at church yesterday. Our new pastor seems to be just what we needed.

Yesterday was the anniversary of my daddy's death. It's hard to realize that it has been fourteen years since he died

My son's children have a new trampoline, and they love it. It really is so funny to see them jumping up and down, like monkeys. I've always been a little afraid of trampolines, so I'm kind of uneasy that they might get hurt.

Well, the Braves lost yesterday, but they say that a team can't win them all, so I'm trying to not be disappointed. Especially since they have the best record in all of Major League Baseball so far this year. They've been awesome. Go Braves!!!

## 13 Aug 2003 - Tomorrow Should Be Special

There were four of us girl cousins on my daddy's side who were born within about two years' time. A few years ago, I met Nancy and Mary Faye in Concord, which is about half way between their homes and mine. We had a great time over lunch, and sat in the cafeteria for about three hours. A year or so later, I met Mary Faye, Nancy, and Anne outside a mall near Charlotte, and we had a really good visit. Well, since that time, Mary Faye has died with cancer. She was the oldest, eleven months older than I. Now I am the oldest, then Nancy, then Anne. We are planning to meet tomorrow morning at a very large mall near Concord. I've never been there, but surely I can find it. We are to meet at about 11:30. I'm really eager to spend time with them. Since I was an only child, my first cousins seem a little bit like sisters to me. My grandson, Jamison, called me after church tonight and asked if he could go with me. So he will keep me company on the drive there and back. He's a really

The Braves won tonight. Yay! I loved it.

Our house is still at a standstill, due to all the rain and mud. I am so eager to see it framed up, but we can only wait. There seems to be a good possibility that they may be able to pour the concrete by the end of the week, and if they do, then the framing would be the next thing. We'll see.

Well, it's getting late, and I have a big day to look forward to tomorrow, so I'll close this entry for this time.

## 14 Aug 2003 - A Fun Day

Well, the Braves just won their game, (Yay!!!) and now I'm all set for bed, but I wanted to write a little about my day. I drove to Concord, to the new huge mall, and met my cousins there. My grandsons, Jordan and Jamison, went with me, and I think both Anne and Nancy were impressed with the boys' behavior. During lunch, Anne talked with the boys about Nintendo games, which she really enjoys, and they were able to give her some information about them. I think they were impressed with her: They never knew a lady that age who loved Nintendo games. It was so pleasant to spend time with my cousins. It seems like we are all girls again when we are together. I was amused that Anne is still unhappy about her freckles after all these years. And we had a good laugh when Nancy showed us her big circle of white hair in the back. She had a spell of her head itching and when the doctor couldn't help her, she put peroxide on the area, thinking that would help. Later, someone asked her what she had put on her hair, and she said nothing. But then she remembered the peroxide. I asked her if she didn't remember when we were girls that peroxide was what a lot of girls used to bleach their hair. Anne asked her if she didn't remember hearing about peroxide blondes. I don't know where she was during that time, but it was so funny. Her hair has always been a natural blonde, and still doesn't have very much gray in it, but it really is white in the back. Well, it was a very good visit. We talked about old times, and we caught up on each other's families. Anne said we should do that at least every three months. I hope we will. I missed Mary Faye today. I'm not sure now how long it has been since she died, but it must have been at least a couple of years. She was with us at our last get-together. She was so special to all of us.

## 22 Aug 2003 - Two Big News Items

We have out 23rd grandchild, born Tuesday morning. Actually, he's our great-grandchild, and his name is Harrison. He's 7 and a half pounds. Of course, he is beautiful too. He has two big sisters who probably will take turns holding him, except at night. Thank God for him. They finally got our cement poured, and now we expect the framing to begin this next Monday. I must get Jami to take a picture to put on here. Irving said that after the framing is done, then the roof is next, then the siding. How exciting is that?

Well, I'm keeping sweet little Joey today, and he just got up from his nap, so I must get off here, because he wants to help me type.

## 24 Aug 2003 - A Totally Good Day

It was a long, full day, and I am exhausted. But it has been great. First of all, everything went so well at church. It was Homecoming Day, and we had a great crowd of family and friends. Our music went perfectly. We did a medley of old songs, very simple but I think everyone really enjoyed it. Lunch was a real treat, as always, not just the food but the fellowship. I strongly recommend belonging and being active in church. Those friends become dearer and dearer through the years, and you can be sure they'll stand by you. Not everyone of course, because there will always be some who are not what they seem to be, but still there are a lot that I would trust and depend on. I love my church. Can you tell?

Later in the afternoon, there was a nap and a Braves game which they won. Yay!! Then I went to my son's church to see the program being performed by the children's choir. Well, let me tell you about my grandchildren. Three of them sang solos and did such a good job. The older two, who are 11 and 9, had lengthy speaking parts, and they were great. I saw no Stage fright, just total confidence. Made me mighty proud.

Now the day is over, everyone is in bed except me, and I'm about to get ready for bed, I just want to reiterate: It has been a totally good day. Thank you for it, Father.

## 6 Sep 2003 - Ballgames

I have four dear little ones playing ball this season. One 11-year-old playing baseball, one 10-year-old playing football, one 9-year-old playing softball, and one 6-year-old playing T-ball. I really must attend some games. So this morning I went to Alex's first game. I enjoyed it. Our team won. I think the score was 7-5. I look forward to seeing them all play, but I must say that I can hardly stand football, but I dearly love the little fellow who is playing it, and I really hope he does well. Little Aaron had his first T-ball game today. His mother told me of two hilarious incidents: A little fellow was playing third base, and when he heard a coach yell "run home," he took off and slid into home plate. Another little guy was running from first to second base when he heard a coach yell "get the ball." He stopped running and got the ball. I laughed my head off at these two stories. T-ball is always so entertaining. Everyone should go see a game at least once. The Braves won their game tonight. I loved it.

The roofer worked on our new roof today. I don't know whether he finished, but I doubt it. He'll probably finish it on Monday. Everything is coming together at last. Irving said this evening that he is starting to feel much better now that so many of the last things are lined up. It will be so good to get finished and move in and hopefully we will feel at home. I really need that.

## 15 Sep 2003 - Just Checking In

Yesterday was my daughter, Paulette's, birthday. I didn't get to see her yesterday, but I did see her Saturday and today. She is
still very sweet and special, and I look forward to being her neighbor.

The next thing on our house will be the insulation, then the sheet-rock. I tentatively chose the kitchen cabinets on Saturday, and I think the men will come out tomorrow to measure for them and to give US an exact price.

The Braves won their game a little while ago. I'm so looking forward to tomorrow's game, because Greg Maddux will be trying to break a very special record. He is now tied with Cy Young for winning 15 or more games in (I think) 16 consecutive seasons and if he can win tomorrow, he will hold that record all by himself.

We had a very good service at church yesterday. The music went so well that when the preacher stood up to preach, he was crying. The song the choir had just sung had touched him so deeply. It was about how it will be when we get to Heaven, and he talked about how thankful he is for all that God has done for him. I am so thankful too. God has blessed me so much more that I could ever have asked for. He is so loving and so faithful.

Well, I must turn this off and get ready for bed. I just wanted to check in.

## 21 Sep 2003 - The End Of A Good Day

We've enjoyed another good Sunday. Sunday School was a time of good fellowship and study, the preaching was very good, the music was too. Then this evening's choir practice went well. We got a lot done there. Then our adult training class was most enjoyable. We had a good number there.

The Braves were awesome this afternoon, and Greg Maddux broke the record he and Cy Young had been tied for. I had a great time watching it, all by myself. So my day has been very full, and I'm glad to be at home now, and through for the day.

Irving has had a really rough five days. He seems to have strained some muscles in his back, but thank God he seems to be getting some better now.

Well, I have two grandsons here for the night, and I'm sure they would enjoy watching some TV before bed, so I'll turn this off for tonight. And it won't be long until bedtime. I'm looking forward to it. One more thing I wanted to say: I just finished reading a book Jami loaned me, and I'd like to recommend it. It's titled "And the Shofar Blew," written by Francine Rivers. She is an outstanding author, and the book is very, very good.

## 27 Sep 2003 - Andrew Got Married Today

My sweet oldest grandson got married today. Everything went well, the bride was beautiful, and the two best men were so handsome. These were my two oldest great-grandsons who are almost 12 and 10 years old. They did double duty as ushers and best men. Every time I looked at them, I felt tearful. It has been a happy day... The one thing that hasn't been happy is that my husband is having a good deal of pain from strained muscles and spasms, but we hope that he is getting better. He has been sleeping in the recliner, and that doesn't make for a restful night. See I ordered our kitchen cabinets Thursday. They should be ready in three to four weeks. The sheet-rock has been delivered, so I expect that will be done on Monday or Tuesday, unless those people are tied up on something else. I'll be so glad when all of this is done. It has really been stressful. I think it was "becoming" who asked me recently whether we would be decorating with all new things. No, we can't do that. We'll use the furniture we already have. But I do want to buy a small table and chairs for the breakfast nook. And I think I want a futon to go in the guestroom. Not sure about that yet. Well, I guess everything will work out, in God's time.

## 14 Oct 2003 - My Uncle Was Abused

He has always been called Golly, he's 84 years old, lost his wife recently. His son and daughter-in-law moved in with him to take care of him. It sounded like a good plan. But I recently learned that they have been really mean to him. They convinced him that the government had quit sending his check. (Their names are on his checking account, so they had full access to his account.) They wouldn't let him eat at the table with them, and the woman even hit him several times. His oldest daughter visited him recently, and found him alone, so she took him home with her for the day. From there, he called his second daughter and asked her if she would come and get him. (She lives in Mississippi.) She and her husband came as quickly as they could, went to the Social Security Office and had his address changed to theirs. From his home he only took his clothes, his Bible, a flashlight, and one other small thing I can't remember. So now he is happy and safe with his daughter, and she is so happy to have him. She said that he feels like he has been let out of jail. I'm just horrified that his own son could allow his own daddy to be mistreated. I want to blame his wife, but he could surely have done something to stop it. My daughter said that charges should be filed against them, and that is probably true, but it would be Golly's word against theirs, so it would be hard to prove it. But God knows all about it, and I don't think they'll get away with it.

## 18 Oct 2003 - A Beautiful Wedding

I just got home a little while ago. First there was a beautiful wedding at our church, then a great reception at the country club. I really enjoyed it all, until the music suddenly changed into a bunch of loud noise. I knew then that it was time to leave. I fear that the next generation will have really bad hearing before they get old, due to listening to such loud music. One thing about the wedding that was so funny. The preacher told me that he noticed a caterpillar on the floor and was careful not to step on it. Then he noticed that it was on his shoe. Soon it was crawling up his pants leg. The bride and groom saw it and nearly laughed. Soon after that, when they walked away from the preacher to light the unity candle, he looked to see where it was and it was on his sleeve near his elbow. He flicked at it and it grabbed onto his finger, kinda wrapped around it, and wouldn't let go. So finally, he flipped it off into the choir area behind him. Now tomorrow, if one of the ladies in the choir sings a particularly high note, we will know what she saw. I sure hope no one sits on it. That could be really messy.

## 25 Oct 2003 - Just Checking In

Our house is coming along very well now. And we have some really special helpers. Last night, Jami and her whole family were there filling nail holes, and getting things ready for painting. Her boys moved a lot of pieces of scrap lumber too. Today they were all back priming and painting. And my son Jon and his wife and two of his children went over there and did a lot of sweeping and cleaning up. They gathered up a lot of cardboard and brought it here. Then Jon burned it. Family is so special. One other thing I forgot. My kitchen cabinets are to arrive on Wednesday. That will be a biggy.

I worked at the jail on Thursday morning. A couple came in to be married by the magistrate, and it seemed sad to me, because they were dressed so casually. She was wearing pants and a plain top, and he was wearing a polo shirt and pants. Nothing really wrong with that, but a wedding is such a special occasion. And neither of them had any family there. The two witnesses appeared to be casual friends. Another striking thing that happened was that a grandmother came in to see about getting her grandson out of jail. He had just been brought in a little while before, charged with drug possession. He is 17 years old. It was going to cost her three hundred dollars to get him out. His car had already been towed, and she was going to have to get it back too. She said she felt like wringing his neck. But she obviously loved

him, and I really felt sorry for her. I so hope he will get his life straightened out.

I found out that our new pastor sings, so I asked him to sing tomorrow, and he said he would. He even thanked me for asking him. He is so sweet, and I am so looking forward to hearing him.

Well, I must get off here and do a few things around the house. It's such a beautiful day in the neighborhood. Thanks be to God for it, and for so many blessings.

## 31 Oct 2003 - The Kitchen Cabinets

They were finished up this morning and I am delighted with them. They are made of honey oak, and the top is a dark green marbly pattern. I love Jami's counter-top and copied hers. The sink is even set in, and now I just lack buying the stove and dishwasher and choosing the tile for the floor. I think the kitchen and the little back porch will be my favorite places.

The down side of this is that Irving is having a great deal of pain again, this time it's like muscle spasms and extreme soreness. He is so frustrated because he is not able to do any work on the house. He still tries occasionally, but it causes him so much pain that he really shouldn't try it.

I really am eager to get settled in for both our sakes. It has been a stressful time for us. Irving was joking this morning and saying that with all this experience we are getting, that maybe we should start building houses to sell. But I'm pretty sure we won't be doing that.

Well, it's time to get ready for bed.

Earlier in this entry I said that all I lacked was a few things in the kitchen. Well, I might have given the impression that I was that near being through with the whole house. That's not the case at all. We lack a good many things, but we are making a lot of progress, for which I am truly thankful.

## 7 Nov 2003 - Friday Again

Another week is nearly over, and we have accomplished a little more on our house, but it will still be a while before we can move in. Our driveway and sidewalk and patio have been poured. And our yard has been leveled and sown with grass, and covered in straw. It rained a little last night, so maybe the grass will come up soon. We hope the garage door will be installed on Monday. Calvin is planning on painting the garage tomorrow, and whatever else he has time for. Our grandsons, Jordan and Jamison, picked up a lot of rocks for us today, and our grandson, Alex, is planning to set our blueberry bushes out for us tomorrow. My son picked up our stove and dishwasher and placed them in the kitchen. Our oldest grandson, Andrew, helped him unload them. That saved us about fifty dollars delivery fee. So we are getting lots of help from our sweet family. I'm beginning to think we'll be ready to move in about three weeks, but who knows? I just know I don't expect to ever try building another house. I may have said all of this in my last entry. I can't keep track any more. It's hard to think of anything else these days.

Irving is still in a great deal of pain when he is on his feet, but he feels like he just has to go to the house and see what else needs to be done. It troubles him so much that he is not able to do all this himself.

We kept our precious little Joey today, but he was just here a little over two hours. He is such a good boy, and so cute. We all love him.

Well, I guess that's enough for today. I'll need to fix supper soon. I need to talk nice to Jami and get her to put a recent picture of my house on here soon.

## 15 Nov 2003 - Two Special Birthdays

Yesterday, our newest great-granddaughter was born. She is so pretty and her name is Adeline. She's our 24th. Amazing...

Today, our granddaughter, Lauren, is 14 years old. She's my son's firstborn, the one who was born in the car. What a story! Now I have 2 granddaughters who are 14, Hannah and Lauren. They are just 4 months apart, they are both taller than I am, and they are great girls.

Our house is still coming along slowly. Maybe we will get it finished soon. We hope so.

## 18 Nov 2003 - An Update On The House

I feel kind of encouraged this morning, because things started picking up yesterday. The heating people connected the gas logs and did some of their other work, and the plumber came back and brought our water heater and toilets and faucets. Today I'm hoping they will get all those things installed. The trench for our water tap is due to be dug today, and my son is going to put up some gutter on the front of the house. My grandson plans to continue painting. That has been a hard job, especially since it is all white. He says you can't see where you've been. But maybe he can be done with it in about two more days. Then we can start on our floors, carpet for the bedrooms and tile for the rest. Then we will be nearly through. It's getting exciting.

Irving is still having so much pain, he's not able to do anything or enjoy anything. He has an appointment to see an orthopedic surgeon next Monday, if he can stand to wait that long. I so hope he can get help. Then we can move into the house and he can have rest and peace. He really does deserve it. He has always worked so hard and provided so well for us, almost never wanting anything for himself. He is a very special man, and I'm blessed to have him in my life.

Well, it's almost 7:30. Time to get busy. I have a house to finish. I've always hated going to Lowe's, but I told Irving yesterday that I'm liable to start liking it if I have many more trips there. And there will be many more.

## 23 Nov 2003 - It Has Been A Good Day.

Everything at church was so good today. Especially tonight at choir practice. We got a lot of good practice done on our Christmas music. And we will have a combined Thanksgiving service on Tuesday night with three other churches. Our choir will sing a great medley featuring "I'll fly away," and we really enjoy that. A group of five men will sing "Beulah Land," and Jami will sing a solo. All the other churches will do some music too, so we should have a good time. Our pastor will preach, then we will have a time of fellowship and finger foods.

One sad note: I called my friend in Charlotte, and her husband told me that she died last month. She had a stroke a couple of years ago, and I've been calling about once a month to ask about her. Her husband told me that she had another bad stroke and died in just a few days after that. He tried to call me, but couldn't find my number. We aren't listed where we are presently staying. Evelyn was a good friend to me. She was always so eager to do anything she could for me or anyone else who needed her. I'm glad that she was a Christian and we know that she is happy now. But her husband will be so lonely without her.

I went to a place yesterday and picked out the lights and ceiling fans for the house. I'm relieved to have that done, and now I'm eager to see them in place.

Irving is no better, but tomorrow he will see a new doctor. I so hope he can help. It really has been a hard several weeks.

Well, I must get off of here, and get ready for bed. Maybe tomorrow will bring blessings.

## 24 Nov 2003 - A Brief Report

I took Irving to the orthopedic surgeon today. They did several x-rays and learned that there were two compression fractures. Those fractures have been the cause of all his pain around his middle, spasms and such. The only thing to do now is to go back to the doctor who has helped him twice before by inserting cement into the fractured vertebras (or vertebrae) I'm not sure how it is spelled. So now we wait until an appointment is made. Afterwards, we will have to begin seeing a specialist on Osteoporosis. The doctor said that Irving needs aggressive treatment for that. So it must be pretty bad. Irving feels like today's trip was for nothing, but at least we did find out what is going on in his spine. And we have high hopes that the cement procedure will give him a great relief. I just hope we get an appointment very soon.

## 27 Nov 2003 - Thanksgiving Day 2003

There is a song titled "Count your blessings" which says we should "name them one by one. And it will surprise you what the Lord has done." I couldn't possibly name them all. I'm sure there are many that I haven't even been aware of. But I will name a few: Tops on my list must be Jesus Christ. What a wonderful Savior and Friend. Then there is Irving. What a blessing he has been for 37 years, a special friend and excellent provider. I have 3 precious children and 2 great step-daughters. Who could ask for more? Then for the icing: Imagine 24 grandchildren, each one so special, one very beloved girl has gone on to Heaven but I won't stop including her on my list. We will always love Christi. The 2 newest ones are Harrison and Adeline (whom we haven't met yet.) I have a church family which means so much to me. There are many special friends there that I know I can count on. I'm thankful for music, with which God has blessed me through the years. He has given me good health and everything else that I need. And now on top of all these other gifts, He has given us a new house which is nearly ready to move into. These are certainly not all of my blessings, but when I begin to count them, I am truly so thankful for "what the Lord has done."

## 2 Dec 2003 - Yesterday At The Hospital

We left home at 6:15 and were still ten minutes late getting to the hospital, due to a train and the heavy traffic. It really was a hectic ride. Soon they sedated Irving for his MRI, because he couldn't lie down without severe pain. The doctor looked at the two crushed vertebrae and thought at first that he probably couldn't fix one of them because it was so flattened. But later in the day, when they started the procedure, it turned out that they were able to repair both of them. The procedure is called vertebroplasty and it is a lifesaver. We didn't get to leave the hospital until about 7:30, because Irving was still mostly asleep and not breathing much. But we finally got home at about 8:30. I really don't like driving at night anymore, but thanks to God we made it safely. Well, today Irving has been so sore he could hardly move, but I'm so hoping he'll be improved by morning. He went to bed a few minutes ago, and I do hope he will be able to sleep.

About the house, the electrical inspector found one small problem which will be fixed tomorrow. Then I must go to the water department and arrange for a meter to be put up. I called today for the carpet people to go out and measure to see how much floor covering we will need. So things are moving right along.

I've been planning for months to go on a trip to the beach this coming Friday. My money has been paid for a month or so, and I want to go so badly. I usually go every year and have a wonderful time. Our former pastor arranges everything: We go down on a nice big bus; in the evening we eat at a fantastic seafood buffet; then we go to see a great show; then on Saturday we usually go to a large mall for shopping and lunch; and after that we go to another show. Then we get back home around 7 or 8 o'clock. I've been in a terrible dither, wondering whether I'll get to go, since Irving has been having such a bad time. But Jami says that her family will look after him while I'm gone. And now I have hope that he'll be feeling a lot better by Friday. Well, we'll just have to wait and see. It's all in God's hands, so everything will be alright, one way or the other.

## 7 Dec 2003 - December 7, 2003

I did get to take the trip to the beach, and it was so pleasant, but I did feel a little guilty about leaving Irving. But everything turned out fine. Jami's boys stayed here a lot of the time, and I noticed a bag from Arby's on the table. Irving said Jami had brought a bag of roast beef sandwiches. And I had left him several things to eat which would be easy to prepare. Se He has really been feeling terrible, still having spasms, still sleeping in the recliner. Calvin's family gave their daddy's lift chair to him, and that has really saved him a lot of strain. I'm grateful for that. He called the preacher yesterday and asked him to bring some of the elders here to pray for him. The Bible says that if anyone is sick, he should call for the elders to pray for him. We don't often do that, but Irving felt that it was what he should do. So today right after church, the preacher and seven of our deacons arrived and they each one prayed for Irving to be healed. That was one of the most precious things I've ever seen. Now we wait and see what God will do for him. We know for sure that God heard each prayer and that He is able to do whatever We need.

Yes the house is coming right along. The cable man is due to be there on Wednesday, and I hope by then I will have gotten the carpet ordered out. We still don't have the final inspection, but that should happen very soon, probably tomorrow or Tuesday, then we will have power in the house. Irving said today that this will be the house that Doris built. He said he started it and that I am finishing it. Aren't we getting a great Christmas gift?

Well, it's bedtime again and I'm so glad. I'm still so tired from the trip, but so thankful that I got to go. I expect that tomorrow will be a very busy day, so I will need a good night's rest.

## 15 Dec 2003 - Another Trip To The Hospital

Since Irving had the last procedure done to repair two vertebrae, he has been in a great deal of pain. So today we went back to the hospital for x-rays to see what was causing his pain. Well, he has two broken ribs. It appears that when they put him on his stomach to do the procedure, it broke the ribs. With Osteoporosis the bones can break so easily. But the doctor said his lungs look good, and that the ribs will heal on their own. So we both feel better just knowing what has been going on.

We have the floors done in the living/dining area and the kitchen and the hall. They really are pretty. I think I did well choosing them. And we now have water in the house. Our only big remaining problem is that we are having to wait for the electricity. I talked to the man this evening, and he said it could possibly take until Jan. 2nd. But I'm hoping it won't take that long. But at least now we can see that it will probably be all ready in ten days or so. I've started packing some things, getting ready to go.

Our Christmas program is taking shape and looking good. We'll have our last practice this Wednesday night. It is titled "His Very Own Star."

Time to stop for this time. Maybe I'll have more news soon about the long-awaited house.

## 22 Dec 2003 - It's Getting Close

We presented our Christmas cantata last night, and everything went so well. There were four soloists, (including Hannah) and they all did very good jobs. Our speakers were all outstanding, and I am so proud of our choir.

teens Now, on to the Christmas gathering for our family. I reserved the church fellowship hall, because we don't have room for the whole crowd at home. We used to always get together in different homes, but for the last two or three years (or maybe more) we haven't done that. So I think it's time we all spent Christmas together again. I'm planning for thirty-five, but probably there will be a couple missing. Things always seem to come up. But I'd love it if everyone could come. I'm providing the meat, and I asked the others to bring a vegetable and a dessert. I think Jami and Jon have planned some kind of games or something entertaining. I hope everything works out smoothly.

About the house, we are waiting for the electricity to be turned on. I still have to get the insides for the closets and the pantry, and the blinds. So we are really in the "home" stretch now. I wish I could show everyone my pretty floors. I'm excited about that, after looking at the cement floors for so long. God is so good to us. He always gives us something to look forward to, and I'm really-so thankful.

Irving is still not well. We believe his ribs are healing, but he still has a lot of pain. He is still sleeping in the recliner day and night. His appetite is very small, and he feels weak. Of course, that is to be expected with so little activity. But we are certainly hoping for better days, and we know that our Heavenly Father is aware of all our troubles, and that He will take care of us.

"God so loved the world that He gave His only begotten Son, that whosoever believeth on Him should not perish, but have everlasting life." (John 3:16)

Thanks be to God for His Unspeakable Gift. Praise the Lord.

## 29 Dec 2003 - Another Update

This has been a sleepless night. I don't know why, maybe too much on my mind. But I finally got tired of trying to sleep, and decided to get up and write awhile... cr I went to the funeral home last night after church, to visit the family of one of our church members who died. He was in his late eighties, a very sweet man, and so loved by his wife and five daughters. He was married for sixty-six years. He'll be missed for a very long time. I guess spending that time with the family has filled my mind with so many thoughts that it's hard to sleep.

Irving has so much pain from Osteoporosis, and this past week he was nauseated and threw up four times. We were afraid there was a blockage. Obviously, there was something wrong. So I persuaded him to go to the emergency room on Saturday. They did blood work and x-rays, and the doctor decided that the sickness was due to gastritis, brought on by a great deal of pain and stress. They put a pain patch on his arm, and he has rested a lot better since, although he is still having to spend every night in the recliner. Osteoporosis is a dreadful illness, so painful.

Now for some good news. I expect we will get to move into our new house at the end of this week, providing the power company gets the power on when they said they would. I hope to go to Lowe's today to find closet and pantry shelves and blinds. That will be all of the major things we need. We have spent more than we sold our last house for, but we will have more room and a much bigger lot. And it will be a better house. So it's worth a little more money. I know that Irving will be relieved when we are settled. He has always been such a good provider, and he really wants me to have that house. It has been so hard for him not being able to get the house finished himself. He says he started it and I'm finishing it.

Well, I've said all I have to say, and I'm still not sleepy. It's 4:15 now, and still time for a good nap, so I think I'll lie back down and at least rest a little more before I start my day.

## 1 Jan 2004 - January 1, 2004

The years are flying by so quickly I can hardly keep up. I can hardly believe that it is actually 2004. Well, the power company is supposed to turn our electricity on tomorrow and that's hard to believe too. So today there was a good deal of moving done. While my grandson Andrew and I were at Lowe's buying the closet shelves and the blinds, my son Jon and his wife and my daughter Jami moved a lot of our things into the garage. So we are almost there. If we can get the most important blinds installed, and a few shelves in the closets, we might possibly spend the night there tomorrow. The cablevision is to be turned on Saturday, and the telephone is to be connected on Monday. So J expect we'll be all moved in either tomorrow or Saturday.

I took Irving to the house this afternoon, and I think he was pleased with all that has been done since he last saw it. He liked the floors, said the kitchen floor was about what he'd had in mind. I so hope that getting moved will give him some peace. He has had such a hard time for a long time, so much pain.

Well, this has been another long day, and I'm thankful that it's time to go to bed and rest awhile.

## 5 Jan 2004 - There's No Place Like Home

We are finally here, and it feels so good. There is still a lot to be done, but there is no real hurry. This is a very comfortable house, and I thank God for it. It seemed to take forever to get it finished, but it was worth the wait. Today they connected our phone, and that was the last major thing to do. My grandson Andrew is coming over tomorrow to do several small things for us. He'll put up two towel rods and two toilet paper holders, and maybe a paper towel holder in the kitchen, if I can pick one up in time.

Irving continues to feel so bad, and sometimes he sounds so discouraged. He told me Saturday that now that we got me into this new house, that if the Lord calls him I'll have a roof over my head. He has always been such a good provider, and he is still thinking of me. We have to go to see his regular doctor tomorrow, then he has an appointment with the V.A. doctor on the 14th, and one with the Osteoporosis specialist on the 29th. I keep hoping there will be some kind of help for him. I'd love to see him enjoy this house.

Well, it's getting late, so I'm about ready to go to bed. It's a great blessing to be able to rest awhile. Tomorrow will probably be another busy day of moving more stuff here and putting it away.

Thanks be to God for His Great Mercy and Love.

## 13 Jan 2004 - Another Busy Tuesday

I started out the day delivering meals to ten elderly people, with Jamison helping me. Then we stopped at our previous home and picked up another small load of things. Then I went to Ladies' Prayer at the church. Later in the afternoon, Irving wanted to go to the other house to look around and see how much we have left there. (We can't find his two or three quarts of honey, and I think he just thought I was overlooking them.) Then after loading up a few more things we headed home. We stopped for gas, and after paying for the gas the van wouldn't start. Three men tried to help us, and we were reminded that there are still some very kind people left in the world. They couldn't get it started, but in a few minutes, a mechanic stopped at the convenience store on his way home. He looked at the van and determined that the trouble was in the starter, and he told us that if it still wouldn't start in the morning, to call him and he would send someone to pick it up, and he would fix it. Jami came and picked us up and brought us home. She offered us her van to use tomorrow when we go to Rock Hill to see the V.A. doctor. But we may try to get Irving fixed comfortably in the car and drive it. We'll see. So today has been full enough for me. But I can't complain. I certainly have more blessings than I could ever ask for. It's so peaceful tonight here in our home. I thank God so much for this house, and for all He has given to me.

## 18 Jan 2004 - Some Improvement

I'm so glad to report that Irving is feeling a little better these last few days. He even went to church this evening. He has been able to lie down in bed for a few hours at a time, and that is just a wonderful blessing after having to sleep in the recliner for several weeks. I just hope that he won't break any more bones.

I went to the funeral home tonight to visit a family who lost a loved one. He was 25 years old and has a baby on the way in March. He had been waiting for a heart/lung transplant, but it didn't come. His grandmother who raised him died nine days ago. I'm so sorry for all of them.

Church was good today, as it usually is. Irving had thought last night that he might be able to go, but then he didn't sleep well and couldn't make it.

Well, we still have several odds and ends to do to the house, and I have a lot of putting away to do, but I'm so delighted with this house. What a wonderful blessing it is.

Jordan and Jamison are watching TV in the den. Now and then I hear them laughing. It will soon be bedtime and I'm looking forward to it. I have a lot to do tomorrow.

## 25 Jan 2004 - An Icy, Cold Day

I had heard that there would be icy weather starting early this morning but I didn't think it would be in our county. Wow, was I wrong! It was sleeting this morning and so cold, but we went on to church. It was the first time Irving has been able to go in several weeks. It wasn't so bad driving there, but about halfway the ice started to form on the windshield. When I parked, we discovered that the pavement was slick, so I drove around to the other side of the building where you can drive under a shelter to let people out. Jami and Calvin came out and helped us in, then Calvin parked the van. It was good to be at church. I didn't have to direct the music today, because it was Baptist Men's Day and the men did everything, including singing in the choir. I enjoyed it a lot. Afterwards, since the roads were getting worse, Calvin drove our van and Irving home, and Jami drove me home in her van. What a relief that was. I can't stand to drive if it is the least bit slippery.

We have spent the afternoon just being lazy, and now the evening is beginning to get long. I may just go to bed early. I wonder what tomorrow will bring. I was planning to keep little Joey, but I don't know whether his mother will bring him if the roads aren't a lot better. I think our schools will be closed tomorrow and I know that will be great for the children. I'm so thankful that we don't have to go anywhere, and that we have plenty of food in the house. I hope folks around here don't begin to lose power. That would be dreadful. Well, we will see.

## 15 Feb 2004 - Sunday Morning Beginning

Well, it's early Sunday morning, about 6:30, and I thought I should take a few minutes to add a brief update to my diary.

My youngest grandchild, Aaron, turned seven on Friday. He will always be our youngest, because our children are all through having babies. He is such a cute little fellow and a smart one. I picked him up yesterday afternoon and took him to the Dollar Tree, where he picked several toys. Then we got ice cream cones to eat on our way back home. Those were delicious. I told Aaron that we had our own private little party.

Later, my granddaughter Miranda and my great-grandson Drew and I went to a party for little Joey. He is the one that Jami and I have kept since he was seven weeks old. He is two today. I had never been to his house before, so he was surprised to see me, and so excited. His parents planned to cook out on the grill, but the weather wasn't fit, so we had pizza and it was very good. Irving had thought he would go, but he didn't have a good day, so he decided he couldn't make it.

Today will be a busy one at church, but I'm expecting it to be very good. Our preacher is going to sing a solo, and I'm really looking forward to that. Then tonight we will have a worship service, and I have invited the son of one of our members to come and sing for us. He has a good voice, but didn't start singing until he was probably past forty years old. I'm looking forward to hearing him.

Well, it's time to get busy. I need to put a chicken in the pot, then start getting ready to go. I hope everyone who reads this has a great Sunday.

## 16 Feb 2004 - Antisemitic?

1 keep hearing so much about Mel Gibson's new movie, The Passion of the Christ, and people are trying to make Mel Gibson seem antisemitic. This is ridiculous. He simply believes the Bible to be the truth, and he has produced a movie that presents the truth about the death of Jesus Christ. It doesn't matter who did the crucifying, it only matters that Jesus gave His Life to save me and you. He didn't have to allow them to crucify Him. But He came to earth for this very purpose. He shed His blood on that cross to pay for my sins and yours, and I'm so grateful for that great love and mercy. Christians can hardly be Anti-Semitic. Jesus Himself was Jewish. These people are special and I could never hate them. I hope that America will always stand by Israel, because I believe that is what God would have us do.

## 18 Feb 2004 - My Third Anniversary

It is three years today since I started this journal, and it has been quite an experience. I'm glad I have taken the time to record a lot of memories, because my children will have them available whenever they want to look back with me. Maybe I can think of some more to tell about later. That is, if my mind will not fail me. Well, that's in God's hands. I do pray that He will preserve my mind, my eyes, and my ears, if that is His will. I'm a little selfish, I know, but I also know that He loves me, and that He will do whatever is best for me.

## 1 Mar 2004 - March Is Here

I'm kind of glad that February is over. Maybe it won't be long now til Spring returns. We've really had a big snow, and it was so beautiful, but I had one major disappointment. My snow cream didn't turn out well because there was sleet in it. I didn't think about that when I brought the pan of snow inside. Then I used my only can of evaporated milk, then I couldn't find my vanilla flavoring. My grandson came driving over on the ice to bring me some. So then I couldn't start over with good snow, because I had no more evaporated milk, and I surely couldn't ask my sweet grandson to bring vanilla again. So I'm left with a craving for snow cream, but I think I can wait til next year. The cutest sight was waiting for me when I got back from church last night. There were two snowmen standing in my yard, a man and a woman. So cute. Irving told me that Colton and Austin had come over and built them.

I went to see "The Passion of the Christ" this past Wednesday, along with my daughter and son-in-law. It was so moving and so heart-breaking to see Jesus being treated so horribly. But I think we Christians need to be reminded what Christ did for us, and that He was willing to pay the price for our sins, because He loves us that much. I can't begin to imagine the kind of love that God the Father showed when "He gave His only begotten Son, that whosoever believeth in Him should not perish, but have everlasting life." But I am so very thankful that He does love us that much.

## 9 Mar 2004 - Painted Posts, Yay For Me

I finally have my front porch posts painted. While the weather was so beautiful on Saturday, I decided I would get started on that dreaded chore. I put one coat on them, and what a job that was. And all night my left arm and wrist ached. Then yesterday I put the second coat on, and now I am so proud. I think the front of my house looks so pretty, I'm eager to show it. So now I must get Jami to come over with her digital camera and put the picture on my diary for me. We also now have four new shrubs at the front of the house. The two gardenias have two buds on them, and I am so eager for them to bloom.

Irving goes today for a bone scan. His sedimentation rate (whatever that means) is too high, so the doctor ordered this scan to try to learn what might be wrong. I'm praying that it won't mean anything serious. He has felt the best lately that he has in a long time, and that is such a blessing. He's able to go to church again, and that means so much. In many ways, life is so good. Even though there are problems, God helps us through them and gives us blessings all along the way. I'm so thankful for this new day.

## 28 Mar 2004 - Just Checking In

It seems that lately I haven't had much to write about, even though I do want to keep this journal going. I guess my life gets into a little bit of a rut. But I thought maybe if I started writing an entry, I would have some kind of thoughts to record.

Well, first of all, today at church was so good. Jami sang Via Dolorosa, which talks about the way of the Cross, and how hard it was for Jesus to walk that last walk towards

Calvary. He paid such a high price to redeem me. I don't know any way to ever repay Him, but then He doesn't require that I repay Him. It's all free. Amazing, isn't it?

Church tonight was good too. Then choir practice went along so well, our Easter music is about ready. I love my choir. They are such a special group, and so faithful. I'm blessed by God to have the privilege of working with them. I wonder how much longer I'll be able to direct the music.

I'm loving the Spring weather we've been having. It's so refreshing. And Irving has had a good-sized garden area plowed up, and yesterday we bought a used tiller for just $50.00. Irving isn't able to use it, but he thinks he can teach the grandsons to do it. We'll see. It really would be a good thing if the boys learned how to grow vegetables, while their Granddad is still able to teach them. We have tomato plants ready to be put in the ground. I do love home-grown tomatoes. And Irving is raising ten young chickens. We hope to have a good supply of eggs along about August or September.

Well, I guess that will have to be enough for this time. It's time to get ready for bed, and I'm glad. It has been a very good day, thanks to God.

## 3 Apr 2004 - Big Week Coming Up

On Tuesday morning early, my granddaughter and I plan to go to visit some special relatives. First, we want to visit my aunt who is in a rest home. She will be 98 years old in July. Then we will head towards the mountains to visit my mother's family. I'm really looking forward to it, but it will really be a full day.

Then on Thursday I plan to go to Atlanta to watch the Braves play. A young couple in our church invited me and another woman to go with them to Atlanta. They know that Eula and I both are big Braves fans, as does everyone who knows me. This has been in the works for probably a couple of months, and awhile back after Eula and I told them to let us know how much we owed for the motel room and ticket to the game, Eric presented us each with our bill. Part of the bill was serious, and told us how much we owed, which was about 41 dollars I believe. It listed the discounts and everything he had worked out. But then there was a charge of 3 dollars for the stress of his riding that far with 3 women. But the funniest item was an 8 dollar charge for a Mets tee-shirt. The Braves will be playing against the Mets that day. I was so glad that he made that charge optional. But the thought of me coming home wearing a Mets tee shirt is really hilarious. I'm so looking forward to this trip, and I'm so touched that this sweet couple would offer to drive us. And we even have rooms so near the ballpark that we can easily walk to the game. And I found out today that Thursday night will be Hank Aaron Night, honoring the 30th anniversary of his record-breaking home run. So exciting.

## 10 Apr 2004 - It's Jami's Birthday!

Forty-one years ago today, I gave birth to such a special baby. The world really gained a prize, I think, but maybe I'm prejudiced. Jami, you've been such a blessing to my life, and I pray that your life will always be blessed.

Se My granddaughter and I postponed our trip to the mountains to visit relatives because my cousin, with whom my aunt lives, was very sick and running a fever. We decided not to go and risk catching something, so we will probably go before very long.

My trip to Atlanta was outstanding. This really special couple at our church invited me and my friend Eula, who is a widow, to go with them to see a Braves game. We left here early Thursday morning, had such a pleasant trip down there. We worried that it might rain or that it might be chilly, but it was perfect. The game was wonderful, especially when John Smoltz came in to close it. I loved seeing the game, and the Braves won. Yay!!! We had a safe and happy trip back, full of new sweet memories. I'm so grateful to the dear friends who took us with them. And I'm so glad that I found Irving well and safe when I got home. Now we are looking forward to a very special day at church tomorrow, when we will be remembering the Resurrection of Jesus Christ. He lives!!! And I'm so grateful for that.

## 30 Apr 2004 - My Day.

Not very eventful, but I did want to write a little before I get totally rusty. I am so glad to say that Irving and I are doing so well and feeling so blessed.

We have a new volunteer to help us deliver meals to the elderly, so I met her today and drove her on our route and told her a little about all of our clients. She plans to deliver the meals next Wednesday.

I went to visit Paulette and two of her grandsons this afternoon. That was good. Earlier today I visited little Joey for awhile. (He was supposed to stay with Jami, but his mother changed her plans, and I needed to see him.) A little while ago, I walked over to Paulette and Steve's house and visited with them for a half hour or so.

Well, now I need to get off from here, and see if the Braves' game has started. I so look forward to seeing them play. But I saw something this morning on the Weather Channel about snow in Colorado, so I'm hoping they will be able to play. It's hard to imagine snow on the last day of April.

## 3 May 2004 - A Surprise Birthday Party

Yesterday evening, I went to the church to get ready for choir practice and there were a good many cars in the parking lot. I saw Calvin nearby and asked him if there was a deacons meeting. He hesitated, then said that there was a bridal shower. That was true, but it should have been over earlier.

I went into the sanctuary and saw that there were already a fair number of choir members there. They don't usually get there ahead of me, but I went ahead getting books from the back, preparing for choir practice. Then the preacher came in and asked if we were busy. He said he needed to get our opinion about something in our old fellowship hall. I looked at my watch and told him that we could spare about two minutes. He said it wouldn't take but a minute or two, so all of us followed him, and when we got to the doorway I got the most wonderful surprise. Everyone shouted "Happy Birthday," and I was immediately surrounded by a group of grandchildren hugging me. I've never felt more loved before. I looked around and saw not only my precious choir members, but all of my children were there, with their families. And there were several special friends who mean so much to me. We ate pizza and had such a great time. The choir presented me with a beautiful bouquet of roses, and there were several other gifts, but the love I felt from all of these wonderful people was the best gift of all. It was awesome!!! The Bible says in Psalm 90 that "the days of our years are three score years and ten," but of course they are often extended for many more years. On Wednesday, I will reach my three score years and ten, and I am so very thankful for all the blessings God has showered down on me through my wonderful family and friends. I really want to live the rest of my days in a way that will please Him. Thank you, Father, and thank you, sweet family and friends.

## 26 Jun 2004 - It's Been A Whole Month!

When I decided to log in and write a little, I was surprised to see that my last entry was on May 26. I seem to have been really busy lately. This week has been kind of full: I had to take meals to the elderly Thursday, then go for a perm at 3:00. Friday I went to a 4 hour instructional meeting for the upcoming primary election, then a little shopping, then to a funeral at 3:00. Today I did a four hour stint at the county jail, minding the visitation desk. (It has been quite awhile since I could make time for that.) At 6:00 this evening we went to the church for a party honoring our pastor, and I ate too much. I wish I had used a little willpower at the dessert table.

So here I sit at nearly 11:00, feeling stuffed and needing to go to bed. Maybe I'll take the time to write again real soon, but so many of my days are just routine and I don't have much to say. But I must say that there is something wonderful about routine days: Things are running smoothly and peacefully. Thanks to God.

## 21 Jul 2004 - Just A Few Items To Tell About

Well, I've let nearly a month pass again between entries. But I really do want to stay in touch. My Aunt Flora died Monday night. She had just had her 98th birthday on July 1st. She was the last of Daddy's siblings, and I'm sorry she is gone, not for her sake but for mine. She was a very good person, a good homemaker, a good mother, a good wife, and a good aunt. She'll be missed.

My next news is happy. Little Mary Hannah is 15 years old today. Hard to believe. She is really a special girl, very sweet, very smart, and very pretty. And she's not bad at playing Rummy. . I worked at the polls yesterday, and I was totally exhausted when I got home. So today I haven't done much except rest.

We have enjoyed so many good things from our garden lately. What a blessing it is to have all this good food. I think our cantaloupes are almost gone. Irving has carried some to church two or three times and given them away. Now our okra is producing and our green beans are blooming.

Well, I've stayed up later than usual, so I must get to bed. Tomorrow is my grocery day. I will probably enjoy that. I like buying the groceries, but I don't like carrying them in and putting them away.

The Atlanta Braves lost their game tonight, but it was really close, 4 to 3. I believe they are still tied for first place in their division. Go Braves!!!

Happy Birthday, Dear Hannah. Nina loves you a lot.

## 3 Aug 2004 - I'm So Behind

So many things have been going on lately, I thought I should at least write about a few of them.

When I last wrote I told about my aunt Flora dying. Well, my granddaughter Miranda drove me to Statesville the next Thursday evening for the visitation and it was so good to see a good many of my relatives. Some of them I hadn't seen for maybe 50 years. My cousin's three children were there, and I had never seen them except in pictures when they were very small. I spent most of the time talking with my cousin, Nancy, who often bit me when we were small. I have fully forgiven her and enjoy her company now. Even way back then I liked to play with her when she wasn't mad at me.

Last week on Wednesday, I rode with Jami and two of her children to Asheville. Her third child, Jamison, had been visiting with his aunt and cousins for a few days. She had to pick him up, so we stayed until Thursday. After lunch with Susie, we visited for awhile, then they took me to meet my cousin, Marlena, who drove me to her house to spend the night. She lives right behind her parents, my uncle Jay and aunt Sis, so I was able to spend time with them that evening and the next morning. I loved that. And Jay even cooked breakfast for us Thursday. His biscuits are excellent. Everything was so good. I was also able to spend awhile with my little cousin who has a very rare disease, citrulanemia. I'm not positive about the spelling. Her liver won't process proteins like it should, so her mother has to measure every gram of protein. I believe they said she can only have six grams a day. But she is so pretty and seems so healthy. She is almost 4 years old and is waiting for a liver transplant. I don't know how long she can wait, but if you believe in prayer please remember Savannah.

I went to breakfast with my Sunday School class this morning. We do that every first Tuesday, and we enjoy it so much. Today there were nine of us there.

I'm so excited about the Atlanta Braves. They are doing so well now. I love it. If only they can continue, they might be able to win their division for the 13th time.

Irving is doing well, thank God. We've have had so many cantaloupes from his garden, but I think they're about gone now.

I need to close this for now and do a little work. So far this has been a super day.

## 22 Aug 2004 - Homecoming Day

We had such a nice morning at church. We always have Homecoming Day on the fourth Sunday of August, and lots of former members and friends and family come to be with us. We had a really big crowd, and everything went well. The music was very good, we had a baptism service (5 people were baptized), and our former pastor preached about David and Goliath. He said that we all have our giants to face in life, and that we can defeat them if we trust God to help us. After the service, we had a covered dish meal together. Great fellowship.

When I came home, I had a little nap, then watched the Braves win the ballgame.

What a nice day, and I'm so thankful for it.

## 4 Oct 2004 - Looking Forward

I've changed my server recently in order to save a bit of money, but it is a little worrisome, because I can only be on for about ten minutes a day; therefore, I don't really have time to make an entry or to make comments. I may have to change to some other plan. But for now, I'm at Jami's house and thought I would do an entry on her computer.

I have several things coming up that I think are newsworthy. First of all, we are expecting two great-grandchildren in the next few months. My grandson, Andrew, has three sons, so we are so hoping for a girl for him. Of course, he would probably spoil her terribly.

Another thing is that my friend and I plan to go to a senior citizens retreat next Monday. It is in a beautiful location, way back in a wooded area. It will last from Monday afternoon until Wednesday afternoon. We go to these every chance we get and really enjoy ourselves. J just wish Irving felt like going, but he did go to one and didn't enjoy it very much. He doesn't mind my going, though.

This same friend and I also plan to go the the NC State Fair in about two or three weeks with a group of seniors. I've never been to this before, so I guess it's about time. I'm looking forward to it. There are some really good things about being a senior citizen. Last month, I took a course in safe driving for senior citizens, which may be really beneficial.

Jami is looking for another cruise for us in December, since we didn't get to go last month. That should be a wonderful time, if God is willing.

Well, that's enough for this time. I need to get back home in a few minutes. God is still blessing me tremendously, and

I thank Him so much.

## 26 Jan 2005 - It's Been Quite Awhile

My WebTV slowed up and finally died on me. So I bought a new MSNTV2 a couple of days ago. It seems to be working fine, but I'm not quite used to it yet. Anyway, I think I'm all set to make an entry again at last. I don't have anything in particular in mind, just odds and ends. One thing that was so exciting to me was the fact that 1 got a new (to me) car about four weeks ago. It's a 2004 Dodge Neon, and a really cute car. I had driven my other one for about 13 years, so I think I was due for a newer one. Another thing that is on my mind a lot these days is the fact that my little third cousin, who is only 5 years old, has had a liver transplant, and she has had a terrible time. But she is beginning to get better, we hope. And we pray that she can have a healthy life. My husband has been feeling so much better these days, with very little pain. We are concerned somewhat about a growth he had removed from his face yesterday, but we'll have to wait for possibly near a month to learn if it was malignant. The doctor said it was pretty deep.

Our weather has been so strange for this time of year. We've had a lot of springlike days, then several very cold days. Now today has been beautiful, but the forecasters are talking about possibly icy conditions over the weekend.

Well, this has been fun, but I need to get off now and do some work around the house. I'll almost surely be doing more entries now.

## 4 Feb 2005 - Back Again

This would have been my mother's 88th birthday. She has been in Heaven for almost 7 years. All of us who loved her will always miss her. But we have confidence that we'll join her in Heaven one special day. I cant ask for anything more wonderful than that. I've had friends who didn't get along with their mothers, who have harsh words and bitterness, and I really have sympathy for them. They have missed one of the most beautiful relationships anyone could have. Mother was not only my mother; she was my sister and my best friend and my favorite teacher. I know that I was so blessed to have her as long as I did. And I am blessed now to have my precious family. I love them so much, and I know they love me... Tomorrow Irving has an appointment with the heart doctor to learn the results of the stress test. We hope for good news..Well, it's time to go to bed, so I'll close this for now. More later, I hope.

## 5 Feb 2005 - A Random Act Of Kindness

I just want to share a nice thing that happened to me last evening. I had a $20 gift certificate from Christmas for the Mayfair fish restaurant and Irving didn't want to go, so I invited my friend, Eula, to go and eat with me. We had a really nice visit and our food was good, and when we were nearly through, we learned that a lady who had been sitting next to us had left $14 to pay for our meals. That only left me owing $5 and some change. So when I gave them my certificate and the change, I got back $15. We were amazed and delighted. What an extremely nice and generous thing that lady did. I wish I could thank her, but since I don't know her, I guess I'd better be looking for a way to pass the kindness on to someone else.

## 8 Mar 2005 - Rough Spots

We've been experiencing some rough spots for a couple of weeks. First Irving fell, then he got really sick the next day: A light stroke and pneumonia. The next weekend our daughter Debbie was in the hospital in danger of a heart attack. She's better now, thank God. One of our little great-granddaughters has had Mono for about a month, and she is not getting better. On top of everything else, I fell in the parking lot at church last night, and I'm still unnerved about it. It's a terrible thing to fall. I'm really sore, but I realize that it could have been so much worse. I'm pleased to announce the birth of our newest great- grandchild yesterday. He is due to come home from the hospital tomorrow, and I can hardly wait to see him. At church tonight, my granddaughter, Hannah, sang the most beautiful solo. It blessed my heart. I think it was her best solo yet. She's only 15, but seems almost professional. Do I sound like a proud grandmother or what?. So obviously, our rough spots don't take away from the wonderful gifts God gives us. He is incredibly good and kind.

## 15 Mar 2005 - Just Another Entry

I'm having a rough time getting over the fall I had in the church parking lot last week. Some things have gotten much better, while others keep popping up. I guess it just takes longer as we get older, but I'm really getting tired of this. Oh well, I'll just have to be patient.

We went over to visit our new great-grandson this evening. He is adorable. So bright-eyed.

Two of our great-grandsons came over this afternoon and helped Irving set out two rhododendrons and one gardenia. Our gardenias and azaleas from last year ought to bloom pretty soon. I'm looking forward to seeing that. I'm looking forward to springtime.

Our chickens are laying the nicest big brown eggs, usually six or seven every day. Irving really enjoys tending to his chickens, and we love sharing the eggs.

Well, Easter is just around the corner. Our pastor prefers to call it Resurrection Day, and I agree with him. It really celebrates the most amazing event. Jesus actually died on that cross, then he came to life again. Now He is in Heaven preparing a place for all who place their trust in Him. And when the time is right, He will come again and receive us. What a day that will be!!

## 27 Mar 2005 - A Wonderful Morning At Church

Our sunrise service began at 6:45 am, and it was very good. At the close of it, Jami sang "He's Alive," and it was amazing. Afterwards, we went to the fellowship hall for breakfast. Several of the men did the cooking, and it was all delicious. Then we had Sunday School, then worship service was at 9:45. We presented a musical program unlike any we've done before. We put together songs from several other cantatas and musicals, and we put in some solos and duets and other groups. We had a lady to do narration between some of the songs. and she and the Lord did an excellent job on that. I was so very pleased with the way it all turned out. Since I got home, I've done almost nothing but rest, and now it is nearly bedtime.

In the morning I'm due at the jail at 8:00, to work at the visitation desk until 12:00, so I guess tomorrow will be pretty full, but that's no problem.

I am finally much better after my fall, and I'm so thankful. I so hope I will never fall again. That's a horrible experience.

In closing, I want to say that I am so grateful that Jesus rose from the grave. We serve a living Savior. And because He lives, we too can live. What a Promise!

## 29 Mar 2005 - A Few Small Items

I don't really have much in mind to write about, but I would like to get back to making entries more often. I think the discipline is good for me. I need to keep using my brain so it will stay strong longer. Of course, I do still work crossword puzzles daily, using a pen like my mother always did. Oh well, enough of that.

I worked at the jail yesterday morning and it was interesting as usual. A woman who was there to visit her boyfriend told us about serving 4 years in jail for shooting a man who, knowing he had AIDS, had sex with a friend of hers. The man didn't die, but she doesn't regret shooting him. I thought that was a little extreme, but she surely did show loyalty to her friend. I signed up to work next Saturday too.

We went to Jami's house this evening for supper and I stayed to watch American Idol with them. There was another family there visiting and I always enjoy spending time with them. I have a favorite contestant: Anthony Federov. I really like his style. Of course, all of the finalists are so talented.

Well, It is getting late, so this will have to do for this time. It has been a beautiful day, and I thank God for it.

## 31 Mar 2005 - A Dreary Day

This day has been damp and gray and I really am longing for the sunshine to return. I haven't been outside except to get the paper and to feed the cats.

We are having our backyard fenced in with chain link fencing. They started the job yesterday, but couldn't come back today due to the rain. I'm looking forward to having this fence, so that if we ever get a dog, we'll have a safe place for him/her. Also, Irving's chickens won't be bothering neighbors. I laughed at the rooster today. Irving let them out as usual to eat some grass, and two of the hens strayed away from the group. We have seven hens, and when the rooster realized that two were not there, he got so upset, he started calling them in a really strange voice. After a while, they both came running around the side of the house. He came running to meet the second one, and I suppose she got fussed at for worrying him. I told Irving I was surprised that he knows how many wives he has. So he is smarter than I gave him credit for. It's amusing to sit at the kitchen table and watch them, but they often come onto our little porch and eat cat food and leave little messes. So we are thinking that our next project should be to screen in the porch.

Well, it's bedtime again, so I'll quit this for now. I so hope tomorrow will be at least partially sunny. But I know I shouldn't complain, because the weather is in God's Hands, and He knows exactly what we need.

## 19 Apr 2005 - Just A Quick Note

Yesterday I had a small tumor removed from my gum, and I really dreaded it. Jami drove me to Charlotte to have it done. I think I am still a little under the anesthesia, so if I make a blaring mistake here just overlook it.

Irving had a skin cancer removed about a month ago, and when he saw the doctor today, he said that it is growing and they will have to go in there a little deeper to get it. That is a little scary, so we'll have to be praying hard about that. His appointment is for May 18th. It's on his cheekbone, so I'm wondering how deep they can go.

So these days are a little worrisome for us, but we know Who holds the future, and we've placed our trust in Him.

## 22 Apr 2005 - What A Day!!

I went to the oral surgeon this morning for the post op checkup. and I was so relieved to learn that the tumor in my mouth was not malignant. Not that I expected it to be, but it is wonderful to hear such good news. I've been thanking God all day. What a blessing. I'm really so eager to get to the place where I can chew solid food. I'm craving salads and fried chicken and hamburgers. When you have to mash up everything or drink liquids, it gets old soon. But I'm really not complaining. I know that many others have a Jot bigger problems than I do. Yesterday morning our preacher came to visit me. Then in the late afternoon, our special friends (The VonStegalls) came to visit and brought a beautiful plant. It's so special to have good friends. And tonight Jami and her family came and brought blackberry ice cream that Calvin made. Yummy!

So it has been a very great day. I've been sort of walking on a cloud all day. I go back to the doctor next Thursday, but I don't expect any problems. I just hope he will say that I can start eating solids again. I'll most likely eat out that day.

## 25 Apr 2005 - Beautiful Sunshine Today

Who could ask for anything more? It's a perfect day. Yesterday was chilly, which is not an ordinary April day around here.

We had a very good day at church: Good Sunday school, good sermon, good music. Then in the evening, we had an enjoyable choir practice, and a good study on one of the Beatitudes. We're told that we are blessed when we are persecuted for Jesus' sake. So many Christians have been horribly treated over the years since Christ was here. It troubles me to think about the things that were done to them. I'm selfish enough to hope that God will spare me from that kind of persecution and of course I hope He will spare my family. I don't deny that I am selfish, but I'm not proud of it.

I'm planning a family get-together at Golden Corral on May 3rd for Irving's 80th birthday. There should be about 30 of us, not counting the little babies. I hope Irving will feel well enough to enjoy it.

Well, I guess I should turn this off for now and see if I

can accomplish something.

## 26 Apr 2005 - A Good Game

I really enjoyed the Braves game tonight. It got so close in the bottom of the ninth, but the Braves won 4 to 3.

I had to do a lot of switching back and forth from 8 til 9 o'clock because I also love to watch American Idol. My favorite is Anthony, but I don't expect him to win. I also like Carrie a lot. Of course, they almost never sing my kind of music, but I can still appreciate their talent.

It has been chilly and damp today, and I think it's due to rain again tomorrow, but we have to appreciate whatever we get. God knows best what we need.

My little cousin Savannah, who had a liver transplant in December, is still having problems from time to time. A couple of days ago she was back in the hospital with a rather high fever.

I went over to see our newest great-grandson yesterday. He's seven weeks old, and so cute. He smiles a good deal now, and his daddy said that he's been trying to talk.

I took a couple of books to little Drew, and read one of them to him. I enjoyed that. He'll soon be four.

Well, I guess that is my news for today, so I'll quit and get ready for bed. God has blessed me again today, and I am thankful.

## 30 Apr 2005 - Was It The Ovaltine?

It's now 4:15 am, and here I sit. I gave up on sleep about an hour ago. I've been trying to figure out what is keeping me awake, and the only thing I can come up with is that I had a glass of milk with Ovaltine about an hour before I went to bed. Now I wonder if it has caffeine in it.

I went back to my oral surgeon on Thursday, and things

are looking good. After ten days of not being able to chew, I am now really enjoying eating again. I love it.

My grandson Jamison will be in a Taekwondo tournament today, and I so hope it turns out well for him. I'm sure he is nervous about it. Irving will celebrate his 80th birthday next Wednesday. I've invited all of the family to meet with us at a local restaurant. I hope most everyone will be able to be there. And I hope he will have an enjoyable day. He surely deserves it. He is a wonderful man. Well, I guess that's enough for this time. I might just lie down and try to rest awhile.

## 5 May 2005 - Cinco de Mayo

What an unusual birthday for me. My birthday came on 05-05-05, and that will never happen again, in this lifetime. Jami and her children came this morning, bringing me a beautiful orchid plant and Jamison brought me a bouquet of roses which he picked. Then they took me to O'Charley's for lunch. I enjoyed that so much. I told the waiter that it was my birthday, and that I was expecting a prize. So when we were nearly through eating, a group of waiters came to our table, clapping their hands and singing to me. And they brought me a small cake with a yellow rose in the center. They probably thought I was a little bit senile, but hey, "Ye have not because ye ask not." I was happy to get that little cake. Hannah asked me if I felt older today. I told her that I don't, that I feel very young. I hope that doesn't mean that I'm getting childish. Then again, that wouldn't be so bad, would it?

## 2 Jun 2005 - Checking In

1 don't really know what I'll write about. I'll probably just ramble a little. Our weather here has been so unusual, so

damp and chilly. It's hard for Irving to be shut in so much. I plan to go to a senior citizen get-together tomorrow. This is an annual thing, held at Cane Creek, which is a really good place for picnics, fishing, swimming, and paddle-boating etc. There is even an area for camping. I'm not sure about what our meeting will be like, but we are all supposed to bring a covered dish. The meat and drinks will be furnished. A quartet will sing, and I expect that will be entertaining. Last year, Irving went with me, but it was really tiring for him, so he decided not to go this year. I just hope the weather will be much better tomorrow. I went back to the oral surgeon yesterday, and he says my mouth is doing great. Excellent, he said. That was good news. Irving has to go next week to a surgeon to have the cancer removed from his face for the third time. They will remove a small bit and test to see if there are cancer cells. If there are any, they will remove another bit and test it. They'll continue this until there are no cancer cell. I don't understand all about it, but in doing this, they will track the direction of the growth. It's just so complicated that I can't make sense of it. Irving is really dreading this, and I feel so bad for him. He has been through so much in the last few years. Well, I guess I should go and get ready to cook supper. I just wanted to write a few lines to keep in touch.

## 9 Jun 2005 - Busy Days

Yesterday, Irving and I went to Charlotte to consult with a surgeon about the skin cancer. He talked with us about things that could go wrong during surgery. It's hard for me to explain, but if either of two certain nerves should be damaged, Irving could lose the ability to wrinkle his forehead, or the ability to close his eyelid. We could choose radiation, but the cure rate is much better with the surgery. Now we wait to hear from the doctor about an appointment. He will be on vacation next week, so it will be at least week after next before the appointment can be made.

We got home from Charlotte at 6:00 yesterday, and by the time we ate supper, it was too late for me to go to Bible School. But I was able to go tonight. We will have commencement tomorrow evening. That should be nice. We've had a very good attendance.

Our 39th anniversary will be this coming Saturday. I don't guess we will do anything special. Maybe we'll go out to eat. I'm due to work at the jail that morning, so it looks like Saturday will be pretty full. Our anniversary next year should really be celebrated big-time. 40 years. It's interesting that his two daughters were married in the same year as we were. I think we all ought to take a nice long cruise together in 2006. Well, I can dream, can't I?

It's getting late, so 1 must get ready for bed. This has been a very good day, for which I thank God.

## 16 Jun 2005 - Nancy

I learned late last night that my first cousin, Nancy, was murdered by her husband on Tuesday night. He shot her. They had married in 2001, and they had had problems, but I thought they were doing alright now. The last time I talked to her, about two weeks ago, she sounded so good. She said that they had decided to sell their house and either buy or build a smaller one. He is 76, and she was going to be 71! in September, so the work of a large house and yard was getting to be too much. I don't know what brought this terrible thing on, but nothing can justify what he did. I have felt stunned all day. Nancy was just 4 months younger that I am, and it's so hard to believe that she is gone. I think if she had been sick or had died of some natural cause, it would not have been such a shock, but to think that she was murdered is really hard to take in. Well, this has been on my mind all day, and I just wanted to talk about it. The one very bright thing about this is the fact that I believe that Nancy was ready to meet Jesus, so we don't have to be worried about her soul.

## 21 Jun 2005 - So Hard To Believe

Nancy has been dead for a week tonight and it's so hard for me to believe. We didn't see each other often in recent years, but I always knew she was there. We talked on the phone occasionally, and the closeness was always still there. The last time I saw her was probably near a year ago, when she and another cousin met me at a large mall about midway between our homes. We ate lunch and talked for a long time. It was great. And we fully intended to do it again soon. Probably 3 or 4 years ago, these two cousins and another one met me at another mall, and the 4 of us had a wonderful visit. In my daddy's family there were about 14 grandchildren, and we 4 girls had a special relationship. Mary Faye was the oldest, then I was 11 months after her, then came Nancy 4 months later. Then Anne came along about 9 months after Nancy. So we were all born within about 2 years time. Now Mary Faye has died from cancer, and Nancy has been murdered. Anne and I are stunned. It's so hard to believe. I have so many memories and funny stories about Nancy and me. One day soon maybe I'll write them down. It's so strange to realize that there is now no one who shares those particular memories.

## 23 Jul 2005 - Grandchildren

I've been so blessed with grandchildren this week. On Sunday, Jordan and Jamison spent the night with me. Then Monday night, Colton and Austin spent the night. On Thursday, Hannah celebrated her 16th birthday. I picked up Lauren to take her to the party, so the two of us had a bit of quality time together. On Thursday night, Alex and Rebecca spent the night. This morning, I went to Miranda's graduation from her surgical tech program. We were so proud when she was announced as the valedictorian. (Made me cry.) It's just wonderful being a grandmother. Of course, it's wonderful being a mother too. It's a wonderful life, and I thank God for it every day.

## 11 Sep 2005 - It's Been Awhile

I just realized it has been since July 23 that I last made an entry. It must be time to update. The last two weeks have been so shocking, with Katrina doing so much horrible damage. I'm so sorry for the people who've been hurt by this. I expect it will be many months before any kind of order will be restored in New Orleans. And today has been a fresh reminder of the terrorist attacks of 9/11/2001. What a tragedy that was. America will never really recover from that. Our service at church today was centered around remembering that terrible day, and praying for all those who had lost loved ones in that attack. May God bless America. Well, my two grandsons who usually always spend Sunday nights with us beat me on all of our card games. I think I taught them too well. We play rummy, gin rummy, and casino. Jordan won at rummy and casino, then Jamison beat me at gin. I enjoyed it, but I would have preferred to win at something. Oh well, there's always next Sunday night. We recently had a dear diary friend to come and visit. That was such a treat. She is known as "Sugarnspice". She brought her teenage daughter, along with that daughter's best friend, and the youngest member of the family, Clarissa. We had talked on the phone a few times, so we already felt like friends, but this was the first time I've ever met a dear diary friend in person. I think we will always be friends. Well, it's almost 11:00, but I had a piece of chocolate pie this evening, and I fear that I won't sleep well.

Oh, the Atlanta Braves' game this afternoon was wonderful, so exciting! I sure do love that team, and I already dread the season ending in about three weeks or so. I would be so glad if they could do well in the playoffs, maybe even go to the World Series and win that. Wow, what a thought!. I'm going to close for now, and get ready for bed, and hope to sleep.

## 22 Sep 2005 - Checking In Again

So often I feel like I should make an entry, but then I just don't feel that I have anything to say. But I do need to say hello from time to time. Well, this week has been super busy and I'm really tired. We've just completed a revival meeting at church, and it was a good time. I think our church has been blessed. Yesterday, Irving had an appointment in Charlotte for an EEG. When we got there, they had messed up our time, so we had to wait extra long. We had not had lunch, so we were starved when we finally left there. We stopped at IHOP for lunch. (1 thought of you and your girls, Sonja.) When we got back home, we stopped by to visit a little while with Jami. She had her gall bladder removed yesterday, and she is still sore and in pain today, but we expect her to be fine in a few days. We couldn't be at the hospital with her because of Irving's appointment. I sure do feel sorry for the people who have been so hurt by Katrina, and for those who are facing hardships now because of Rita. Many are praying daily for their safety. Well, it's almost 10:30, so I need to get ready for bed. Tomorrow promises to be another busy day. After thinking about the people in New Orleans whose homes were destroyed, I feel really humble and thankful that

I have a home and so many blessings.

## 10 Oct 2005 - Not Much To Say

Just making an entry, probably boring to read. The highlight of the day was a trip to the dentist to have my implants cleaned. Afterwards, I went by Bojangles and got two biscuits and two coffees to bring home. That's about it. Seems so negative on the surface, but let me be sure to point out the positive side. My mouth appears to be healthy; I had the money to pay the dentist; the biscuits and coffee were very good. We have been getting some much needed rain And I feel very well. What more could I ask for. Well, I hate to mention it, but my Braves lost their game yesterday, but they played so valiantly for 18 innings. I'm so proud of them, win or lose. Now I must wait til spring training comes again. I've been watching some of the Yankees game this evening, but I don't know who to pull for. Church was good yesterday, as it usually is. I'm so thankful to be a part of a good church, with a dear church family. Well, it's past 10:30, so I think I'll get ready for bed, then watch a little more baseball. One other thing, it won't be much longer til we get back to Standard Time. I don't think I'll ever like Daylight Savings Time. Maybe I'm A little bit "set in my ways."

## 13 Nov 2005 - I Wrecked My Car

On Nov. 2nd, I was going home from church at about 8:30, and I guess I must have blacked out and I drove into a yard and hit a tree. It was one of the most horrible moments of my life. The seat belt really bruised me badly, but the CT scan showed no broken bones or injured organs. The greatest blessing was that my two great-grandsons were with me and they didn't get hurt. Thank God. I went to church today, and it was good. Jami is taking care of the music for me. And today a young man who is one of my favorite people sang a beautiful song called "Here comes a Miracle." That blessed me. My sweet uncle that we call "Golly" has Alzheimer's and prostate cancer. His daughter told me that they are calling Hospice in to help him. So he probably doesn't have long to live. He was a big part of my childhood. Well, that will do for now. I'll try to stop by soon for an update. Remember that God is good all the time.

## 18 Nov 2005 - My Uncle Died

Last night, just when I was ready to go to sleep, my cousin called to tell me that my uncle "Golly" died. He has suffered from Alzheimer's for maybe three or four years, and he also had prostate cancer, which caused his death. He was my mother's younger brother, and I have a lot of memories of him when I was a child. We stayed with him and his family for a period of time when I was around seven. I loved to help him work in the barn. We would shell dried corn and I enjoyed it, but it made my hands sore. So at Christmas one of my gifts was a pair of gloves for shelling corn. I was proud of them. And that same Christmas, Mother made Golly a purple hood to keep his head warm while he worked outside. I remember him parching some of that dried corn in a big skillet on a little heater in their living room, and what a feast that was. It was like "corn nuts" that we buy today. And we would sit around and sing while we ate our corn. Simple pleasures mean so much through the years. Well, Golly was good to me, and he will be missed, but I'm glad that he has gone on to be with Jesus now. There were ten children in my mother's family, and now there are three left, one uncle and two aunts. By the way, Golly was not his real name. It was Clifford. He got the nickname as a boy, and it always stuck. He served honorably in the Navy during World War II, and was always a decent, hard-working man. Well, I haven't slept hardly any and it is now about 3:45, so I think I'll lie back down for awhile.

# Contents

| | |
|---|---|
| Starting at last | 1 |
| In the beginning | 1 |
| After the Wedding | 2 |
| Just Rambling | 3 |
| Days of Radio and Rummy | 4 |
| Free as a Bird | 4 |
| Music Hath Charm | 5 |
| First Love | 6 |
| Tell a child the truth | 8 |
| Temporary Housing | 9 |
| I Remember Jimmy | 10 |
| World War II, as I saw it | 11 |
| One Wonderful Day | 12 |
| Jeep | 13 |
| The Runaway | 15 |
| Great-grandparents | 15 |
| S.A.L.T. | 16 |
| The Accident | 17 |
| Snuff and Sacrifice | 18 |
| A School Volunteer | 19 |
| Grandma | 19 |
| Mamaw | 21 |
| More About Mamaw | 22 |
| More Training for SALT | 23 |
| Visiting Aunt Pearl | 24 |

| | |
|---|---|
| Puerto Rico | 25 |
| A Few of the Things I've Learned | 27 |
| My First Chinese Food | 28 |
| Another Small Memory | 28 |
| Another SALT Session | 29 |
| Golly | 30 |
| Uncle Bill | 31 |
| I Love Baseball | 33 |
| Put Off The Bus | 33 |
| Another SALT Class | 34 |
| I Enjoyed Charlotte | 35 |
| Responses to Comments | 36 |
| Scary Things | 36 |
| Extra Innings | 37 |
| Ladies' Jubilee | 38 |
| Mary Faye | 39 |
| SALT Graduation! | 40 |
| Mother Loved To Fly | 41 |
| A Few More Pleasant Memories | 41 |
| Two Very Interesting Hours | 42 |
| Special Times With Children | 43 |
| His Eye is on the Sparrow | 43 |
| My Uncle James | 45 |
| A Few Fun Things | 45 |
| The Salvation Army | 46 |
| I Nearly Forgot | 47 |
| China is not our Friend | 47 |
| Still Thinking of China | 48 |
| Mustard Sandwiches | 48 |
| I Never Got Enough | 49 |
| Easter Sunday | 50 |
| A Little About Daddy | 50 |
| A Big Adventure | 51 |
| The Yard Sale | 52 |
| The Free Puppy | 53 |

| | |
|---|---|
| Believe it or Not | 53 |
| House for Sale | 54 |
| Two More Overnight Guests | 54 |
| A Long Evening | 55 |
| Rebecca | 55 |
| The Journal Jar | 56 |
| My Favorite Writers | 57 |
| Mother Had A Fur Coat | 57 |
| It Was Scary The First Time I Saw It | 58 |
| Mother's Shoes | 58 |
| One Of My Lessons | 59 |
| What A Nice Compliment | 59 |
| An Adventure Trip To Florida | 60 |
| Prune Whip | 61 |
| A Workshop And A Concert | 62 |
| Cinco De Mayo | 63 |
| A Surprise Phone Call | 63 |
| Mother Was Right On Time | 64 |
| Billy | 65 |
| Quilts and Aprons | 66 |
| I Can't Stand Bullies | 67 |
| I'm so Thankful | 68 |
| Mother | 69 |
| My Trip To Caraway | 70 |
| Yellow Jackets Attacked | 70 |
| About Yesterday's Entry | 71 |
| Still Thinking About Mothers | 71 |
| An Answered Prayer | 72 |
| The Soldiers | 73 |
| Bad Language | 73 |
| Two Really Big Announcements | 74 |
| A Big Scare | 75 |
| More About My Boy | 76 |
| NEPOTISM | 76 |
| Memorial Day | 77 |

| | |
|---|---|
| A Couple OF Rough Days | 78 |
| One Day At A Time | 78 |
| Bits and Pieces | 79 |
| Another Long Day | 80 |
| Uncle James Died | 80 |
| A Very Full Day | 81 |
| A New Kitty | 81 |
| The Words Of My Mouth | 82 |
| An Update | 83 |
| Uncle | 83 |
| Daddy Taught Me To Drive | 85 |
| Daddy's Birthday | 85 |
| Just Rambling | 86 |
| Short Stories About Clothes | 86 |
| Aunt Flora | 87 |
| Uncle Claude | 88 |
| Aunt "Buppie" | 89 |
| Uncle Clyde | 90 |
| The Choir Social | 91 |
| July Birthdays | 91 |
| Aunt Bert | 92 |
| Animal Stories | 93 |
| Aunt Edith | 94 |
| My Aunt Louellen | 95 |
| I Can't Resist Sharing This | 96 |
| Beauty Parlor Or Jewelry Store | 97 |
| My Aunt Sis | 97 |
| How To Handle Stress Or Maybe Not | 99 |
| A Mostly Good Day | 99 |
| Phi Theta Kappa | 100 |
| Imagination | 101 |
| A Nice Evening Coming Up | 101 |
| Visiting Loved Ones | 102 |
| Remembering | 103 |

| | |
|---|---|
| The Hideous Attack | 104 |
| A Letter To Paulette | 104 |
| A Morning With SALT | 105 |
| Alzheimer's | 106 |
| Superstitions | 107 |
| Go Braves! | 108 |
| Just Checking In | 108 |
| Contrasts | 109 |
| This Has Been A Good Day | 110 |
| A Nice Day | 110 |
| A Really Nice Short Vacation | 111 |
| The Lady Was Discarded | 112 |
| The Braves Lost Last Night | 113 |
| Forgiveness | 113 |
| My Second Visit With Eleanor | 114 |
| I'm So Thankful | 114 |
| I Am Thankful I Can Walk | 115 |
| Erma Bombeck | 116 |
| I Can Hear Music | 116 |
| S.A.L.T | 117 |
| Thankful For Freedom | 118 |
| Lost In The Country | 119 |
| Another Reason To Be Thankful | 119 |
| Lauren Is Twelve | 120 |
| A Big Day | 121 |
| A Good Thanksgiving | 121 |
| A Busy Day, But A Good One | 122 |
| This And That | 123 |
| SALT Christmas Party | 124 |
| Working At The Jail | 125 |
| A Very Nice Trip | 125 |
| Thoughts About Christmas | 126 |
| Counting My Blessings | 128 |
| Yesterday Was Busy But Great | 128 |
| Lost In The City | 129 |

| | |
|---|---|
| I Think I'm Ready | 129 |
| Christmas Eve | 130 |
| I Can't Sleep For Some Reason | 131 |
| Getting Back To Normal | 132 |
| A Family Affair | 133 |
| New Year's Eve, And All's Well | 133 |
| Beginning A New Year | 134 |
| All Set For Snow | 135 |
| Such A Pretty Day | 135 |
| A Good Samaritan | 136 |
| Finally Able To Drive Again | 137 |
| Mixed Emotions | 137 |
| It's A Boy!!! | 138 |
| Ladies' Jubilee | 138 |
| Our Preacher Resigned Today | 140 |
| Choose To Be Happy | 140 |
| A Special Visitor | 141 |
| Changing Carpet | 142 |
| The Carpet Looks Great | 142 |
| A Few Of My Favorite Things | 143 |
| I Heard A Funny Joke | 144 |
| Mrs. G. | 145 |
| A New Member's First Impression | 146 |
| Barry | 146 |
| Cruising | 147 |
| Another Tragic Suicide | 148 |
| A Sad Anniversary | 148 |
| Aaron, A Real Cutie | 149 |
| Giving Credit For A Kindness | 150 |
| Our Preacher's Last Day | 151 |
| I Need To Vent | 151 |
| Dustin | 152 |
| Grandparents Day | 153 |
| A Visit From Four Boys | 153 |

| | |
|---|---|
| Working At The Jail | 156 |
| Dear Diary | 156 |
| Learning To Appreciate | 157 |
| Bits And Pieces | 158 |
| A Good Morning | 159 |
| Eleanor Seems Worse | 159 |
| The Braves Won!!! | 160 |
| A New Job | 160 |
| April 10th, A Special Day | 161 |
| Little Joey | 161 |
| Another Routine Day | 162 |
| Sundays Are Pretty Full | 162 |
| Calvin's Dad Died Today | 163 |
| The Graveside Service Was Today | 164 |
| A Happy Birthday | 164 |
| The Fishing Trip | 165 |
| Mother's Day 2002 | 165 |
| Rayne Has A Mind Of His Own | 166 |
| A Wonderful Rain | 167 |
| A New Mower | 168 |
| Home Again | 168 |
| Shopping At Wal-mart | 169 |
| More From The Reunion | 170 |
| June 11th Is A Special Day | 171 |
| Father's Day | 171 |
| Two Birthday Parties | 173 |
| Allegiance | 174 |
| Rebecca Had A Birthday | 174 |
| A Proud Grandmother | 175 |
| My First Cruise | 175 |
| Perilous Times For Children | 176 |
| A SALT Day | 177 |
| Too Busy To Think | 178 |
| Lots Of Sad Things | 179 |

| | |
|---|---|
| An Enjoyable Day, Full Of Blessings | 180 |
| Farther Along | 181 |
| A Mostly Very Good Day | 182 |
| Rayne's Poem | 182 |
| What A Week This Has Been! | 184 |
| A Visit With A Friend | 185 |
| The Blind Can Lead Sometimes | 186 |
| First One Thing, Then Another | 186 |
| Number 300. Wow!!!! | 187 |
| Missing The Braves | 188 |
| Just A Little Talk About Memories | 188 |
| Super Saturday | 189 |
| Bedtime At Last | 191 |
| A Full Weekend | 191 |
| Election Day | 192 |
| If I Should Ever Get Old | 193 |
| My Aunt Is Probably Dying | 193 |
| Lizzie Died | 194 |
| Lizzie's Funeral | 195 |
| A Very Easy Day | 196 |
| A Happy Thanksgiving Day | 196 |
| The Wedding Trip | 197 |
| Traveling Again | 197 |
| The Myrtle Beach Trip | 198 |
| Another Good Sunday | 198 |
| A Very Blessed Day | 199 |
| Visits With Friends | 200 |
| Shopping And Loving It | 201 |
| Another Year Ending | 201 |
| Darla's House Burned Today | 202 |
| Quite A Mixture Of Emotions Today | 202 |
| It's Jon's Birthday | 203 |
| It's Beautiful Outside | 204 |
| Mrs. Alma | 205 |
| Great To Feel Better | 205 |

| | |
|---|---|
| My Mother's Birthday | 206 |
| Just Got Home From Church | 207 |
| Two Deaths Today | 207 |
| The Third Death | 208 |
| Brrr, An Icy Day | 209 |
| My New Cell Phone | 209 |
| Calvin's Mother Died | 210 |
| Our Variety Hour | 211 |
| My Florida Trip | 211 |
| A Few Jumbled Thoughts | 212 |
| What A Beautiful Day | 213 |
| The Braves Are Back!!! | 213 |
| A Very Special Day | 214 |
| I Have To Brag | 214 |
| Easter Sunday, 2003 | 215 |
| Such A Pleasant Day | 215 |
| Mother's Day, 2003 | 216 |
| Monday Morning | 217 |
| Our Vacation Bible School Was Great | 218 |
| I Have Clay's CD. | 219 |
| A Little Progress | 219 |
| Daddy's Birthday | 220 |
| More Birthdays | 221 |
| Cara's Wedding | 222 |
| Another Blessing | 223 |
| Sleepless in Carolina | 223 |
| Tomorrow Should Be Special | 224 |
| A Fun Day | 225 |
| Two Big News Items | 226 |
| A Totally Good Day | 226 |
| Ballgames | 227 |
| Just Checking In | 228 |
| The End Of A Good Day | 229 |
| Andrew Got Married Today | 229 |

| | |
|---|---|
| My Uncle Was Abused | 230 |
| A Beautiful Wedding | 231 |
| Just Checking In | 231 |
| The Kitchen Cabinets | 232 |
| Friday Again | 233 |
| Two Special Birthdays | 234 |
| An Update On The House | 234 |
| It Has Been A Good Day. | 235 |
| A Brief Report | 236 |
| Thanksgiving Day 2003 | 237 |
| Yesterday At The Hospital | 237 |
| December 7, 2003 | 239 |
| Another Trip To The Hospital | 240 |
| It's Getting Close | 240 |
| Another Update | 241 |
| January 1, 2004 | 243 |
| There's No Place Like Home | 243 |
| Another Busy Tuesday | 244 |
| Some Improvement | 245 |
| An Icy, Cold Day | 246 |
| Sunday Morning Beginning | 247 |
| My Third Anniversary | 248 |
| March Is Here | 249 |
| Painted Posts, Yay For Me | 249 |
| Just Checking In | 250 |
| Big Week Coming Up | 251 |
| It's Jami's Birthday! | 252 |
| My Day. | 253 |
| A Surprise Birthday Party | 253 |
| It's Been A Whole Month! | 254 |
| Just A Few Items To Tell About | 255 |
| I'm So Behind | 256 |
| Homecoming Day | 257 |
| Looking Forward | 257 |

| | |
|---|---|
| It's Been Quite Awhile | 258 |
| Back Again | 259 |
| A Random Act Of Kindness | 260 |
| Rough Spots | 260 |
| Just Another Entry | 261 |
| A Wonderful Morning At Church | 261 |
| A Few Small Items | 262 |
| A Dreary Day | 263 |
| Just A Quick Note | 264 |
| What A Day!! | 264 |
| Beautiful Sunshine Today | 265 |
| A Good Game | 265 |
| Cinco de Mayo | 267 |
| Checking In | 267 |
| Busy Days | 268 |
| Nancy | 269 |
| So Hard To Believe | 269 |
| Grandchildren | 270 |
| It's Been Awhile | 271 |
| Checking In Again | 272 |
| Not Much To Say | 272 |
| I Wrecked My Car | 273 |
| My Uncle Died | 274 |

Made in the USA
Columbia, SC
07 April 2023

1e8eb7d4-7b41-42d3-84b2-1cb471cf033cR02